SEARCHING FOR TRUTH

Principles of Biblical Investigation

JEFF ADAMS

Published by Reality Living Publishing, Inc.
5460 Blue Ridge Cut-off
Kansas City, Missouri 64133
816-358-1515

Printed in the United States of America
Library of Congress 93-090212
ISBN 10: 1-888-220-29-5
ISBN 13: 978-1-888220-29-2

Contents

Dedication

To the countless men and women who daily put their lives on the line to serve and protect.

Acknowledgements

Police officers tend to have certain "hang outs," restaurants and coffee shops where the food is good, abundant, reasonably priced and where they feel safe and welcome. They are a very close fraternity and stick together. I am pastor of a church that is blessed by a number of officers who like to hang out with us.

In many discussions over the years, I have observed that certain elements of good detective work bear a remarkable similarity to sound principles of Bible study. For years I have wanted to commit to writing some basic Bible study principles for our church family, and it seemed to me that it might be interesting to use these common investigative techniques as a framework.

A brief conversation several years ago with Officer Kelly Sapp of the Kansas City Missouri Police Department confirmed what I had suspected about commonalities of investigative technique between law enforcement and Bible study. After settling on the principles I wanted to include, I enlisted the help of my friend from high school, Tina Lewis Rowe, a captain with the Denver Police Department before the President of the United States appointed her in 1990 as the United States Marshal for Colorado (now retired). Tina provided valuable research from law enforcement textbooks and fascinating insights that enhanced my understanding of investigative techniques. She read each word of the rough drafts several times, offering both corrections and suggestions that make this work much more valuable.

Members of my own ministry team have been both helpful and encouraging. Their help has made it possible to see this project through to completion, putting my raw thoughts and rough words into published form. I give my deepest thanks to Tim Mensendiek, Cathy McGaughey, Jeff Cox, and Ken Bretches.

June Kolkmeier made the final edits and assured that you, the reader, might think that I can write fairly decent English. Thanks, June!

Finally, thanks to my wife, Cheryl, whose great patience endures hours of seeing me sitting at my desk or with my laptop computer on my knees working full speed ahead into the late hours of the night. Thank you, Honey!

Introduction

I love to read and study the Bible! Since putting my faith in Christ when I was a university student, I have had a passion for God's word. I wrote this book imagining that you and I were sitting across a table, and I was sharing with you some of the principles, truths and practical suggestions I wish someone would have shared with me back then. The language and scope are purposefully very basic, with the image of a new believer in my mind, yet taking into account that some readers may have been studying the Bible for years. If that is the case, maybe the perspective of a different personality or approach will open your eyes to things you might not have noticed.

The format of the book is designed to lead you in interacting with the biblical text itself. Relax and read at whatever pace is comfortable. You may be using this as study guide with a small group, or you may be going through this material on your own. Either way, you will do yourself a favor and enhance your learning if you actually write out the answers to the questions.

You need to know that my personal study Bible is the King James Version (KJV). I cut my biblical wisdom teeth on it, have a massive amount of notes in it that I don't want to transfer to another Bible, and have spent a lifetime memorizing verses in it. You might be using another version of the Bible, but I think most of the time you will be able to follow along quite well. Keep in mind that I am using the King James Version to develop the questions for you to answer, so you might want to compare the version you are using to the KJV, if something seems confusing.

Even though I use the King James Version for study in English, I am bilingual and also minister weekly in Spanish. My study or "work" Bible is English, but for my personal time with God each day I read the scripture, pray and write my daily journal in Spanish. The Bible I use for those purposes is the Reina-Valera of 1960.

There is no end to books that have been written about the study of the Bible and I have several of them in my office. They range from heavily academic to very basic, like this one. Most of them are good and helpful, and some of them are outstanding. Why write another one? I believe God uses individual personalities and gifts in order to reach a diversity of people. One author may appeal to some people, while leaving others disinterested.

This book is primarily intended for the congregation of the church I pastor and those in our orbit of influence via internet and television broadcasts, written material and our conferences and mission activities. My prayer is that whoever stumbles across this material will have a passion for the Bible, too, and that this will serve as a foundation for further study in God's word.

Relax and read at whatever pace is comfortable.

CHAPTER ONE

The Intrigue of Investigation

What is it about detective work that fascinates us? Generations of fans have followed the adventures of Sherlock Holmes and Doctor Watson. Long before the *National Enquirer* and other supermarket tabloids, there were flamboyant police tabloids that provided sordid details of spectacular cases. Old-time radio shows entertained the public with whodunits—a trend that continued into television. *Dragnet*, featuring Sergeant Joe Friday ("Just the facts, Ma'am.") was a hit on both radio and television for more than 20 years. No matter the most recent incarnation, police dramas are popular on television and the big screen.

With twenty-four hour news channels we don't even have to wait for a case to be solved and then written for news sources. We can follow the details of the latest "case of the century" by listening to speculation from authoritative "talking heads" on the TV screen, or we can simply have the Internet homepage inform us any time there is a new development in a case that interests us.

I suppose many people have an urge to imagine themselves living what they perceive to be the adventurous life of a police detective as seen in the movies or television. Many of us enjoy solving puzzles, whether it is a crime, a crossword puzzle, or other kinds of "brain teasers."

Fortunately, most of us are mature enough to draw a line between fantasy and reality and understand that what we see on a screen or read in a book is often far removed from the day-to-day reality of police officers. Most officers have some memorable cases and exciting experiences during their careers, but usually not enough to fill up an entire weekly television program! I have many friends in law enforcement, and I know that a detective's job is tough and not nearly as glamorous as some might imagine.

While speaking one day with some of those friends in law enforcement, a thought suddenly crossed my mind: there are many similarities between good principles and practices of police investigation and Bible study. The more I thought about it and discussed it with the officers, the more convinced I became of these shared principles.

Even the best of analogies breaks down at some point, but there are enough similarities between police investigations and Bible study that I will occasionally use them in this workbook. I will quote from real officers and the books they study to show how some of the same principles of investigation apply to both law enforcement and Bible study—which I

> *There are many similarities between good principles and practices of police investigation and Bible study.*

believe is the greatest adventure and mystery with which you could ever be involved!

And, the great thing about the mysteries of life and the truth revealed in the Bible is that God wants to give you the answers you need!

We will begin our investigation, then, by meeting the Author of the Bible.

One of the frustrating things about detective work and human investigation is interviewing witnesses and suspects, who often won't talk, can't talk, or part with information that is inaccurate or untruthful. In the case of biblical investigation, its Author is not only willing to communicate with us but is anxious to do so. He will always tell the truth.

Meet the Author

Have you ever read a good book and wished you could actually talk with the author? Even the best books provoke questions, or cause us to wonder what the author was thinking when he or she was writing.

The Bible is the best of all books—in a league of its own!

The Bible is the best of all books—in a league of its own! Reading the Bible can lead to many questions and even bewilderment at times. The good news is you can still talk to the Author, although the Bible was written centuries ago. In fact, the best way to understand the Bible is to read it prayerfully and to maintain a constant dialogue with God. God *wants* you to understand the Bible, by learning principles of biblical investigation. Doing that is how to begin this amazing adventure! Success in the adventure requires a growing, personal relationship with the Author.

This chapter will lead you to properly assess and grow in your relationship with God. You will learn some essential principles to make certain you get the maximum understanding and benefit from your Bible study. You also will consider some very practical issues, such as your choice of a Bible for a lifetime of biblical investigation. More than intellectual understanding or academic learning, the attitude with which you approach Bible study is the key that opens the book. The Bible claims to be a living book, capable of supernaturally penetrating your heart to transform your life. We must approach Bible investigation by first realizing that the Bible is no ordinary book.

Begin With a Sense of Awe

God Wrote the Bible

Pick up your Bible. You hold in your hand the very words of God Almighty. Over the centuries, many have written about the inspiration and inerrancy of scripture.[1] The Bible is unique, because it was written by human beings directly under the influence of God's Holy Spirit.

Some say writers like Shakespeare, Homer, or Thoreau were "inspired." They were certainly great writers. However, this is not how the word "inspired" applies to the Bible or theology. Biblical inspiration is God's supernatural way of putting into the Bible what he wants you to learn about him.

- *Read 2 Timothy 3:16–17. Paul speaks of both the purpose of scripture and its origin. According to Paul in this passage where does scripture come from?*

  _____

  _____

- *According to this same passage in 2 Timothy 3:16–17 what portion of scripture is inspired?*

  _____

  _____

Paul's forceful statement includes "all" scripture. The word "scripture" comes into our English language from the Latin word for "writing." In the biblical context, scripture means holy or divine writing. By including all scripture, Paul affirms the entire Bible is inspired. This is a powerful claim! This inspiration extends to the 66 books forming the Old and New Testaments. By the way, these 66 books of the Bible do not include those books called *The Apocrypha* in the middle of some editions of the Bible. The sidebar in the box explains why they are not included.[2]

Paul said all scripture is given "by inspiration of God." That phrase is the correct translation of a single Greek word literally meaning "God-breathed." In English that same meaning is conveyed by using the word "inspiration." In other words, Paul's word choice indicates scripture is the product of God breathing His words into the men who put them in written form. This does *not* mean God mechanically dictated the words to men while they were in some strange trance-like state, but rather used the richness of their personalities and life experiences to give us exactly the message he wanted us to have.

- *Read Genesis 2:7 where God made man's body from the dust of the ground. From this same verse, what did God do that caused man to become a living soul?*

  _____

  _____

The verse forms a beautiful parallel with the inspiration of the Bible. Just as God breathed life into man and man became a living soul, he breathed life into the Bible and it became a living book. The Bible is a book of living words, words of life.

NOTES

The word "apocrypha" comes from a Greek word meaning "concealed" and literally points to writings not published, since the Jews never published these writings on an equal basis with scripture. Neither Jews nor early Christians considered these books part of the Bible. Certain Bible publishers include them because of the valuable historical and cultural information they furnish about the 400 years that separate the Old from the New Testament. While the Bible claims to be inspired of God, The Apocrypha never does. Jesus and His disciples constantly quoted from the Old Testament scripture, but never from The Apocrypha. Even a casual reading of The Apocrypha reveals a quality of content that in no way measures up to the Bible.

God Used Men to Write the Bible

In the above verse from Genesis, God breathes the breath of life into man's body and man becomes a living soul. Man's three components appear in this verse:

1. A body from the dust
2. A spirit, symbolized by the breath of God
3. The resulting human soul

These three elements correspond to the Trinity: God the Father, God the Son and God the Holy Spirit. This also explains why God could say (Genesis 1:27) that he made man in his own (God's) image.

The word "inspiration" also appears in Job 32:8 and suggests how God carried out the process of breathing life into the words of scripture; just as he breathed life into man.

- *Read Job 32:8 and answer what God's inspiration does for man?*

  _____

  _____

- *In what part of man does God interact in the inspiration process?*

  _____

  _____

Job 32:8 suggests a fusion of man's spirit and God's Spirit in the process of inspiration. The Hebrew word translated "breath" in Genesis 2:7 is the same word rendered "inspiration" in Job 32:8.[3] God communicates with man and gives understanding by means of his Spirit interacting with man's spirit. You might think of your spirit as God's breath of life within you. Just as the Greek word Paul used in his letter to Timothy implied God breathed the very words of scripture, the Hebrew word used in Job is also strongly connected to the concept of breath. Inspiration has to do with God's Spirit breathing in and through man.

The context of this verse in Job is not directly connected to the writing of scripture. Job was probably the first book of the Bible committed to writing. Read Job 32:1–10 to get a better idea of the context of the words we examined in verse 8. Elihu, who spoke these words, is simply saying that God's truth and our understanding of it come from the interaction of divine inspiration and our own human spirit, not just experience and age. Elihu was a younger man than Job and his three friends who have dominated the action of the book until this point. Elihu respectfully waited until they had spoken their piece and then dared to add his own thoughts. His point is that even though they are all older than he, God can give wisdom to a younger man just as to one who is older.

> **You might think of your spirit as God's breath of life within you.**

The concept of God's Spirit supernaturally breathing his words through man is consistent with the Apostle Peter's description of how we got the Bible.

- *Read 2 Peter 1:20–21 and describe how scripture came to be.*

  _____

  _____

- *Is biblical interpretation a totally private matter?*

  _____

  _____

God could have carved the Bible into a granite cliff on the side of a great mountain. He could have dropped the entire Bible down from Heaven unfettered by human hands. Instead, he did something far more amazing. He spoke through some 40 humans on three continents, writing in three languages over the course of about 1600 years. He retained their distinctive personalities, backgrounds, and cultures, yet gave us precisely every word he wanted us to have, and he made it all fit together as though following the outline of a single mind. Not only that, the human authors had an awareness of the supernatural character of what they were writing.

- *Read 2 Samuel 23:2 and tell who David says gave him the words to speak.*

  _____

  _____

Peter makes a fascinating statement about Paul's writings at the conclusion of his second letter.

- *In 2 Peter 3:16 Peter includes Paul's writings with what other group of writings?*

  _____

  _____

Paul was still alive and writing other parts of the New Testament, yet Peter was already putting them on the same level with "the other scriptures."

Not everything Paul wrote was divinely inspired or considered to be scripture. For example, even before writing the letter we call 1 Corinthians, Paul had written a prior letter mentioned in 1 Corinthians 5:9. No one ever seriously suggested that earlier letter was inspired of God. Peter, though, clearly recognizes some of Paul's writing as being part of the divine scriptures. This awareness of inspiration and transcendence on the part of the human authors, and the confirming witness of other believers, set the books of the Bible apart as unique. Though forged in

The purpose of the Bible is to reveal God's truth to those who put their faith in Him and are guided by His Holy Spirit

the hearts of ordinary human beings, the Bible you hold in your hand is God's special revelation of his truth to mankind.

God Wrote the Bible to Be Understood

The Bible is God's revelation to mankind. A revelation is an unveiling, an unfolding, or revealing of something. The Bible is God's revelation of his truth to us, not an attempt to hide or conceal it.

Some, however, approach the Bible as though God's truth were hidden somewhere in its pages. They look for some secret code or a hidden message beneath the surface. We have already remarked how the Bible is a book of infinite depth written by God's infinite intelligence. No one of us will ever understand it all! But, this is simply due to the depth of the content and subject matter, not some divine design to hide life's secrets from all but the few who discover the code. The purpose of the Bible is to reveal God's truth to those who put their faith in him and are guided by his Holy Spirit.

While the depth and complexities of the Bible have occupied countless generations of students, the central truths of sin, forgiveness, eternal life and basic life principles are accessible to a child. Regardless of personal background, academic training or the lack of it, *you* can understand the Bible. God wrote the Bible to be understood.

We thank God for teachers and gifted scholars through the ages who have invested their lives learning Hebrew, Aramaic, and Greek, the languages in which the Bible was originally written. God uses their skills to be certain the words translated into our birth languages accurately communicate the same meaning as the original languages. Theologians labor to help us catalogue, systematize, and understand the teachings of the Bible. God calls preachers and teachers to help us understand this truth and apply it to our lives. These gifted individuals though, should never stand as a barrier between the Bible and everyday people. No matter who you are, you can learn to understand and apply the Bible to your life. The Bible was written for people just like you and me. Teachers and scholars assist us to understand the Bible for ourselves; they should never be seen as mediators speaking to us on God's behalf.

- *Read 1 Timothy 2:5. How many people (or mediators) do you need in your life between you and God?*

  _____

  _____

- *Who is the only mediator you need?*

  _____

  _____

Almighty God has chosen to reveal himself to mankind. Through an amazing, supernatural process he measured and selected every word in the Bible you hold in your hand. And, he wrote it so you could understand everything you need to know about this life and eternity to come.

Lean on God's Spirit for Understanding

The Bible Is a Living, Supernatural Book

While the Bible was written for man to understand, there is a prerequisite. As a supernatural book, it should be properly interpreted by God's Holy Spirit. Paul explained this aspect of God's truth to the Corinthians.

- *Read 1 Corinthians 2:14 and describe how the natural (physical) man views the things of the Spirit.*

  _____

  _____

- *Why is this?*

  _____

  _____

The Bible is to be spiritually discerned (scrutinized or determined). God's Holy Spirit can guide us to correctly understand and apply biblical truth to our lives.

- *Read John 16:13–14 and answer who actually teaches us the truths of the Bible?*

  _____

  _____

In the context of this passage, the truth Jesus speaks of is God's truth, his Word, the Bible. Following these instructions to his followers, Jesus prayed to the Heavenly Father and gave us a biblical definition of truth.

- *Read John 17:17 and answer the question, "what is truth?"*

  _____

  _____

The Holy Spirit Teaches Us the Bible

The Holy Spirit is our primary Bible teacher. One of the primary aims of the Holy Spirit's ministry is to lead us into an understanding of God's truth, the Bible. Even those who have not yet become followers of Christ can understand what they need to know to place their trust in Jesus Christ as Lord and Savior.

- *Read John 16:8 and give another function of the Holy Spirit's ministry.*

_____

_____

Faith became a personal reality for me during my freshman year in college. Alone in a dormitory room, I became a follower of Christ reading Billy Graham's book *Peace with God*[4], and checking out passages of Scripture in a Bible I had received as a small child. Before that time, I respected the Bible, occasionally read the Bible, and yet had little understanding of its content or application to my life. I had read portions of the Bible related to assignments in English and Philosophy classes. I was even a student preacher for "Student Day" in the church where I was raised. But, my understanding of the Bible was purely intellectual. Following my conversion to Christ, I discovered a level of understanding I never knew existed. The Holy Spirit of God within me became my Teacher and the Bible came alive. I was in awe of God and His book!

Even before I truly understood what it meant to be a follower of Christ, the Holy Spirit was already working in me every time I was exposed to the Bible, reproving, convincing, and convicting me of my need and God's truth. Long before you got serious about studying the Bible, I am sure that God's Spirit was working in *your* life, too, lovingly drawing you to God. From the moment we place our faith in God, the Holy Spirit comes to live within us and constantly works to lead us into life-long discovery and application of God's truth in every part of our lives as his children.

A Right Relationship with God is Essential

Correct understanding of the Bible depends in large part on your relationship to God. Be certain you are a genuine follower of Christ and have a living relationship with him. No church or denomination can forgive your sin and guarantee your eternal destiny. No amount of effort or good works can bring about salvation from the penalty of sin. Conversion to Christ begins with a moment in time when you recognize the reality of how sin has separated you from God and accept his grace by putting your trust in him and committing to be his follower.

There is nothing you can do to solve the problem of sin. Jesus Christ paid the penalty for our sin when he died on the cross. On the third day

No church or denomination can forgive your sin and guarantee your eternal destiny.

he rose again from the dead, proving he was God in the flesh and gaining victory over sin and death. The moment you place your faith and trust in him, you can begin a lifetime of spiritual growth.

If you have any question or doubt about the reality of your relationship with God, immediately contact someone who can help you. Speak with the pastor of your church, a trusted Bible teacher, small-group leader, or someone else you know who has a solid walk with God. They will be happy to discuss this with you and show you clearly from the Bible how to be certain of your eternal life and the presence of God's Spirit within you.

Once you have settled the issue of eternal life, you are ready to grow in your walk with God. Just as the Bible gives the necessary information for eternal life, the Bible gives the instruction you need to face the issues of daily life.

God equips us with a mind to comprehend the Bible's message. But, as we saw previously in 1 Corinthians 2:14, the Bible must be spiritually discerned or understood. God's Spirit enables us to go beyond mere intellectual understanding. This is how the Bible becomes a living book to us. Paul praised the Thessalonians for their correct attitude toward God's word.

- *Read 1 Thessalonians 2:13 and describe what you must do for the Bible to begin working in (or changing) you.*

_____

_____

The biggest challenge we face in learning principles of biblical investigation is not understanding **what** the Bible says, but **believing** what it says. The Bible works effectually in those that believe. Approach it with a skeptical heart and your skepticism will be reflected back in your face. Approach the Bible with a believing heart and the Holy Spirit of God will lead you on a life-long adventure.

Each time you open your Bible, open your heart toward God in prayer. Learn to carry on a continuous conversation with God as you read and study. As a follower of Christ, be sure your life is in submission to and under the total control of God's Holy Spirit.

Avoid Two Extremes Common in Biblical Investigation

The Search for "Hidden" Meanings

Some try to discover a hidden or secret meaning in scripture. They use the Bible as a springboard for their own opinions, rather than simply accept the clear meaning and sense of the Bible. Bible teacher John Phil-

*John Phillips'
"Golden Rule"
Of Biblical
Interpretation
"If the plain sense
makes common sense,
seek no other sense.
That is the golden
rule of Bible
interpretation."*

19

lips rightly says, "If the plain sense makes common sense, seek no other sense. *That* is the golden rule of Bible interpretation."[5]

Prior to Christ, certain Jewish scholars such as Philo (ca. 20 B.C.–A.D. 54) looked for hidden meanings and symbols in the Old Testament by mixing Greek philosophy and metaphysics with the Jewish scripture. By the Third Century, Origen of Alexandria (ca. A.D. 185–254) was instrumental in developing what is often called the "allegorical method"[6] of biblical interpretation.

This effort to unite Greek philosophy and Scripture resulted in incredibly fanciful interpretations of the Bible. Basically, proponents of this method paid little attention to the context and clear meaning of scripture, but used the Bible to represent whatever was convenient to their individual purposes. Origin's mentor Clement, for example, took the story of Jesus feeding the 5,000 with five loaves and two fishes and made each element of the story a symbol. He taught the five loaves represented preparatory training of Jews and Greeks and the two fish symbolized the philosophy and curriculum of Hellenistic philosophy. Absolutely nothing in the Bible substantiates or even suggests this symbolism. This teaching is rooted in Clement's imagination, not the Bible. Unfortunately, variations of this method predominated until the end of the Middle Ages and the dawn of the Protestant Reformation.

Even today some still try to discover the supposed secrets of the Bible while ignoring the obvious. A few years ago, Michael Drosnin, a journalist, wrote a book claiming to be based on the work of the famous Israeli mathematician, Eliyahu Rips, who has searched for encoded messages in the Hebrew Bible using mathematical models.[7]

Though his book is heavily attacked from many quarters, Drosnin claims Rips' mathematical model can be manipulated by a sophisticated software program to reveal great events of history, from the rise and fall of Hitler to the assassination of President Kennedy. While I have no doubt about God's ability to hide encoded messages when, where, and how he desires, the most amazing feature of all in this story is the fact this man professes to be an agnostic! He sees all sorts of dates, names, events, and keys of history hidden in the Bible, speculates this might be the product of advanced alien intelligence, and yet totally passes over the simple message of God's love, grace, mercy, truth, salvation, and future judgment right on the surface where any grade school child can find them. Don't let this happen to you!

The Failure to See Beneath the Literal, Historical Surface

There is an opposite and equally wrong extreme approach to Bible study. This extreme sees nothing past the literal, historical and grammatical surface. Certainly, we must begin study by understanding the literal, historical and grammatical context of the words on the pages of scripture, because the Bible is a completely accurate historical document. However, though there are no "hidden" meanings, God definitely has a purpose far beyond the surface of the literal words.

- *Moses wrote the first five books of the Bible. According to Jesus in John 5:46 who did he write about?*

_____

_____

Not once does Moses mention Jesus directly in these first five books of the Bible. However, our Lord Jesus Christ appears constantly in word pictures. For example, Abraham offering up his beloved son Isaac is a beautiful picture of God the Father offering up his only begotten son, Jesus Christ.

- *Read John 3:14 and Numbers 21:5–9, and tell what Moses did in the book of Numbers to cure those bitten by scorpions?*

_____

_____

- *What does John 3:14 say this is a picture of?*

_____

_____

There is symbolism in the Bible. The meaning of that symbolism, though, does not depend upon our imagination but the clear teaching of scripture. Paul, for instance, compares the church to the human body, a building, and a bride. We don't have to search for those images because Paul tells us directly what they are.

Later in our study we will discuss the whole issue of symbolism, word pictures, and images in the Bible. For now, just understand that any imagery in the Bible will be defined in the Bible itself, not by our imaginations.

- *Think about this question carefully, and then answer concisely in your own words. What is the difference between the "allegorical method" we discussed earlier, where people simply apply their own imagination to the Bible as they wish, and the genuine symbolism that exists in the Bible?*

_____

_____

If your answer in some way discussed a difference between reading something into the Bible and symbolism that is defined clearly in the Bible itself, you answered correctly.

Paul, for instance, compares the church to the human body, a building, and a bride.

Take Your Bible Seriously

You Can Depend On Every Word of Scripture

Earlier, we discussed the Bible's claim to be divinely inspired. You have probably heard those who complain the Bible has been greatly changed through the centuries as it has been translated from one language to another and copied multiple times. Maybe you've had those concerns yourself. Rest assured, we have more evidence to confirm the accuracy of the Bible than any other ancient document. The Old Testament was written in Hebrew with a little Aramaic thrown in for good measure, while the New Testament was written in Greek.

There are so many faithful copies of the Hebrew and Greek manuscripts available today that conservative scholars have no reasonable doubt as to their complete accuracy. For example, Josh McDowell, in his book *Evidence That Demands a Verdict*, quotes scholar F. F. Bruce as saying,

> **It cannot be too strongly asserted that in substance the text of the Bible is certain: Especially is this the case with the New Testament. The number of manuscripts of the New Testament, of the early translations from it, and of quotations from it in the oldest writers of the Church, is so large that it is certain that the true reading of every doubtful passage is preserved in some one or other of these ancient authorities. This can be said of no other ancient book in the world.**

> **Scholars are satisfied that they possess substantially the true text of the principal Greek and Roman writers whose works have come down to us, of Sophocles, of Thucydides, of Cicero, of Virgil; yet our knowledge of their writings depends on a mere handful of manuscripts, whereas the manuscripts of the New Testament are counted by hundreds, and even thousands.[8]**

Evidence or not, God promised he would preserve every one of his words to us. Jesus said in Matthew 5:18, *For verily I say unto you, Till heaven and earth pass, one jot or one tittle shall in no wise pass from the law, till all be fulfilled.* Later, we'll learn more about those "jots" and "tittles," but for the moment you have God's promise to preserve what he has spoken—not just the idea, but the very words.

Understanding the process of how the Bible was written will underscore your confidence in every word of God. You can see this process illustrated in the life of the prophet Jeremiah, chosen by God as his writing instrument.

- *Read Jeremiah 1:9 and answer who gave Jeremiah the words to write in the Bible book that bears his name?*

_____

_____

This is the way God gave us the Bible. He put His words in human mouths and those words were then put in writing.

- *Read 2 Peter 1:20–21 and answer who gave the men writing scripture the words to write?*

_____

_____

Sometimes, the prophet through whom God spoke was not the actual one to commit the words to writing, but spoke them to another person who in turn wrote them down. This other person was like a secretary taking dictation. The technical name for such a person is *amanuensis*.

- *Read Jeremiah 36:1–4 and answer who was the amanuensis that wrote a portion of the Book of Jeremiah?*

_____

_____

The Apostle Paul also used another person to write down much of his material. In the concluding remarks of Paul's letter to the Romans, his amanuensis sent his own greetings. In New Testament times, the amanuensis would often serve as mail carrier, physically delivering the letter to the intended recipients.

- *According to Romans 16:22 what amanuensis wrote concluding remarks in the book of Romans?*

_____

_____

- *The Apostle Peter also used this same technique. According to 1 Peter 5:12, Peter's secretary recorded the words of the book. What was his name?*

_____

_____

Why is this so important? We learn from these passages that God supernaturally transmits words from his heart to the hearts of men who then either faithfully commit these words to writing themselves or through another person. **This places the focus of the process on God himself**, not the human instruments. For some books of the Bible, God communicates word-for-word to one man who speaks to another man

God preserves his Word, even when men try to destroy his written record.

*Our job is to
learn principles
of biblical
investigation
and determine
which versions
of the Bible are
most appropriate
for more
in-depth study.*

who puts the very words of God to paper. If God can do this, God is able to oversee the entire process of transmitting those same words from copy to copy, from language to language, and from generation to generation.

God preserves his Word, even when men try to destroy his written record. The book of Jeremiah is a good example.

- *Read the whole chapter 36 of Jeremiah, paying special attention to verses 16–24, and answer what King Jehoiakim did with the scroll on which God's words were written?*

_____

_____

The original manuscript was destroyed. What happens now? Not to worry! In verses 27–32 God simply tells Jeremiah to take another scroll and write "*all the former words that were in the first roll.*" Unlike most of us, God never forgets what he said.

Some worry that all the original manuscripts of the Bible are long gone. But, just as in Jeremiah's day, God will faithfully preserve his words despite man's attempts to destroy them. If we could see the original manuscripts behind a glass case in a museum, we would probably be worshipping them instead of God! God has everything under control, just the way he wants it.

Do you remember that passage we saw in 2 Timothy 3:16–17 where Paul told us all scripture is given by inspiration of God? Right before that, in verse 15, Paul reminded Timothy that he had known the "*holy scriptures*" from the time he was a child. Obviously, the original manuscripts of the Bible were not kept in Timothy's house for safekeeping! Paul refers to the copies of scripture to which Timothy had access as the "holy scriptures." Paul had total confidence in God's ability to preserve his words in the copies of scripture passed down from generation to generation. You can, too. You can depend on every word of the Bible!

The process is clear. God's words are supernaturally transferred from his heart into the mouth of the prophets and other human writers of the Bible, onto the pages of scripture, and into the hands of believers, who are then responsible to receive them into their hearts.

Your Choice of a Bible Version Is Important

Buying a Bible can be rather intimidating and confusing because you are confronted with a flood of different translations, versions, study Bibles, and special editions. Let's see if we can cut through some of the confusion. God faithfully oversaw the transmission of his words from Heaven to each human writer who put the words on paper or delegated that duty to an amanuensis. Then he preserved the same words from copy to copy. Therefore, he is fully able to oversee the process of translation from one language to another.

Going into the details about each Bible translation is beyond the scope of this book. Our job is to learn principles of biblical investigation and determine which versions of the Bible are most appropriate for more in-depth study. I don't want to oversimplify a complex subject, but we can say that basically Bible translations take one of two broad approaches. Let me explain these approaches and what you need to know to make an intelligent Bible version for your personal study.

Formal translations aim to translate scripture as literally word-for-word as possible while maintaining the integrity and accuracy of the original language. The best-known example of a formal translation in English is the Authorized Version of 1611, commonly called the King James Version (KJV), the standard Bible in the English-speaking world for almost 400 years. Another familiar example is the New American Standard Version (NASV) used by many serious Bible students. Other examples are the New King James Version (NKJV) or the New Revised Standard Version (NRSV).

If you speak more than one language, you understand there are times when it is impossible to be completely literal and still accurately communicate the same meaning. For example, I can speak a single Spanish word, *vámanos*, and those Spanish-speakers with me know I'm saying, "Let's go!" But, I have to use at least two words in English to say the same thing. In more formal English I might use three words, "Let us go!" Whether I used two or three words in English, I can say that each word in English is the accurate translation of the Spanish, since the Spanish word combines both pronoun and verb, and English requires both be expressed as separate words. But, the meaning of the words remains exactly the same.

Many formal translations such as the King James Version italicize most words added to give an accurate rendering of the Hebrew or Greek. Those italicized words are no less scripture than others. Each word is necessary to communicate precisely the same meaning in good English. Sometimes the inverse is true, and two or more words of Hebrew or Greek can be literally communicated in a single English word. That is just the way languages work.

The differing grammar of languages often changes the word order in a sentence or the use of punctuation marks. When one speaks of a "word-for-word translation," we must understand the number and order of words may vary from language to language, even though the meaning is exactly the same. A formal translation such at the KJV or NASV aims to take each word of the Hebrew and Greek manuscripts and give a totally accurate translation with each word in the translation representing a formal equivalent meaning for each word of the ancient manuscripts.

Those who speak a single language often have difficulty grasping how the translation process works. I know it is hard to understand something you have never experienced, but consider this. The gospels in the New Testament were translated before they were put on paper! Jesus and his disciples spoke Aramaic in their daily lives. When God was ready to have those words and events put down in written form, he inspired Matthew, Mark, Luke, and John to write them in the Greek language, the language of commerce in the Middle East at that time. So, the very presence of the four Gospels in the New Testament is a testimony to God's faithfulness to communicate from language to language and culture to culture. If God could do that then, don't you think he is capable of overseeing the translation process today, as we work to translate the Bible into the more than 2,000 languages that still do not have even a portion of scripture?

Free Translations have a different focus. They are more concerned with finding an equivalent ***thought*** rather than finding precisely the right ***words*** to represent every word in the original. For example, a paraphrase takes more liberty with scripture, attempting to express the ideas of scripture "in other words." All of us paraphrase when we repeat something without much thought for a literal rendition of the message. A paraphrase can be particularly gripping and cause us to hear or understand something from a different perspective. Due to nuances of language and idiomatic expressions, a formal translation is sometimes not as easily understood by some readers, especially those with little Bible knowledge. A paraphrase often can help you grasp the intent of a scripture passage.

When it comes to a deeper study, though, freer translations can make it harder to comprehend the meaning of individual words. A paraphrase, by virtue of its nature, sometimes sacrifices accuracy, can omit certain details, or inadvertently give a misleading emphasis or meaning. Some paraphrases of scripture are so loose and free that many experts categorize them as interpretations of scripture rather than actual translations. One of the earliest paraphrases of the Bible in the English language was commonly called "The Living Bible" and became widely popular in the last half of the twentieth century. There are other examples of paraphrases, such as Phillip's New Testament in Modern English.

Other versions of the Bible attempt to be more accurate than a loose paraphrase, yet still lean heavily on an ***equivalency of thought*** rather than ***individual words***. Often, the phrase "dynamic equivalency" is used to represent the idea of trying to communicate in contemporary language the equivalent phrase, idea, or concept in the original. Again, this method poses a problem for deeper study when the philosophy of dynamic equivalency dominates an entire translation. The process of searching for words and phrases that are the dynamic equivalent of the Hebrew or Greek can often result in a translation that misses the mark of the original full meaning. The degree of liberty taken by translators who use dynamic equivalency varies wildly.

In an extreme example of a dynamic equivalency, a translator working to translate the Bible in an Asian culture might elect to translate Jesus' statement "I am the bread of life" as "I am the rice of life." In many oriental societies rice, not bread, is the staple of life. In those cases "rice" would be the dynamic equivalent of "bread." Granted, this is an extreme example, but it illustrates the danger. While "rice" may be more culturally relevant to the readers, you lose the texture, nature, and other senses of the word "bread" that can greatly affect the meaning and symbolism of the author.

When Jesus later spoke of his body being broken for us, we can visualize the breaking of a loaf of bread, but "breaking rice" just doesn't convey the same meaning. Also, should the translator choose "rice" instead of "bread," we can't easily cross-reference other scriptures that use the same image, as when Jesus said," I am the bread of life."

Though certainly not guilty of such a radical approach as in the example above, an example of the translation philosophy of dynamic equivalency in English is the very popular New International Version (NIV). While enormously popular in many circles and providing sometimes gripping contemporary language, the NIV takes a freer, dynamic equivalency approach that presents formidable challenges for those ready to do deeper study that aims to seek out the meaning every word of God. Another widely available translation based on dynamic equivalency is *Today's English Version*, also known as the *Good News Bible*.

This workbook intends to introduce you to deeper Bible study. Should deeper Bible study be done with a formal translation such as the KJV, or a freer translation?

- *Read Proverbs 30:5; Psalm 12:6; Revelation 22:18–19; and Deuteronomy 4:1–2. Having read these scriptures, is the emphasis on the "**thoughts**" of God or his "**words**?"*

_____

_____

_____

So, what's the answer? If the Bible is the book of God's words, not just his ideas, and every word is inspired, deeper study requires a formal translation with every word translated literally and accurately. A paraphrase and to some degree a dynamic equivalency aims to get the point across, but often at the cost of the precision and accuracy of individual words. You need to know that even the formal types of translations mentioned above such as the KJV and the NASV also make use of dynamic equivalencies and paraphrases in certain situations where difficulties in translation would make a more literal translation inappropriate. There are situations where a literal, word-for-word translation would convey a totally different idea in English.

Every preacher and teacher paraphrases by taking scripture and expressing it "in other words" so listeners might better understand. Preachers often illustrate their sermons by giving listeners a "dynamic equivalent" of the words of scripture in contemporary terms. That's effective communication, but never a substitute for the authority of the actual words of scripture.

This workbook intends to introduce you to deeper Bible study.

The basic issue is one of final authority in our lives. A paraphrase or dynamic equivalency can be helpful to a new believer, a child, someone just learning a second language, or a seasoned believer wanting to look at a passage from a fresh perspective. But, when it comes to our final authority, we look to the very words of God, not just His ideas. Ideas are composed of individual words and changing words can drastically change the idea.

When we want to say something extremely important, we measure every word. What God says in the Bible is eternally important, and he meant every word! Therefore, when you do more in-depth study of the Bible, I suggest that you use a formal translation such as the KVJ or NASV.

If you read the introduction, you already know this workbook is designed to be used with the King James Version of the Bible. There are a few old English words we will need to learn, but as a formal translation combining literalness, accuracy, and eloquence of language, it still has no peer. In fact, this translation has shaped our English language in many respects. Many of its memorable phrases have been common expressions in our language for centuries.

Your church, pastor, or Bible study leader may use a translation other than the KJV. My objective is not to cast doubt on anyone's love for God or biblical understanding because they use a different translation. I have used the KJV my whole life in study, preaching and teaching. I continue to appreciate the KJV's accuracy, authority, beauty, and centuries of influence. There are other more technical reasons I still use the KJV, many of which are beyond the scope of this book.[9] Whatever version you use in your church, Bible study, or personal life, you should study it, believe it and obey it! As you study and interact with this workbook, I highly recommend you give the KJV a try since that is the source of the questions you will be asked to answer.

While I use the KJV as my primary Bible, I constantly read through the Bible in various Spanish translations, and English translations to give me a fresh perspective. And, I regularly consult with various Greek and Hebrew texts, and occasionally compare passages in German, French, or Portuguese. (No, I do not speak those last three languages, but I have studied them enough to be able to work my way through a few verses of scripture to see how the translators dealt with it.) I am not an expert linguist, but from personal observation I can report that God speaks *your* language!

Before You Go Bible Shopping

Are you relatively new to Bible study? Let me tell you what I wish someone would have told me a long time ago. Before you invest serious money in a new Bible, wait! Get a cheap Bible with easy-to-read type and margins wide enough to hold some notes. As you progress, you will learn how to make notes in your Bible and which notation system works for you. Make your mistakes now on a cheap Bible. Later, you will want to invest in the best Bible you can afford—genuine leather cover, wide margins and good paper.

Even then, when you get your good Bible, don't carry it around everywhere, accidentally spill coffee on it, smear it with chocolate stains, and generally wear it out. Keep it for your study times. You will want it to last for many years so you won't have to copy all those notes into a replacement Bible.

Instead, have other Bibles for specific purposes. Have a lighter-weight, thinner Bible to carry to church or when you travel. I like to do my daily Bible reading from a Bible *without* notes. This keeps me focused on the text of the Bible and not my notes. This practice frees me to receive a fresh word from the scripture and not just rehash what God has shown me previously, although, there are many times I greatly benefit from reading my personal study Bible. Doing that refreshes my memory and allows me to get reacquainted with precious lessons from the past.

Not only is there practical value in learning to take good care of your Bible, there is even more at stake. The Bible, after all, is God's word, his special revelation to mankind. We should treat it with respect. There is nothing magical about its pages and there are no prescribed rituals in the Bible regarding handling it. But, if we can give proper honor to our national flag, we should give no less respect to the way we treat our Bible.

Those of you who have been raised on computers may be comfortable enough to save your permanent Bible study notes digitally in a Bible software program, totally bypassing physical notes in the margins of a real Bible. I already had a couple of decades of wonderful study notes in my Bible before I became computer literate. However, I do enjoy doing my daily Bible reading out of my handheld Personal Digital Assistant (PDA).

Do you ever feel overwhelmed by too many choices? How about choosing the right paint for the living room? You enter the store wanting a nice off-white color and find enough off-white colors to make your head spin.. Worse yet, each of them has a name sounding like exotic places in a travel brochure. Or, consider the ritual we go through to order in a restaurant. Salad or soup? Which dressing? Potatoes, mixed vegetables, or rice? Potatoes? What type of potatoes? French fried, baked, mashed, twice-baked, tater tots, hash browns? How would you like your meat cooked? What do you want to drink?

Buying a Bible involves more choices than you might imagine. While many of the choices concern price, size of the Bible, size of the type font, leather, imitation leather, hardback, paperback, color, zipper or not, thumb index for each Bible book, red letters for the words of Jesus, on and on. However, other choices are crucial, not trivial.

Once you decide on the translation (version), you will often be asked if you want a study Bible. A study Bible is one that has notes, commentary, charts, and/or other study aids in addition to the biblical text. There may be a wealth of information, maps, and charts in the appendices. Each

Buying a Bible involves more choices than you might imagine.

Keep in mind that the Bible is divinely inspired, but the notes are not.

book of the Bible may be accompanied with summaries and historical information. Some contain insightful devotional guides. Many well-known Bible teachers, pastors, or others have published their own study Bibles. Most of them offer valuable information; all of them are limited in some ways since they are written by human beings.

Keep in mind that the Bible is divinely inspired, but the notes are not. What you have is simply the opinion, experience, and knowledge of those who publish their own study Bible. Before you buy a study Bible, find out who published it and whether or not they represent a particular viewpoint that might bias their comments. Ask your pastor, Bible study leader, or others for their thoughts on selecting a study Bible. Any study Bible can provide much helpful material, but don't automatically assume all experts agree on all the information and historical data in the notes and margins. For my serious study Bible I prefer one without someone else's commentary, but room in the margins for my personal notes. However, a study Bible with good notes, summaries and historical data may be a great help for beginner and expert alike.

Get a Plan

As you get serious about learning principles of biblical investigation, nothing is more important than to set some objectives and have a plan. It is easy to get excited and establish totally unrealistic expectations such as reading through the Bible in a couple of months. Some people actually can do that, but not everyone reads at the same speed. Even those who read fast may not be absorbing very much.

The real issue is not how many times you read through the Bible, but how well you allow the Bible to read you! Failure to reach expectations often leads to discouragement and abandonment of the practice of daily time in the Bible. I would much rather someone consistently read and apply a single chapter a day than try to do too much, get discouraged and quit altogether. You can always increase the amount you read later, as you become more familiar with the Bible and principles of biblical investigation.

Now, let's talk about objectives. We talk to God in prayer, and He talks with us through His word. Every follower of Jesus Christ should spend time daily in prayer and Bible reading. That is realistic objective number one.

As to the amount of scripture you read each day, every person is different. What would be realistic for you? Almost anyone can read a chapter each day. If you are reading-challenged, never be afraid to ask for help. There are many wonderful adult education programs available in local communities, high schools, colleges, and civic organizations. Ask your pastor, Bible study leader or librarian for help. Do *NOT* be embarrassed! Be embarrassed only if your pride keeps you from getting help. Some Bible students can read several chapters a day without much of a challenge. Start with a realistic goal, and then adjust it as necessary to assure that you can reasonably expect to do it every day.

Where should you begin? If you are a new believer, I recommend you start with something easy to read in the New Testament like the Gospel of John or the First Epistle of John. You might want to follow that with the exciting Book of Acts to learn about the early spread of the gospel. Then read the four Gospels to survey the life of Christ. Next, move on to the epistles (letters) Paul wrote: Romans through Philemon. Then, go back and read through the entire New Testament in order beginning in Matthew. Enhance this reading with a simple devotional guide available at many churches and Christian bookstores. Others are available on the Internet.

As you progress in your biblical understanding, accept the challenge to read through the whole Bible. There are several ways to attack this. There are guides on reading through the Bible in a year. Some alternate readings between Old and New Testaments. Others combine a reading schedule with devotional helps.

I strongly believe every Christian should try to read the whole Bible in a year. Reading only a little more than three chapters a day you can finish the entire Bible in a year, a goal well within the reach of just about anyone. For more than 30 years I have read through the Bible from Genesis to Revelation several times a year. I would not trade this experience for anything, as it has given me a "big picture" of the whole Bible. Reading the whole Bible in a year also keeps the content of the Bible fresh in my mind and heart.

I like to distinguish between Bible reading and serious study. Early in the morning I enjoy just reading my Bible as I follow my plan to read it through from Genesis to Revelation. Since I am already familiar with much historical background and other technical information, I rarely stop to investigate particular details. I *DO* stop when the Spirit of God brings some truth to my attention and convicts my heart to listen. I also write this down in my journal. We'll talk more about keeping a journal later.

There are other times in my routine to engage in deeper investigation and study. For the moment, simply set realistic goals to read your Bible daily and stick to them. If you are a beginner, reading a chapter or a few chapters each day allows you to pause, study, and investigate at the same time you are reading. Just remember that both elements are necessary—reading and study.

Now, let's put all this together and come up with a plan that will work for you. Prayerfully consider the following:

My relationship with God
- *Am I absolutely certain I have eternal life, forgiveness of sin and a personal relationship with God?*

I strongly believe every Christian should try to read the whole Bible in a year.

- *If not, I will speak to a pastor or other mature Christian before this date:*

_____

_____

My personal commitment to Bible reading and prayer

- *I will commit to read my Bible and pray every day (Yes or no).*

_____

_____

My personal plan to read my Bible

- *My initial objective in Bible reading is to (Choose one of the following):*

  _____ *Gain a basic understanding of the New Testament by following the above plan for beginners or another plan that takes me through selected books of the New Testament.*

  _____ *Follow a reading schedule to read through the Bible in a year.*

  _____ *Read completely through the New Testament or Bible by reading chapters a day.*

My commitment to evaluate

- *On the _____ day of _____, 2____, I will prayerfully evaluate my Bible reading and prayer habits. I will make any necessary adjustments in order to maintain consistency.*

Choose a date at least two months or more in the future, so you will have established daily Bible reading as a habit. This evaluation is only to determine if you should cut back on the number of chapters you read daily, add to that number, change the plan you are following, or make some other course adjustment.

Final Advice

Don't make this commitment unless and until you intend to honor it. Ecclesiastes 5:5 tells us it is better not to make a vow to God at all than to make one and not do it. Learning principles of investigating/studying the Bible and embarking on a life-long relationship with God and his word is serious business.

If you do miss a day for whatever reason, don't get discouraged and quit. Grab hold of God's grace and forgiveness and jump right back into the routine. Let me give you some important advice: If you do miss a day or even a few days, don't be so concerned to "make up" what you missed. The most important thing is to get back on schedule *today*.

Notes

1   A thorough discussion of the doctrine of the inspiration and inerrancy of scripture is beyond the scope of this book. Josh McDowell gives a good outline summary of the basic issues regarding the inspiration and trustworthiness of the Bible. See Josh McDowell, *Evidence That Demands a Verdict* (San Bernardino, California: Campus Crusade for Christ, 1972), 15–79. See also Mal Couch, ed., *An Introduction to Classical Evangelical Hermeneutics: A Guide to the History and Practice of Biblical Interpretation* (Grand Rapids: Kriegel Publications, 2000), 15–31.

2   If you want to explore this issue further, good material abounds. For example, Merrill F. Unger gives beginning Bible students a brief summary explaining why *The Apocrypha* is not part of the Bible, giving a brief historical synopsis of each book. Merrill F. Unger, *Unger's Bible Handbook* (Chicago: Moody Press, 1967), 456–459. See also McDowell, 37–40.

3   This same word is sometimes translated also as "spirit" or "wind." In a general sense this word is used by extension to mean life or anything that is alive. This knowledge helps us understand the depth of meaning this word possesses and the intimate connection between God's breath, spirit, inspiration, and human life.

4   Billy Graham, *Peace With God* (New York: Pocket Books, 1966).

5   John Phillips, *Bible Explorer's Guide* (Neptune, New Jersey: Loizeaux Brothers, Inc., 1987), 15.

6   See some basic historical information about the allegorical method in Couch, 95–103; and in Robertson McQuilkin's *Understanding and Applying the Bible* (Chicago: Moody Press, 1992), 37-47.

7   Michael Drosnin, *The Bible Code*, (New York: Simon & Schuster, 1997).

8   McDowell, p. 45–46.

9   A major concern is the tendency of some translations to cast doubt on the authenticity of certain verses or phrases or eliminate them altogether, verses or portions that have been in the Bible for centuries. I find this unfortunate and unnecessary.

CHAPTER TWO

It's Not About You!

For some reason the article about Seattle's Green River Killer burned deep into my consciousness. I was fascinated by the investigative process and how similar it was to effective Bible study. Here's what caught my attention:

> **Marcia Chapman's hand seemed to be waving in the river's current when Detective David Reichert first saw her partially clothed body on the Sunday afternoon, Aug. 15, 1982. It was a gruesome welcome to what would turn out to be the most harrowing case of the Seattle cop's career. In the water, beside the body of 31-year-old Chapman, was another body...**

> **An hour earlier, Reichert had been coming home from church with his wife Julie and three small children. Now he was standing on the bank of the Green River thinking out the first steps in a murder investigation, trying to ignore the flies biting his skin.**[1]

This would not be the last time David Reichert would stand on the bank of the Green River. Not until November 30th, 2001 would police arrest Gary Leon Ridgeway as the one police had called the Green River Killer. Two years later, November 5th, 2003, Ridgeway would plead guilty to the deaths of at least 48 women. Police are sure there are more—maybe many, many more. Reichert would find himself drawn time and again to the bank of the Green River, sometimes just staring for hours without looking for anything in particular, but at everything in general, in hopes of seeing something, anything that would lead him to break the case.

The reason I made a connection between this case and effective Bible study is a critical element of good detective work exemplified by Detective Reichert—the ability to patiently size up the whole scene before focusing on any one piece of evidence. A good detective understands that the "big picture" will most likely piece together individual clues that may lead to clues that otherwise could be overlooked.

Cadets in most police academies learn two basic steps in crime scene investigation: survey, then search.

Cadets in most police academies learn two basic steps in crime scene investigation: *survey*, then *search*. Charles O'Hara established these two elements in his classic law enforcement textbook which is still quoted in college classes even though it was written in the 1950's.

Elaborating on these two stages of investigation, O'Hara says:

> **The investigator must restrain himself from taking physical action. The natural inclination is to form a quick opinion and endeavor to verify it by physically examining the various articles.**

The most advisable measure at this point is to stand aside and make no estimate of the situation.[2]

Before jumping in to take apart a particular book or verse of the Bible, the Bible "detective" (student) should restrain himself or herself, stand back and take in the big picture. To use O'Hara's words, we should survey before we search. This workbook will follow that plan. The first four chapters are dedicated to the survey and the rest of the book to the search.

The analogy of a crime scene to Bible study is less than perfect, except to say that it is a crime what sin has done to twist God's original plan for his kingdom! As a supernatural book, the Bible will always have an element of mystery and awe, but it was never intended to be an unsolvable mystery. To a new believer reading it for the first time without some basic orientation, the Bible can certainly *seem* like an unsolvable mystery. That is why the purpose of this chapter is to give you a "big picture" view of the Bible. You will need this overall perspective later as you dig deeper into individual passages sections of scripture. Hopefully, this "investigative" approach will make the adventure of Bible study less overwhelming and intimidating, as well as much more satisfying.

Sometimes I have seen even seminary graduates miss the mark when they jump into a Bible passage. They can read Hebrew and Greek and possess many other wonderful Bible study tools. Yet, they fail to take into account the context of the Bible as a whole.

Let me quote another old police textbook by B. W. Gocke. Here is a simple list of five principles to follow when coming upon a crime scene:

1. Waste no time beginning the investigation.
2. Make a survey of the crime scene in order to obtain a broad picture.
3. Avoid preconceived theories; approach the problem with an open mind.
4. Act on the simplest view of the situation; do not create elaborate theories as to how the crime was committed.
5. Obtain a broad view of the entire scene, then begin a search in a logical manner.[3]

Substitute "Bible study" for "crime scene" and these become solid principles for Bible study. The fact that these principles are still in use today underscores their truth and utility. The same is true of the principles of Bible study we will learn in this workbook.

Even seasoned students of scripture often fail to remember the big picture. With our self-centered human nature it is tempting to view the Bible as *MY* personal resource to solve *MY* personal problems and meet *MY* needs. It is true, of course, that every word of the Bible has tremendous benefits for our lives. But, though the Bible is immensely valuable for personal application, it is not a book about us; it is a book about God

Even seasoned students of scripture often fail to remember the big picture. With our self-centered human nature it is tempting to view the Bible as MY personal resource to solve MY personal problems and meet MY needs.

35

and his purposes. To the degree we understand God's purposes and plan in the Bible, we will succeed in finding our place in his kingdom. Discovering purpose and meaning for our lives in God's eternal plan is a great remedy for most everyday problems.

President John F. Kennedy inspired my generation as he concluded his January 20, 1961 inaugural address by saying, "And so, my fellow Americans: ask not what your country can do for you; ask what you can do for your country." That's the attitude we need for Bible study. Ask not what God can do for you; ask where your life fits into God's great plan as revealed in the Bible.

Please do not misunderstand this point. Every need in your life can be met by the truth of scripture. There is nothing wrong and everything right about meeting God in the Bible to face every challenge, need, and problem of your life. The Bible is all this, yet so much more. The Bible is not about you and me; it's about God!

The Bible is not about you and me; it's about God!

The Bible Is a Book about a King and a Kingdom

Of Kings and Kingdoms

God is God. He is complete within himself and absolutely without need. He does not need us. He did not need to create the universe. He did so because he chose to do so. He owes us nothing; we owe him everything.

For whatever reason, God decided to create a universe with beings to love, worship, praise, adore and serve him. God created a universe so vast that its perimeters remain beyond the scope of human discovery. Into this time/space continuum God placed angelic beings and human beings on which to lavish his love and with which he could interact. He did not want robots or androids. He created men and angels to experience feelings and emotions. They can reason and make intelligent decisions. This makes their worship and praise all the richer. There was never a doubt, though, who would rule as Lord and King.

- *Read Deuteronomy 4:39 and Isaiah 45:5–6.*

- *What other gods does The Lord recognize in these passages?*

_____

_____

Over this vast kingdom, our God reigns as the King of kings and Lord of lords.

The Fall of Lucifer

The Bible does not provide much information about angelic beings. We do know that the original masterpiece of God's angelic work was named Lucifer, "bearer of light." He was a special type of angelic being called a "cherub" in the Bible. His beauty and might were far beyond our comprehension. When God rebuked the King of Tyre through the prophet Ezekiel, there was a point when he obviously addressed the evil spiritual power controlling the earthly king.

- *Read Ezekiel 28:12–17 and describe the creature in this passage.*

  _____

  _____

- *Where did he walk?* _____

- *What was found in him?* _____

- *What sin do you think was found in this beautiful cherub?*

  _____

  _____

Isaiah's prophecy contains a similar situation when God rebuked the king of Babylon. The technique is the same as in Ezekiel as God's words clearly transcend the mortal man, the king of Babylon, to address the evil being empowering him.

- *Read Isaiah 14:12–15.*

- *Who did Lucifer want to be?* _____

- *In your Bible, circle all the times the phrase "I will" appears in these verses.*

- *Whose will or desire does Lucifer want to see fulfilled?*

  _____

At issue was a throne and who would sit on it. God positioned Lucifer as the crowning touch of creation. Yet, Lucifer was not satisfied to serve God; he wanted to *be* God. Do you think that same spirit might be around today?

With the sin of Lucifer, sin entered the universe and Lucifer became the Devil, Satan. The kingdom had become contaminated by the cancer of sin. God's masterpiece, Lucifer, sinned. He missed the mark of God's loving plan for him, and the universe was changed.

The Fall of Adam

Putting the details of Lucifer's fall aside for the moment, let's observe how God Almighty created man from the dust of the earth and placed him in the pristine purity of a garden one might say was designed literally as "Heaven on earth." There was one big difference between the angelic beings and this man that God created. The man, Adam, was the founder of a race of people with the ability to reproduce, to bear children. This is a major distinction between men and angels. Angels do not reproduce.

- *Read Genesis 1:26–28. In this passage, what did God give to man, or "let" him have?*

_____

_____

God created man in his own image and likeness and gave him "dominion," or rule, over the kingdom of Eden. God intended Adam to exercise this dominion in a kingdom both physical and spiritual. The Garden of Eden provided for Adam and Eve's every need, both physical and spiritual.

- *Read Genesis 3:8. According to this verse, who walked with man in the Garden?*

_____

_____

Openly accessible to Adam was the Tree of Life that could have eternally confirmed him in a position of worshipful submission to God. Instead, he consciously chose to eat from the wrong tree, the only tree God specifically set apart as being off limits. The choice of trees was God's loving opportunity to confirm that the power of choice was real and to give man the ability to return God's love by making the right choice.

As Adam and Eve confronted the choice of trees in the garden, the "anointed cherub" we met in Ezekiel 28 was there tempting them to sin, not leading them in worship as God originally intended. Now, you need to understand that what happened by the Tree of the Knowledge of Good and Evil that day was far more than a morality play. This was part of the battle for the kingdom. Thwarted in his own design to usurp the throne of God, Satan was dead set on stopping God's plan to have Adam choose to lead a race of human beings to worship God in the kingdom of his creation. The battle still rages to this day.

In Isaiah 14 Satan wanted to be *"like the most High."*

- *Notice carefully how he chooses his words to Eve in Genesis 3: 5. Who does Satan tell Eve she will be like if she eats the fruit?*

_____

_____

Adam and Eve learned the difference between good and evil by hard experience, not by faith. The result was the same as it was in Lucifer's case—instant spiritual death. Again, sin contaminated the kingdom. The humans became a race whose offspring would be "still born" spiritually. Physically, the specter of death would haunt every future human being. From birth, people would begin to die. Spiritually, they would be dead already, no longer reflecting the fullness of God's image. Failing in his first attempt to capture the throne of God, Satan thought to do so vicariously through the man and woman God had created.

And so, the battle for the kingdom raged. The Devil had no idea what God would do to counteract the blow of man's sin, nor could he imagine God would ultimately accomplish all he originally intended and more. God knew exactly what he had to do and had known it all since before the beginning.

The Battle for the Kingdom

The Bible chronicles the battle for a throne and a kingdom. The core of the matter has to do with pride and jealousy as the Devil enlists mankind in his struggle. Satan tempts Adam and Eve to be as gods without God. Ironically, to be like God is God's plan for every one of us! As followers of the Lord Jesus Christ we are to be conformed to his image! In the beginning, God created man in his own image and likeness (Genesis 1:26). The problem is not the desire to be God-like, but to be God-like without God! Mankind struggles with this temptation to this day. An essential part of the survey stage of your biblical investigation is to see the unifying theme that unites the 66 books of the Bible. It is the battle for the kingdom of God.

God has a plan for an eternal kingdom of beings to voluntarily worship Him. The full effect of this plan has been temporarily delayed as God deals with the sin problem in the universe. Do *not* view this battle as though God is desperately reacting to a blow-by-blow attack from the enemy. From before the beginning, God foresaw everything that would happen. He counted the cost of equipping his beings with a free will and deemed it worth the effort to allow these events to unfold. Despite the intervening heartache, God would lovingly and patiently be orchestrating all things to lead ultimately to this eternal kingdom of loving beings worshipping Him for eternity. God has never ceased to be God, has never lost control, and has never been at a loss to know what to do. He is God!

The death, burial and resurrection of our Lord Jesus Christ that makes possible our salvation from sin is an integral part of God's overall plan for his kingdom. God's plan, though, does not center on us. We are merely part of something bigger than all of us put together!

A New Race to Inhabit the Eternal Kingdom

It is easy to be overwhelmed by the many events, people, stories, wars and miracles recorded in the Bible. This discussion of God's kingdom is to remind you to never lose sight of God's constant movement toward that kingdom.

- *Read Luke 3:38 and answer what title is given to Adam in this verse?*

  _____

  _____

- *Now, read Luke 8:28. Who else has this same title?*

  _____

  _____

Created in God's image, Adam sacrificed that sacred image through his sin. No other man in the Old Testament is specifically called the "*son of God.*" Since Adam, the son of God, sinned, all history has prepared the human race for the coming of Jesus, the Son of God, to be founder of a new race of human beings and recover what Adam lost. The New Testament, then, begins with Jesus the second "*son of God,*" just as the Old Testament began with Adam, the son of God. Born of a virgin so as not to inherit sin from an earthly father, Jesus came to deal with sin once and for all.

- *Read John 1:12. Who else is referred to a "son of God" in the New Testament?*

  _____

  _____

- *How do they get this title?* _____

- *Read John 3:1–18 and tell how someone enters the kingdom of God.*

  _____

  _____

A newborn baby is pretty much the center of his or her own universe. Not much thought is given to anything except addressing basic needs such as "I'm hungry. I'm thirsty. I'm wet. I'm happy. I'm comfortable. I'm uncomfortable." Only as the child grows can he or she consider the deeper questions of dealing with others.

New believers in Christ often have a similar self-centered view of life and the Bible. "It's all about me!" That is normal and not a problem unless you fail to grow. Now that you have decided to learn principles of investigating the Bible, it is time to mature in your approach to the Bible and develop the kingdom perspective described here. Instead of seeing the Bible as a toy box or feeding center to see what God is going to do for you today, you should be considering where you fit into God's great plan for his kingdom.

From this point forward, resolve to approach the Bible each day with a sense of awe and discovery to learn more about how you fit into God's kingdom plan.

- *Read Psalms 119:18. What was the prayer of the psalmist as he approached scripture?*

_____

_____

You and I would do well to pray a similar prayer as we open our Bibles each day, confessing that it is all about our great God. We will, of course, discover wonderful application for our lives daily. We will find exactly what we need to meet our every necessity. But, we will do so in the context of learning God's greater purpose for having placed us here on this earth.

There Is Order in the Bible, But It's Not Chronological

Genesis is not the oldest book in the Bible. Most conservative scholars give that honor to the Book of Job. Why, then, is Genesis the first book in the Bible and not Job? The order of the Bible books is not chronological but rather according to logical groups of books having something in common. This is very important to keep in mind for someone who is ready to read through the Bible for the first time. We will discuss those groupings and their order a little later in this chapter.

Since the individual books of the Bible were written centuries apart, it should be no surprise the order of their placement was done after their writing. The Jewish scriptures are word for word the same as our Old Testament, though the order of the individual books is quite different.

The rest of this chapter is dedicated to a brief tour of the books of the Bible and how they relate to God's kingdom. With 66 books there will not be time for many individual comments about each book. The purpose of this survey is to give you the overview that will guide your detailed search later.

Your attitude is the greatest asset you can bring to this survey of the Bible. Relax, observe, and enjoy. Do not allow yourself to get anxious and think you have to remember, or even understand everything you are reading. Just get an idea of the big picture of the Bible. Remember survey first; search later.

Speaking of the similitude with investigative detective work, Charles O'Hara had some wonderful advice that is just as valid for Bible students as it is for crime scene investigators. "Enterprise, initiative, perseverance, ingenuity and an insatiable curiosity are among the characteristics needed, in addition to a rational method of procedure."[4]

Then, he added an invaluable paragraph that bears repeating:

> **Investigation is an art…. The key idea may come suddenly when he is not consciously thinking of the case or it may arrive dramatically when his mind is weighing the available information or following a routine chain of investigative thought. It may spring**

God's plan does not center on us. We are merely part of something bigger than all of us put together!

involuntarily to the conscious mind from a subconscious that is saturated with the data of the case and is occupied with the many facets of the problem. Intuition is not to be despised. The conditions of relaxation and even distraction, which often encourage this phenomenon, should be sought. There are times when sheer plodding work and deductive reasoning are no longer fruitful and where hope would appear to lie in intuition or chance.[5]

So, step back and survey. Seek relaxation to the point of distraction from any competing interest so that your mind and heart may be open to the leadership of the Holy Spirit as you consider the wonder of the Bible. We have something far better than hope in intuition or chance. God's Spirit lives within us to guide us into his truth. Sometimes, though, we are so frantically busy studying the details, we get in the way of God's Spirit directing our attention to the larger picture to see what we overlooked.

For the beginning Bible student this is a good time to mention those study Bibles we spoke about in the previous chapter. If you have one, take the time to read the summary of each book of the Bible before you read it for the first time. Other helpful tools exist as well, including "Bible handbooks" designed to give that big picture overview so critical to understanding the individual parts. When we get to chapter ten, I will describe some of these different tools and give some recommendations.

We are momentarily departing from our interactive format, and I advise you to wait until you can read through the following material in a single setting to see better how it all fits together. If you are new to Bible study, you might find it helpful to open your Bible to the table of contents, or even physically turn to each book of scripture as you go along. This will help you become familiar with the size of the books and their positions in the Bible as we trace the kingdom story from Genesis to Revelation.

The Old Testament: God Promises to Restore His Kingdom on Earth

The Pentateuch

These are the first five books of the Bible. "Pentateuch" comes from the Greek word meaning "five books." Sometimes, we simply call these the "Books of Moses," since he is the human author of all five. The Jews call them the "Torah," or law. Whatever you call them, they begin both the Christian and Hebrew scriptures. In the scope of the battle for the kingdom, the books of Moses show the kingdom disrupted by sin and God selecting a people through which he would reclaim the kingdom. God's calling and establishment of Israel as his people through whom the Messiah would come is paramount to understanding both the mean-

"Pentateuch" comes from the Greek word meaning "five books."

ing and placement of these five books of Moses in the whole of scripture. God chose the nation of Israel, not because they were better than others or because he wanted to bless them to the exclusion of others; he chose to bless them that they might be a blessing to all the peoples of the earth. He did this by giving to them the prophets, the scriptures, and the Messiah that are for all people.

Genesis means beginnings. Many major doctrines (teachings) and themes in the Bible find their beginning in the first twelve chapters of this book. Without going into great detail about creation itself, God puts the focus on the man, Adam, to whom he gave dominion over creation. Upon Adam's sin, God's plan for his kingdom shifts gear. With man spiritually dead, God begins his repair work on the physical level, covering man's nakedness with the skins of innocent animal sacrifices (Genesis 3:21), a prophetic picture of Jesus, the Lamb of God, who would one day appear to offer the one sacrifice for sin once and for all. Among the many important elements of Genesis, God promises a virgin-born (of the woman's seed, not man's) Savior to deal with sin and defeat the Devil (Genesis 3:15). As sin reigns over the race of man, God cleanses the earth with the Flood. Noah and his family are spared and God gives Noah dominion over creation as he gave Adam. Until the Lord Jesus Christ deals with sin, though, there will be no lasting, righteous kingdom on earth. Shortly, sin re-establishes itself upon the earth, and God calls out a race of people through whom he will eventually send the Savior. The balance of Genesis tells the story of Abraham, founder of the Hebrew race, and his descendants, Isaac, Jacob, and Joseph. Genesis ends with Abraham's descendants entrenched in Egypt where they had taken refuge in time of severe drought.

Exodus recounts God calling out the Hebrew people under Moses' leadership from slavery in Egypt. The Jewish Passover celebrates God's intervention for Israel during the tenth divine plague upon Egypt. God had declared that the death angel would kill the firstborn of every house that did not have a sacrificial lamb's blood on the doorposts. Only the Jews followed God's command and the death angel passed over their houses without killing their firstborns. This "Passover" of the death angel gives a prophetic picture of Jesus, the Lamb of God, dying for us that we might live. Exodus beautifully pictures our personal salvation by the blood of Jesus Christ.

Exodus also tells how God gave the Ten Commandments and the law to Israel. The law served as a contract, (or testament, as in Old Testament) between God and Israel. They were to serve God as his people so that he, through them, might offer his promise of life and blessing to all. God also gave to Moses the plans for the tabernacle that was to serve as the center for worship.

Leviticus is the book of things pertaining to the Levites, the priestly tribe of Israel. Since every New Testament believer is a "priest" (1 Peter 2:9; Revelation 1:6) with direct access to God (1 Timothy 2:5), this book has many lessons for us regarding holiness and a right relationship to

God. The New Testament book of Hebrews explains many of the word pictures of Leviticus. In Leviticus God provided a sacrifice, a priest, and a place to meet with his people. In return, we as his people are to be a living sacrifice (Romans 12:1–2), priests, and the place in which God's Spirit dwells (1 Corinthians 3:16–17; 2 Corinthians 5:1, 4; 6:16). Also in Leviticus are instructions for five types of offerings, all illustrating different aspects of Christ's sacrifice for us and what he expects from us in return.

Numbers details the tragic consequences of sin. Having been saved from slavery in Egypt, Israel continued to sin, which doomed them to the 40 years of wilderness wanderings described in Numbers. From Israel's perspective it must have seemed that the promise of a kingdom would never come to pass. Actually, God was preparing a new generation of Israelites to enter into the Promised Land and establish the kingdom. Today, the Israelites again wander among the nations of the world, and many wonder if God's promised kingdom will ever come to pass. God is not finished with Israel, nor has he abandoned plans for his kingdom.

Deuteronomy is a funny-sounding name derived from Greek words meaning the second giving of the law. Moses is facing the end of his life and prepares a new generation of the tribes of Israel to enter the land and set up the kingdom with Israel becoming a political entity. The book contains three discourses by Moses, reviewing the wilderness wanderings, explaining the Ten Commandments and other laws, and listing the blessings and curses that would come as a consequence if Israel failed to obey the law.

As the Pentateuch ends with the death of Moses, God has begun the human lineage leading to the virgin's "seed" and birth of the Messiah. God called out a man, Abraham, to begin that lineage. In the Pentateuch we see that man's children evolve into twelve tribes and then become the Nation of Israel.

Historical Books

Look at the table of contents in your Bible. Beginning with Joshua and continuing through 2 Chronicles you are looking at what we often call the books of History. Having called out a people God now leads them across the Jordan River to establish a kingdom in the land of Canaan which he previously gave to Abraham. The historical books in the Old Testament are arranged to trace the establishment, development and deterioration of that kingdom. The battle for the kingdom rages on!

Joshua leads Israel into the Promised Land, and describes the victorious conquest in this book bearing his name. More than fascinating history, this book is a prophetic word picture looking forward to the day the Lord Jesus Christ returns to conquer his enemies and establish his kingdom on earth. Joshua is the Hebrew form of the Greek name "Jesus." In a personal application Joshua pictures Christ conquering sin and death and establishing his kingdom, the spiritual promised land, in the heart of each believer.

In the Pentateuch we see that man's children evolve into twelve tribes and then become the Nation of Israel.

44

Judges describes the apathy of the second generation of Israelites in the land. The apathy is soon followed by apostasy and anarchy. In a series of cycles of sin, Israel repeatedly rebels against God, suffers at the hands of oppressors, cries out to God for help, and God raises up "judges" or deliverers. By the end of the book, we see a kingdom without a king and every man doing *"that which was right in his own eyes"* (Judges 17:6; 21:25). In terms of Christ's coming kingdom, Judges foreshadows a coming time of great tribulation on earth immediately before the Second Coming of Christ when spiritual anarchy will again prevail. The book warns against the personal anarchy resulting when a believer fails to allow Christ to control his or her life.

Ruth is like an appendix to Judges since this great love story takes place as a bright light against the dark days of the judges. A young Moabite lady (Moabites were natural enemies of the Jews) marries into a Jewish family seeking refuge in Moab from a time of famine in Israel. Following the death of the male members of the family, Ruth, the Moabite, accompanies her mother-in-law, Naomi, back to Bethlehem.

In one of history's greatest love stories, Boaz, a relative of her deceased husband, marries her to redeem her husband's family name. The story is a beautiful illustration of our Jewish redeemer, Jesus Christ, who became human flesh (our kin), in order to take himself a bride (the church), which is made up today of predominately non-Jewish people, all of whom should have been natural enemies of God. Historically, the story is vital in giving us the lineage of David, a descendant of Ruth and Boaz, and the coming king of Israel.

1 and 2 Samuel are a transition from the days of the judges, laying the foundation for the kingdom of Israel. The first king, Saul, is the people's choice, contrasting with David, the second king and the man God picked, a man *"after his own heart"* (1 Samuel 13:14). Christ will be known as "the son of David" underscoring the importance of David in the genealogical lineage of the Messiah. David's life itself is like a battlefield, as Satan constantly attacks the Messianic lineage trying to prevent the fulfillment of God's promise of redemption and the establishment of his kingdom.

Kings and Chronicles give the history of the Hebrew monarchy from its high point under David and Solomon to the civil war and divided kingdom that followed with ten tribes in the north (called Israel or Ephraim) and two in the south (called Judah). These books conclude with the eventual destruction of the kingdom in both the north and south.

Around 721 B.C. the Assyrians conquer the ten northern tribes. The last vestige of the monarchy vanishes around 606 B.C. as Nebuchadnezzar of Babylon takes the remaining tribes into captivity.

On the surface, it would appear Satan has won a victory with the downfall of the monarchy. Just as God, through his prophets, predicted

NOTES

45

this judgment for sin, he also predicted the return and restoration of the nation from captivity, as documented in the next two books.

Ezra describes two waves of Hebrews returning to the Promised Land to rebuild the city of Jerusalem and the temple following years of captivity in Babylon and Persia. God made promises about this land to Abraham and the people who would descend from him. God was not finished with Israel after the collapse of the monarchy, and God is not done with Israel even today. There is no verse in the Bible to indicate that God's plan to set up a kingdom on earth has changed. This book is a great reminder that even when it seems like the enemy has won the battle for the kingdom, God is always at work, always has a remnant of believers prepared, and always has a plan to fulfill his promise of the kingdom.

Nehemiah tells of a third wave of returning Jews. This time the focus is rebuilding the walls of the city. Just as God's people returned from captivity in the days of Ezra and Nehemiah, we have witnessed a new return of Jews to Palestine, with the Zionist movement beginning in the late 1800's and culminating in the miraculous birth of the modern Nation of Israel in 1948. That part of the world is still a battlefield in preparation for the kingdom to come!

Esther is set in the years of Hebrew captivity at a time when their conqueror, Babylon, had itself been conquered by Persia. History is filled with wars in the quest for the kingdom! Esther was a Jewish girl who became Queen of Persia. God used her to providentially prevent the extermination of her people at the hands of a wicked enemy who foreshadows the coming Antichrist. Think of this history as yet another satanic attempt to destroy Israel and prevent the arrival of the promised Messiah. Just as the Jews could not be exterminated in the past, Hitler could not exterminate them in the last century. Nor will the coming Antichrist be able to exterminate Israel. God will honor his promises and set up his throne in Jerusalem when the Lord Jesus Christ returns. The Bible is all about his kingdom.

Poetic Books of Wisdom

The books from *Job* through *Song of Solomon* form another block of scripture called the Poetic Books. Hebrew poetry is more than meter and rhyme. Robertson McQuilkin says, "The distinguishing mark of Hebrew poetry is a correspondence in thought, or parallelism, between one line and the following line; or between one section and the following section."[6] Taking this into account, some scholars estimate more than half our Old Testament can be considered poetry, though "some of that poetry is lost to us in most translations, because not all poetic form in Hebrew is readily or gracefully translated into a poetic form in English."[7] The books of *Job* through *Song of Solomon*, though, are clearly poetry in any language!

The significant contribution these books make to the kingdom theme is to introduce us to the King. The incredible trials of Job have much in common with the future tribulation predicted to come upon Israel just before the return of Christ. Job had so many questions and issues! But, when God finally appeared in the final chapters of the book, Job was all but speechless and in awe. I imagine this is much like our experience will be when we finally see our King face to face. All our questions, problems and issues will evaporate in the light of his glorious appearing!

Though David did not write all the psalms, the Book of **Psalms** is tightly identified with him as a picture of our Lord Jesus Christ, often called the "son of David." This is a book that takes us into the very heart of God, our King, and the reality of the struggle in the building of the kingdom. The wisdom of **Proverbs** and **Ecclesiastes** gives us the mind and soul of our coming King, helping to us to see life as God sees it. **Song of Solomon**, the great love story celebrating Solomon's marriage to a Gentile bride, is an intimate and tender word portrait of King Jesus' love for his bride, the church.

Major Prophets

As a whole, think of the prophetic books that complete our Old Testament as giving us the King's strategy to establish his kingdom. From a purely historical perspective, these prophets are classified according to whether they wrote before, during or after Israel's captivity in Babylon and Persia. The issues they dealt with were real as they delivered messages of God's judgment against his rebellious people, then ministered to them in captivity, and guided the returning remnant to rebuild the temple, the city and its walls.

Biblical prophecy often follows what some have called the "principle of double fulfillment." This means the prophecy has a historical fulfillment not far from the time of the prophetic utterance and a final, complete fulfillment in a future time. Many of these prophecies look to the life of Christ for their final fulfillment, and still others point to his Second Coming. Many of them are quoted by Jesus and the writers of the New Testament, revealing their prophetic nature.

The Old Testament Prophets are arranged in two groupings, major and minor. These terms describe the length of the books, longer or shorter, not the importance of the material.

Isaiah is often called the "Miniature Bible" with its 66 chapters organized in a way that mirrors the 66 books of the Bible. Isaiah wrote of the coming judgment for the sin of the nation, foreseeing the time when Israel would be taken into captivity by Babylon. He also saw God's grace in bringing Israel back to their land. Isaiah's prophecy contains many direct and indirect references to both the First and Second Comings of Christ.

Jeremiah is the "Weeping Prophet" who also preached about judg-

Biblical prophecy often follows what some have called the "principle of double fulfillment."

ment to come. He lived to see his prophecy fulfilled in the beginning of the 70 years of captivity of the Jewish people in Babylon. A good portion of Jeremiah's prophecy has a future application in the coming time of tribulation predicted to come shortly before Christ's Second Coming. The little book of *Lamentations* is an appendix to the larger book describing Jeremiah's anguish and grief as he witnesses the destruction of Jerusalem by the Babylonians. In a prophetic view of the future, this book is a preview of the coming destruction during the time of the Antichrist.

Ezekiel writes as a captive in Babylon and predicts the Jews' return to the land. The prophet experiences some remarkable visions of the coming Christ. Many of his prophecies await final fulfillment in the kingdom our Lord will establish in his Second Coming.

Daniel was a young noble in Jerusalem taken captive by the orders of the king of Babylon in an effort to educate, brainwash and use young Hebrews eventually to help the Babylonian government control and administrate their own people. Daniel became one of the most powerful men in the Babylonian Empire and also in the Persian Empire that followed. The book contains some wonderful stories of Daniel and his Hebrew friends that have great meaning and application for us all in the battle for the kingdom. His prophecy is unique in that it gives a remarkable panorama of God's plan for Israel and the Gentile kingdoms of the world for the past 2,500 years and for the future. His prophecy includes the defeat of Antichrist and the fulfillment of Christ's Kingdom on earth.

Minor Prophets

As mentioned earlier, there is nothing minor about the content or importance of these twelve little books. As do the Major Prophets, the Minor Prophets all contain valuable information about the battle for the kingdom and God's fulfillment of his kingdom plans in the First and Second Comings of Christ.

Hosea is a beautiful, living parable of God's unconditional love for his people.

Joel is a dramatic pronouncement of coming judgment for sin and points prophetically to the events preceding the return of Christ.

Amos was a herdsman (shepherd or rancher) to whom God gave a message of God's impending judgment for sin. Many of his words await final fulfillment in Christ's coming kingdom.

Obadiah addresses the Gentile nation of Edom, not Israel. The significance is how God will judge the nations in light of their relationship to Israel, then and in the future.

Jonah, a reluctant prophet in need of a serious attitude adjustment, took God's message to the Jews' archenemy of the day, Nineveh. While Jonah's experience inside the whale is a picture of Christ's death for us (Matthew 12:38–41), the short message Jonah delivered to Nineveh resulted in the greatest revival of human history.

Micah prophesied to Judah and saw the birthplace of Christ in Bethlehem (Micah 5:2) centuries ahead of time. Many of Micah's prophecies will be fulfilled in the coming tribulation and the Second Coming of Christ.

Nahum, like Jonah, is a prophecy to the city of Nineveh after the spirit of revival was overwhelmed by wickedness. Like Obadiah, Nahum is a stern reminder to all Gentile powers that their relationship with Israel is God's criteria for future judgment as he prepares to usher in his kingdom.

Habakkuk was another witness of Jerusalem's decay and foresaw the coming destruction. In a future sense, Habakkuk saw the remnant of Jews coming out of tribulation and entering into Christ's coming kingdom.

Zephaniah, another prophet to Judah, repeatedly announces the coming of the "*day of the Lord*," both in the Babylonian judgment and in the future time of tribulation immediately preceding the Second Coming of Christ.

Haggai ministered to the remnant of Jews returning from Babylon to rebuild the temple. Fulfilled partially in the return to Jerusalem, Haggai's prophecies also look for a final, complete fulfillment when the temple is rebuilt again in Jerusalem and Jesus Christ returns to set up his kingdom on earth.

Zechariah was a contemporary of Haggai who gives a series of absolutely incredible and sometimes hard-to-understand visions. Portions of his prophecy were fulfilled by Christ in his earthly ministry, such as his triumphant entry into Jerusalem on the foal of a donkey (Zechariah 9:9). Others prophesies await fulfillment when Israel recognizes and receives her King in the future.

Malachi ends our Old Testament and represents God's final words to Israel before the voice of the prophets would grow silent for 400 years leading up to Christ's birth in Bethlehem. Full of rebuke for the corrupted priesthood of his day, Malachi ends with a magnificent vision of Christ coming in glory in the figure of the rising of the Sun of Righteousness. The Old Testament closes with a poignant reminder that God's plan for his King and his kingdom will never be subverted.

The New Testament: God Puts His Kingdom in Individual Hearts and Promises a Future Kingdom on Earth

The Gospels

Through the Old Testament we witnessed God's desire to establish a kingdom on earth that would be his channel to repair the problem of man's sin and restore what was lost with Adam's fall. Repeatedly, the lineage of the coming Messiah and his kingdom were attacked by the Devil and complicated by man's sin. Yet, God never wavered in his plan, even in dark times when it appeared all hope was lost.

The prophets promised a coming King who would set up a literal, physical kingdom in Jerusalem. God became flesh, born of a virgin, so as not to inherit a sin nature from a human father. The King's arrival on earth, though, was not as most had imagined. While many did believe on him, the religious leaders of Israel, with their power, comfort, and traditions threatened, rejected him and eventually delivered him up to the Romans to be crucified.

With Jesus Christ dead on the cross, even his closest disciples assumed the promises of the kingdom died, too. Though he told them clearly, no one really expected him to come out of the grave alive on the third day. In doing so, he conquered sin and death once and for all, offering his grace freely to all who put their faith in him.

When Israel's leaders rejected him as the one promised to be the king of Israel, the Lord Jesus Christ did something no one suspected. He put his kingdom into the hearts of those who believe (Luke 17:21)! This is the kingdom message of the New Testament.

God has not, however, abandoned his promise for a literal kingdom on earth. All that will be completed exactly as promised when our Lord returns again, and Israel will turn to God in spirit and in truth.

The Gospels tell the story of Christ's life. While they are placed first in order in the New Testament as a book, there is an important fact to bear in mind. The New Testament as God's promise or covenant does not actually take effect until the death of Christ. *"For where a testament is, there must also of necessity be the death of the testator"* (Hebrews 9: 16). In other words, a person's "last will and testament" does not go into effect until that person dies.

The Gospels, then, are a transition from the Old Testament to the New Testament. Christ's offer of a kingdom and new covenant was genuine. Rejected by his own, Christ opened his grace to all who believe in his great victory through his death, burial and resurrection. The full effect of the kingdom of God inside believers did not take effect until his death and resurrection. Much of the material of the Gospels, therefore, is directly applicable to Jesus dealings with the Jews and not intended to be blindly applied to the New Testament church, since the New Testament does not properly begin until his death. The principles of God's truth taught by Jesus, of course, apply to believers in any age.

Why four Gospels? With four different but complementary perspectives, we have a complete view of Christ and his life. Few police investigations are conducted by only one detective. It usually takes a team of investigators, each with their own perspectives, to tie a complex case together. To properly view an object with multiple dimensions, one must move around the object. We view a beautiful painting looking square on. To view a three-dimensional work of sculpture, we walk around it to see it from various perspectives. Christ is not one-dimensional and God has provided in the four Gospels what we need to appreciate the fullness of Christ's person and personality.

Matthew writes from a distinctly Jewish point of view. His concern is to present Christ as the promised Messiah, the fulfillment of all the prophets. The offer of the earthly kingdom to the Jews takes center stage in Matthew's Gospel.

Mark has a style that is crisp and to the point like a good journalist, wasting no words in showing Jesus Christ as the servant who came to die that we might live. The content of his Gospel parallels much of what Matthew and Luke present.

Luke offers us a closer view of the humanness of Jesus Christ, the Son of Man predicted by Daniel, yet sacrifices none of his deity. Luke's style is that of a medical doctor: professional, educated, caring, and compassionate. Matthew, Mark, and Luke are often called the "synoptic" gospels, because their material and outlines are so similar. Luke writes this gospel to a Roman nobleman, Theophilusa, and therefore, has much more of a Gentile perspective than either Matthew or Mark.

John is totally different, yet in no way contradictory to the other Gospels. In John 20:30–31 he clearly states that his purpose is evangelistic, that the reader might know Christ as the Son of God and find eternal life through that belief. He highlights only seven of Christ's miracles, using them to illustrate different aspects of the salvation offered to us. While Matthew wrote with a very Jewish audience in mind, John's Gospel targets all people.

The Book of Acts

The acts recorded here are those of the apostles of Christ. This is the history book of the New Testament. Before ascending to Heaven, the Lord Jesus Christ issued a commission to his disciples to take the message of this gospel of the kingdom of God in individual believers' hearts to the very uttermost part of the earth. The task he gave is to make disciples, or learners, of every ethnic group on the planet. Jesus Christ did not abandon his followers, but sent the Holy Spirit on the special

Like the Gospels, Acts is a book of transitions. The early disciples were all Jewish.

mission of being his presence in the lives of believers and equipping them for this great mission.

Like the Gospels, Acts is a book of transitions. The early disciples were all Jewish. Years would pass before God gave a special revelation to the Apostle Paul teaching that his plan was to make Jew and Gentile one new creation in Christ. In Acts we trace the transition from an earthly, visible kingdom Jesus offered to Jews in Jerusalem, to the worldwide announcement of an invisible kingdom of the heart. During this time, the Old Testament is transitioning to the New Testament, and the law is transitioning to grace. Also, Israel is transitioning to the church as God's focal point of earthly ministry in the battle to build God's kingdom in the hearts of those who put their trust in Christ.

Paul's Letters

From Acts until Hebrews, the books in your New Testament are all epistles, or letters, of the Apostle Paul either to churches or individuals. Paul is a "Hebrew of the Hebrews," as he says in Philippians 3:5. But, he also is fully aware of God's call on his life as the Apostle to the Gentiles. Though the entire Bible is written for us as believers in Jesus Christ, this is that part of the Bible uniquely written *to* us, instructing individual believers and churches how to live and promote the kingdom of God in this age.

Romans is the foundation of New Testament teaching and written with the precision of a legal brief. Paul sets forth man's lost state without Christ and the doctrine of salvation. He explains God's unique relationship to Israel, past, present and future. Finally, he gives practical guidelines for Christian living today.

1 Corinthians was written to a primarily Gentile church in Greece to correct some serious problems and bad teaching. Paul began the church himself, but after he departed a series of problems arose, making this book a model of how to deal with problems in a local church.

2 Corinthians is a follow-up to the first letter and one of the most intensely personal views of Paul we have in scripture. This book shows what it is to have a heart for ministry.

Galatians is Paul's response to a serious situation in the Roman Province of Galatia (part of modern-day Turkey) where Paul had begun several churches. False teachers had invaded the region, trying to convince believers to return to the Jewish law. This book teaches Christian freedom and the need to walk in the power of God's Spirit alone.

Ephesians is an intensely spiritual book written to believers in Asia Minor (modern Turkey). Here, Paul explains what it really means for us to be "*in Christ.*"

Finally, he gives practical guidelines for Christian living today.

Philippians is a book of unabridged joy written from Paul's prison cell shortly before he died as a martyr, executed for his faith in Christ. Philippi was the Macedonian city (part of modern Greece) where Paul and his team began the first local church in Europe after crossing the Aegean Sea from Asia Minor.

Colossians was written to a church not far from Ephesus. Though Paul had never visited there, it is believed the church in Colosse was started by the influence of the ministry in Ephesus. While similar in content to Ephesians, the emphasis in Colossians is not on our being *in Christ*, but Christ *in us*.

1 and 2 Thessalonians are addressed to another church in Macedonia not far from Philippi. Acts 17 describes how Paul began this church. In the first letter, Paul encourages them in their growth and commends them for being a positive example to other churches. The second letter deals with a problem of false teaching in the church which frightened believers into thinking they were already in the prophesied time of tribulation. Though short, this epistle contains crucial prophetic information about the last days leading to Christ's return.

1 and 2 Timothy and *Titus* are often called collectively the "Pastoral Epistles." In them, Paul gives very practical instruction to these two men whom he mentored as pastors in ministry and encourages them to do the same.

Philemon rounds out Paul's letters and is addressed to an individual. Imprisoned in Rome, Paul won to Christ a runaway slave named Onesimus. Discovering he had run away from a friend and fellow believer named Philemon, Paul sends Onesimus home to submit and reconcile. Besides being a great lesson on friendship, this little letter beautifully illustrates how Christ paid our sin debt, giving us freedom and putting our sin on his account.

Letters to Hebrew Believers

The four books that follow the Pastoral Epistles in your New Testament have in common the fact that they are all addressed to believers coming from a Hebrew background. The very title of Hebrews gives us that information without having to read another word. Sometimes they are grouped with the little epistles of 1, 2, 3 John and Jude and called the "General Epistles."

I prefer to consider the Hebrew epistles apart, taking into account that the authors assume their readers are well versed in the Old Testament scriptures. This understanding helps Bible students to take the teaching in proper context and avoid misapplication.

Hebrews is remarkable for the way it opens up the Old Testament. Though no authorship is given in the book itself, many assume Paul was the author although other theories exist. Other than Paul, few writers would have been qualified to write such a masterful work with such amazing insight into the Old Testament scriptures. Every Christian should see this book as key to understanding the New Testament application of the Old.

James is a pragmatic book written to challenge the reality of the spiritual walk of believers coming from a Hebrew background, the "*twelve tribes scattered abroad*" (James 1:1). James does not, as some assert, teach that salvation is by faith plus works. His aim is to show that true faith is always evidenced by works.

1 and 2 Peter also target Hebrew believers and show how the Holy Spirit of God had transformed the formerly rough, impulsive, and proud Peter. His first letter teaches that this transformation is made possible by learning to deal biblically with our trials. The second letter is a follow-up to the first, warning against false teachers and looking to the future coming of the King and his kingdom, just as God promised Israel.

Letters from John and Jude

The same apostle who gave us the Gospel bearing his name also wrote the three letters of *1, 2 and 3 John.* The first epistle is a wonderful encouragement to new believers and especially addresses the assurance of our salvation and the confirmation of God's love in our hearts. The second letter instructs how to deal with the spirit of Antichrist. Third John gives specific application for dealing with a bad spirit in the local church.

Jude warns of false doctrine and false prophets in the last days shortly before the return of Christ the King.

The Revelation

Often mispronounced and misunderstood as "Revelations" (plural), this book is the revelation of Jesus Christ. This book tells how it will be before, during, and after our Lord Jesus Christ returns to earth to establish his kingdom in the city of Jerusalem. As the book ends, we see the Bible does not "conclude" but cycles back to the very first chapters of Genesis, as God fulfills the plan he intended from before the beginning. Finally, there is a kingdom, both spiritual and physical, with the proper King on the throne, surrounded by the praise and worship of his creation.

Our tour of the Bible has been both brief and superficial. As you continue to study of the Bible you will learn many more fascinating and important details. Let me encourage you to read, read, read. Most importantly, I pray you will always see the Bible from God's perspective, understanding it's all about Him, not us. As you do, you will discover purpose and meaning you never thought possible!

Interaction Time!

Before putting this chapter aside, try out your growing Bible study understanding by tackling the following questions. Feel free to turn back to earlier parts of the chapter to find or check your answers.

- *Having read through this brief survey of the Bible, do you remember all the information you just read, and do you understand it all?* _____

- *If your answer was "no," is it really that important that you remember all the information you just read?* _____

- *What is the most important lesson you can learn from this brief survey of the Bible?*

_____

_____

- *Remembering what we learned about classic technique of investigation, before we can do a thorough "**search**" we should _____. If you don't remember, go back and check the first quotation from Charles O'Hara.*

- *What is the one theme that ties all 66 books of the Bible together?*

_____

_____

- *Is this theme all about you and your needs?* _____

- *Just before we began our survey of the Bible, I gave you another quotation from police writer Charles O'Hara. It begins with the words, "Investigation is an art." Carefully read that paragraph once again. Can you see how this applies to the way we discover God's truth in the Bible? List one or two ways you can apply this information to YOUR life. (There is no one right answer).*

_____

_____

Good job! Now that you have done this survey of the books of the Bible, we will learn some other ways to consider the Bible as a whole and how its contents all fit together.

Notes

1   Terry McCarthy, River of Death, TIME Magazine, June 3, 2002

2   Charles O'Hara, *The Fundamentals of Criminal Investigation* (Springfield, MO: Charles Thomas, 1956), 43.

3   B. W. Gocke, *Police Sergeant's Manual* (Los Angeles: O.W. Smith, 1943), 27.

4   O'Hara, 20.

5   O'Hara, 21.

6   Robertson McQuilkin, *Understanding and Applying the Bible* (Chicago: Moody Press, 1992), 199

7   Ibid., 200

CHAPTER THREE

Fitting the Pieces of the Puzzle

Completing the border of the puzzle is somewhat comparable to getting the "big picture" of scripture we have been discussing. Certain organizational elements of the Bible serve as a "frame" in which we can begin to fill in the other pieces.

Several times over the years I have heard people compare Bible study to putting together a large jigsaw puzzle[1]. This illustration brings back fond childhood memories.

As a child I loved to help my mother put puzzles together. Like all kids, I had those little "kiddy" puzzles that entertained me only until I grew tall enough to pull myself up to Mom's card table where she was working on a "real" puzzle, and stretch a sticky hand where it was least appreciated, scattering carefully sorted puzzle pieces. As I grew older, more coordinated and a little smarter, I gradually became a "partner" in Mom's puzzle assembly enterprise.

During my childhood the puzzle industry came out with what seemed to me to be huge puzzles—1,000 pieces or more! Just looking at the box was intimidating. When opened and turned upside down, those 1,000 little pieces overwhelmed me until, Mom taught me the secret. First, separate the border pieces, the ones with the straight edges. As you look for the pieces with edges, you discover the four, all-important corner pieces. Putting together the frame as it flowed out from the four corners gave me an immediate sense of accomplishment. Plus, the completed frame would be the key to putting the rest of the puzzle together.

Completing the border of the puzzle is similar to getting the "big picture" of scripture we have been discussing. Certain organizational elements of the Bible serve as a "frame" in which we can begin to fill in the other pieces.

After the frame, the next step in puzzle assembly is to sort the pieces according to color or other distinguishing features. Don't you just love it when there's something like a telephone pole in the picture and you can track down those little pieces of puzzle having a portion of the pole? I contend the Bible has distinguishing features somewhat like those telephone poles that enable us to get our bearings and fill in the remaining pieces.

The puzzle analogy also illustrates a crime scene investigation, which we have compared to Bible study. The entire investigation is a puzzle, beginning with a 911 call, followed by the first response to the crime scene, the crime scene investigation itself, witness interviews, follow-up investigation and leads, laboratory analysis of physical evidence, chemical analysis, medical examination and reconstruction. When and if all of those "puzzle" pieces are put together and have linked the physical evidence to the crime scene, to the victim, and more importantly to the suspect, the investigation is considered complete.

The Bible is infinitely deep. But we can fit almost all of the pieces together to the point it no longer seems to be an unsolvable puzzle. This chapter builds on the survey of the books of the Bible we did previously and aims to put the rest of the "edge" pieces of the Bible together. As the edge of a puzzle begins to take shape, you will notice the remaining pieces usually share some common distinction that will help you sort them out. In this process, it is not really important which piece you pick up first. You pick up the one that is in front of you or one that catches your attention for whatever reason. Once you pick up and examine enough pieces, you begin to see similarities, patterns, lines and angles that connect to other features.

This is much the same way a good detective goes about gathering information at a crime scene after making an initial survey of the big picture. He or she begins focusing on the particulars of the scene, looking for pieces that fit together. There is no feature that must be examined first. The detective's mind is taking in data and looking at details until patterns and other "links" began to emerge.

Most crime scene searches are concentric, from inside to out, then back again. This is like working from the pile of puzzle pieces outward toward the frame, then back again, familiarizing one's self with textures, colors, lines, and other features along the way.

Whether thinking of fitting together pieces of a puzzle or investigating a crime scene, we will learn and use principles that enable us to better hear the voice of God's Spirit as we humbly and reverently approach the study of the Bible. These truths will equip us to see life better from God's perspective, but not to totally "figure out" the Bible by putting every little piece of information into a box and smugly thinking we have learned all there is to know.

Thinking of the puzzle, I suggest that each day we can see the image and reflection of God emerge more clearly as we continue to fit pieces together. Unlike a box that announces a puzzle contains 1,000 pieces, God's book, the Bible, contains an infinite number of pieces and will keep us busy discovering new truths daily for a lifetime!

Allow me to share yet another analogy for a moment. What makes a great masterpiece of art so compelling? In some way it is alive. I remember the first time I saw Leonardo da Vinci's *Mona Lisa* in the Louvre in Paris. The room was stuffy from the presence of hoards of tourists. As I peered over their heads to catch a glimpse of the masterpiece, there it was. Instantly, I knew this was more than a pretty picture. This was life hanging on the wall.

I made my way toward the back of the gallery where there was more room, but I could still see her. I walked from one side to the other and her eyes followed me. They did! I had read about this, but now I experienced the reality of a truly great work of art. I have no reason to believe

No matter how you go about putting the puzzle pieces of the Bible in the right places, you will end up with a masterpiece.

that da Vinci was anything approaching what we would recognize as an evangelical believer. But the Bible tells me in James 1:17 and 1 Timothy 4:4 that whatever is good and true comes from God. I should not be surprised to see God's truth and goodness all around me, even in the most unlikely places. The *Mona Lisa* is good! And good art is a remarkable testimony to the masterpiece of God's creation of mankind, even when tainted by the curse of sin.

No matter how you go about putting the puzzle pieces of the Bible in the right places, you will end up with a masterpiece. The picture that emerges from proper Bible study is one that lives, one whose eyes follow you wherever you go and pierces your soul to the core. That's when you realize you never "master" the Bible. God masters you and me as he speaks to us through his living word. Never lose sight of this.

God's Order Reflected in Scripture

- *Read 1 Corinthians 14:33. This verse says God is the author of what?*

  _____

  _____

- *God is NOT the author of what?*

  _____

  _____

Paul makes this statement in the context of clarifying the confusion often surrounding the exercise of spiritual gifts. The principle, though, is universal. God is not the author of confusion. He is the God of peace, as in harmony, rest, things set at one with each other, and order. We should expect to see this peace, harmony and order in the Bible as a reflection of the author.

The Bible is not merely an assortment of stories, proverbs, parables and religious thought. Once we grasp the theme of God's kingdom threading its way through history, we see God's purpose unifying and coordinating the thought of the many human writers through the centuries. With order and structure God reveals his mind to us in the Bible. Perhaps the most incredible fact of all is to think that God has a specific plan for you and me in his kingdom!

- *Read 1 Corinthians 2:16. What does this verse say about the mind of God?*

  _____

  _____

Spread out like a myriad of puzzle pieces, God's truth is stacked in layers through the Bible. As we stand in awe of his brilliance, let me suggest some simple ways to find those "edge pieces" that can help us bring structure to the rest of the pieces. These are not the **only** "edge pieces," These are only examples to show you that there are, in fact, pieces that, once in place mentally, can help you understand the rest of the picture.

Dealing with Dispensations

What's a Dispensation?

While sounding somewhat ominous or theological, "dispensation" is a word that is directly from the Bible. This is not one of those "archaic" words people sometimes complain about, though its use is rare enough to confuse us if we are not careful. Some synonyms for "dispensation" as it occurs in the Bible are economy, stewardship, or administration. In some religious circles the word "dispensation" has sometimes been used to mean an exemption or exception granted by a church official. This is not the sense in which the word is used in the Bible.

Let's take the synonym "administration" as an example and see if we can approach a biblical understanding of dispensations. Every four years in the United States we elect a President. On January 20th after the November elections, a new "administration" begins. The country itself does not change. The borders do not move. The Constitution doesn't change, though the new administration may work for new legislation or even push to amend the Constitution itself. Each administration is totally different. The names of Cabinet members change. Key players in many facets of government change. Most importantly, there is a new direction, a new attitude, and a new approach to many areas of government. Even when a sitting President is re-elected, his second term is clearly a new administration in key aspects, depending on the players and the circumstances. With each new dispensation there are many changes, although the basic elements of the nation remain the same.

God does not change. God's truth does not vary even a little bit. Through the centuries of human history, however, God has varied his approach from time to time in the way he relates to mankind. Though God's global plan has not changed, there have been different "administrations" of God's dealings with the human race, or different ways that he has "dispensed" his grace to man.

Taking some examples of the way the word "dispensation" is used in the Bible will help us understand its use and meaning.

- *Read 1 Corinthians 9:16–17. According to these verses, a dispensation of what is committed to Paul?*

_____

_____

In these verses Paul is saying he did not choose the ministry as a vocation. He was called, or chosen, to preach the Gospel. He doesn't mean he is unwilling ("against my will") to preach; only that he does this because God called him to do it, not just to receive the "reward" of a pay check or because he made a career choice to become a preacher.

He understands that a "dispensation of the gospel" is committed to him. In other words, this is his "administration" to preach the Gospel, a divine duty assigned to him by the call of God.

Today, the Gospel remains unchanged, but this is ***our*** "dispensation" of the Gospel, even though the world has changed in many ways. We have the same divine responsibility to share the good news ("Gospel") of Jesus Christ with those who need to hear. What we do with this dispensation is up to us.

- *How is the word "dispensation" used in Ephesians 1:10?*

_____

_____

This verse in Ephesians teaches us God was moving toward a new day, a new "dispensation" when our Lord Jesus Christ would bring everyone and everything together in Himself. God has not changed, but what Jesus Christ did enabled God to deal with mankind and dispense his grace in a new and better way.

- *How does Paul use the word "dispensation" in Ephesians 3:2?*

_____

_____

Paul was a leading Jewish scholar. One day he met Jesus Christ on the road to Damascus, and his life was changed forever. God gave Paul a special mission of being the Apostle to the Gentiles. In Ephesians 3:2 Paul explained to the predominately Gentile congregation in Ephesus, that God had given him a *"dispensation of grace"* toward Gentiles. He had not come to dispense law but grace. He said something similar to the Colossians.

- *Read Colossians 1:25. What does this verse say Paul was made according to the dispensation God gave him?*

_____

_____

Putting all this together, let's come up with a working definition of "dispensation." Biblically, a dispensation is a time period when God is dispensing his grace and truth through a certain method. There was a time when God dispensed his truth through the law. In another moment of history God dispensed his truth directly through the Lord Jesus Christ on earth. Today, God dispenses his truth by grace through faith through the Bible and the church.

Understanding Dispensations Gives Form to the Big Picture

Though God never changes, he clearly has varied some of his dealings with man through the ages. Most rational people can agree on the existence of at least two different "dispensations" of God's relationship with mankind—Old Testament and New Testament. Without doubt, the death, burial and resurrection of Christ changed history and changed God's dealings with the human race. Things were simply different in Old Testament time than they are now. Even in the Old Testament itself, God related to man differently before scripture came into existence than afterwards. Also, there was clearly a difference in the relationship between God and man before man's sin and after man's sin.

- *Read Ephesians 2:11–12. What was the spiritual condition of Gentiles in times past?*

  _____

  _____

- *Following the phrase "But now" in Ephesians 2:13, what has changed and why?*

  _____

  _____

- *We may not agree on all the details, but how we divide, handle, or cut up the Bible is important. Read 2 Timothy 2:15. What did Paul tell Timothy in this verse about dividing the Bible?*

  _____

  _____

This is a well-known verse of scripture. What does it mean to "rightly divide" the Bible? I am bilingual and teach these same principles in Spanish. One older Spanish version I often use gives good insight to this verse. Loosely translating to English, the sense it gives is to "properly cut up" the Bible.

Years ago a man in our church in El Salvador was a quality tailor of men's clothing and had many professional clients. Though he employed a number of tailors in his shop, he insisted on cutting out all the material himself. No matter how skilled the tailors were who sewed the pieces

Biblically, a dispensation is a time period when God is dispensing his grace and truth through a certain method. There was a time when God dispensed his truth through the law. In another moment of history God dispensed his truth directly through the Lord Jesus Christ on earth. Today, God dispenses his truth through the Bible and the church by grace through faith.

Some want to cut up the Bible into neat little boxes and becoming so ordered they order God right out of the Bible! God won't fit in any of our boxes!

together and gave them the finishing touches, if the individual pieces were not cut from the bolt of cloth correctly, the suit would not fit well or look right, and fabric would be wasted. Cutting the fabric personally was his way to get maximum value from every bolt of material, as well as to maintain quality control.

It is just as important to "cut up" the Bible correctly. When we make a bad cut in one place, everything is thrown off kilter. How we cut up the big pieces of the Bible affects our total understanding. We do not want to make mistakes in cutting out these "dispensations." The Bible is a massive book, and we will never agree on all the minute details due to our human limitations. However, I do think there is a way we can agree about the things that are most important.

Determining different dispensations in the Bible is a matter of personal observation not divine inspiration. In theological circles what is often called "dispensationalism" can be a controversial topic. There are extreme positions on both sides of the issue. Some people call themselves "dispensationalists" and want to cut up the Bible into neat little boxes with no room for overlap. Sometimes they become so ordered in the process they order God right out of the Bible! God won't fit in any of our little boxes! Others take issue with "dispensationalists" and want to toss out the whole idea of different dispensations of God's dealings with his creation. Remember, "dispensation" is a biblical word. "Dispensationalist" and "dispensationalism" are not.

I can explain this to you so you will understand. Some may measure the distance between two points in miles while others measure the same distance in kilometers. The distance is exactly the same. The only difference is the unit of measure an individual may choose. In most applications the unit of measure is not critical as long as we agree on what unit to use for a particular purpose. If a German asks me how far it is from Kansas City to Wichita, I might answer that it is about 200 miles. If a look of consternation comes across my German friend's face, I might say, "That would be about 322 kilometers." Hopefully, that would bring a smile of relief. The distance, however, is the same. It is exactly the same! But, to say "200" or "322" does not communicate anything but confusion, unless we agree on a common unit of measure to express the distance.

I serve on a board whose lone Canadian is often the object of good-natured kidding from his American colleagues. One day someone said something about all Canadians living only 10 miles from the US border. My Canadian friend immediately responded in mock indignation, "That's not true! We all live within 15 kilometers of the border!"

What is correctly called "dispensationalism" is nothing more than human attempts to discover and communicate how God happens to be "dispensing" his grace and truth at a certain point in time so we can know where we have come from, where we are, and where we have yet to go. Different Bible teachers have suggested different dispensational structures through the years. There is no "right" or "wrong" way to do this as long as we communicate clearly about the units of measure. Does my tailor friend cut every bolt of cloth exactly the same way? Of course not! It depends on the size and style of suit he is crafting. A bolt of cloth is a bolt of cloth and he simply needs to be certain he is consistent with the units of measurement while he is cutting, whether inches or centimeters. You can cut the bolt of cloth in many different ways, but you must cut it correctly.

Earlier, we agreed on at least two basic dispensations: Old and New Testaments. Some Bible teachers like to put more marks on their tape measure. Some speak of five dispensations, others nine, fourteen, or whatever. Let me put it this way: the distance from Genesis to Revelation stays the same. We can cut that distance many ways to measure it as long as we are consistent and communicate what we are doing. There is no one right way to mark off the distance from Genesis to Revelation, or from eternity past to eternity future. You may be more familiar with miles than kilometers, but I would hope you wouldn't argue with someone from another country that only miles are "divinely inspired," and anyone who uses kilometers is obviously of the Devil!

I have heard people speak of being freed from dispensationalism as though they were healed from a fatal illness. I have also heard certain dispensationalists speak with such confidence one might think they had invented the time frames, then informed God. In Bible study, our goal should not be to discover a new way to measure God's interaction with humans or to verify the truth or error of someone else's ideas, but rather to discover God and his will for us on every page of the Bible.

Seven Commonly-Taught Dispensations

Having said that we should not become fixated on the idea of dispensations, let me introduce you to one of the more common schemes you may hear about. This one suggests seven major periods of God's work with mankind. You might want to cut up the distance between Genesis and Revelation in a different manner, but I offer the following as an example of what has been taught to Bible students for many years.

The Dispensation of Innocence

This first measuring unit of the Bible extends from Genesis 1:1 through Genesis 3:5, right before Adam and Eve partake of the forbidden fruit and plunged the human race into sin. God places the man and the woman in the Garden of Eden, giving them dominion over his creation. They are to have children and begin the process of populating the kingdom. Before reproducing they sin, thereby assuring their offspring will be born with a sin nature.

Prior to sin, the man and woman enjoyed a relationship with God based on the purity of their innocence. Without scripture and without a church, they directly related to God with no sin to separate them from him.

Seven Commonly Taught Dispensations

Innocence
Conscience
Human Government
Patriarchs
Law
Grace
Millennium

63

The Dispensation of Conscience

Following their sin, Adam and Eve begin to reproduce. Their children, though, are not born in the image of God but in the image of Adam (Genesis 5:3). The Old Testament law has not yet been given. Abraham and the Hebrew people exist only in God's mind. Mankind now relates to God on the basis of the conscience God put in every human breast. This section of scripture extends from Genesis 3:6 to Genesis 8 and the flood of Noah's day.

Even with the witness of conscience, the human race stumbles headlong down the spiraling and descending staircase of sin until the world has been corrupted more than God chooses to bear. The result is the judgment of the great flood, another defining landmark of history, forever changing both the physical and spiritual landscape of the world.

The Dispensation of Human Government

As they leave the Ark, God gives Noah and his descendents the same commission given earlier to Adam to exercise dominion over God's world. The characteristic feature in this portion of the Bible, from Genesis 9 through Genesis 11, is the emergence of human civilization and government.

The judgment of the flood only beat back the compounding consequences of sin for a season, but did nothing to eradicate the root problem within man. God's plan for mankind was the same as it had been for Adam and Eve—to replenish the whole earth. Man's concern, however, is to make a name for himself and to band together for mutual strength in opposition to God. This is the motive causing God to confound the human race with different languages at the Tower of Babel.

Still, no written scripture exists. No "chosen people" have been chosen. Following God's intervention at Babel, the human race spreads out upon the face of the earth, organizing itself by language groups, tribes and nations.

The Dispensation of the Patriarchs

Genesis 12 marks another major point of time along God's tape measure stretching from eternity to eternity. Here, God calls out a man to be the father of a people that would establish the human lineage of the Messiah. God will eventually rename Abram "Abraham," meaning "father of many nations." Not only Jews, but Arabs trace their ancestry back to this man. The rest of Genesis, from chapter 12 through 50, follows the story of Abraham's descendants.

A patriarch is the head of a family. From Abraham comes Isaac and, later, Jacob. Jacob (renamed "Israel" by God) is the father of twelve sons who each later become heads of the Twelve Tribes of Israel. Collectively, these men are the patriarchs of the tribes that will grow to become the Nation of Israel. From this point forward in the Old Testament, God will deal with mankind through Israel. He will give his truth, his prophets and, eventually, the Messiah through this people. And, God chose this people to be a blessing to all peoples.

The Dispensation of Law

The book of Exodus opens with Israel in bondage in Egypt. As God selects Moses to lead them out of Egypt toward the Promised Land, another world-changing event occurs. Through Moses, God gives a written law. Besides the Ten Commandments, this law encompasses an entire society revolving around loving, worshiping and serving God. For the first time in human history, man relates to God based on a written revelation from Him. This is a different way in which God relates to man, and this dispensation characterizes the rest of the Old Testament from Exodus through Malachi.

The Dispensation of Grace

As you might suspect, this dispensation encompasses most of the New Testament. No event in history changed the world more that Christ's death, burial and resurrection. This time, God's Son Jesus Christ dies on a cross and comes back from the grave to deal with the very root of the sin problem, not just the consequences.

Though God will ultimately fulfill all his promises to Israel, man no longer comes to God though Israel and the law. Today, we come to God directly through Jesus Christ on the basis of his grace alone, and both Jews and Gentiles who become followers of Christ are one in him. Today, the Holy Spirit seals and indwells believers in a way never before known.

The Dispensation of the Millennium

In the final three chapters of the Bible, Revelation 20–22, another of those transcendental happenings is forecast to take place as Christ returns to earth in his Second Coming. In the city of Jerusalem, just as promised by the Old Testament prophets, Christ sets up his throne and rules the world. This earthly reign is said to last 1,000 years (Revelation 20:1–6). Following a short-lived rebellion by Satan, the spiritual and physical kingdom on earth merge as one, and God's plan from the beginning is realized. We are right back at the beginning of Genesis.

All we have done is to break the story down our discussion of the kingdom theme in the previous chapter into edge pieces, called "dispensations," based on the method God was using at any particular time to dispense his truth. We traced the same story using dispensations instead of books of the Bible.

This particular arrangement of seven major administrations or dispensations of God's grace are those many have used through the years to show how the Bible fits together. You may choose to divide the Bible up differently, to use different landmarks that make more sense to your way of thinking. The distance from Genesis to Revelation remains the same, no matter how you measure it.

Remember, the whole point is not to compartmentalize God, but to discover how at any moment of human history, in any culture or circumstance, God is always there and at work dispensing his unchanging love, grace, and truth. He always has been, and he always will be. This is the same God who, when Moses asked for his name, said, "I am" (Exodus 3:13–14).

Feasts of Israel

Focusing on the Feasts

No matter how you view or arrange the various dispensations, they are but one type of edge piece of the Bible's puzzle. Now, we are going to learn another type of edge piece. Once you understand the concept, you will immediately identify these puzzle pieces every time they appear in the Bible.

Throughout its history, nation of Israel has observed seven divinely commissioned feasts.[2] Instructions for all seven can be observed in Leviticus 23, but they are described in other passages also. From a purely historical perspective, these feasts match the harvest cycle. The first three occur in the spring, one in the summer harvest, and the final three around the fall harvest.

All these feasts illustrate important aspects of God's relationship with Israel, and all foreshadow prophetically significant events in Israel's future and the coming Messiah. Being familiar with these feasts, their history, meaning and significance will come into play time and again as you put together the individual pieces of the Bible, both Old and New Testaments. Israel celebrates other important feasts throughout the year. These other feasts do not stem directly from the law but from history and tradition, and there are some references to these other feasts in the Bible. For the moment, we will concentrate on the series of seven divinely instituted feasts that are another common thread uniting the individual parts of the Bible. Examine carefully the following description of the seven feasts with a key word that points to the primary prophetic symbolism.

The Feast of Passover—Salvation

First observed on the eve of Israel's exodus from Egypt, this feast commemorates the Death Angel passing over those Hebrew homes where the blood of the Passover lamb was applied to the doorposts. Let's see an example of how the Bible interprets the Bible as we learn the symbolism of the Passover.

- *Read Exodus 12:1–30.*

- *Read Leviticus 23:5.*

- *Read 1 Corinthians 5:7. This verse clearly states that the Passover is a picture of what?*

_____

_____

Many details described in Exodus 12 symbolize various aspects of Christ's ministry of redemption. As you grow in your biblical understanding, you will be able to return to passages such as Exodus 12 and find many parallels between what happened that important night in Israel's history, as God saved Israel from the slavery of Egypt, and how it points to the future when Jesus, our Passover Lamb of God, would save us from the slavery of sin.

- *Read Matthew 26:2 and underline the word "Passover."*

- *How would you make the connection between Exodus 12, 1 Corinthians 5:7, and Matthew 26:2?*

_____

_____

- *There are other benefits from understanding these Hebrew feasts. Read John 2:13; 6:4; and 11:55. Considering the three Passovers mentioned, Jesus ministry lasted at least how long?*

_____

_____

- *Read John 19:14, another reference to the third Passover of Jesus' ministry. What time of year was Jesus crucified?*

_____

_____

The Feast of Unleavened Bread—Communion

This feast follows the Passover immediately, lasting seven days. We will learn that leaven in the Bible symbolizes sin. So, the absence of leaven indicates the absence of sin. The unleavened bread symbolizes the body of Christ offered up on the cross for our sin, the sinless (unleavened) Bread of Life offered in our place. From the perspective of our Christian life, the Feast of Unleavened Bread pictures the communion or fellowship with God made possible on the basis of this sacrifice. Following immediately after the Passover, this feast demonstrates there should be no break between the moment of our salvation and our walk in fellowship with God.

- *Read Leviticus 23:6–8.*

- *Read again 1 Corinthians 5:7, remembering that Christ is our Passover.*

- *Now, read the next verse, 1 Corinthians 5:8. What feast do you suppose Paul has in mind in this verse?*

  _____

- *If Christ is our Passover, what should Paul's reference to the feast of unleavened bread represent to us, or how should we apply Paul's words?*

  _____

  _____

The Feast of First Fruits—Resurrection

Coming a day after the Sabbath day of the Feast of Unleavened Bread, the Feast of First Fruits on the first day of the week speaks of Christ's resurrection on that Sunday morning. The Sabbath was normally on Saturday, so the next day would be Sunday, the first day of the new week. On this day the priest waved a sheaf of grain before the Lord in action of thanksgiving.

- *Read Leviticus 23:9–11.*

- *Read 1 Corinthians 15:19–23. Do you think Paul's use of the word "firstfruits" in this passage has any connection with the feast by the same name? How, or why?*

  _____

  _____

- *Read what Jesus said in John 12:23–24. What connection do you see, if any, between the priest waving the sheaf of grain on the Feast of First Fruits and what Jesus says here in John 12: 23–24?*

  _____

  _____

The Feast of Pentecost—The Church

Forty-nine days (seven times seven) from the end of the Feast of First Fruits is the Feast of Pentecost on the fiftieth day. Gentiles use the name "Pentecost" from the Greek for "fiftieth." Jews speak of the Feast of Weeks as it is called in the Law. The sheaf of grain waved before the Lord in the Feast of First Fruits appears now as two loaves before the Lord. Many New Testament believers understand this to be a prophetic picture of both Jew and Gentile, two different loaves becoming equal in Christ before God that day the Holy Spirit came to seal and indwell believers. Acts 2 tells the story of the coming of the Holy Spirit in special ministry to believers, fulfilling the symbolism of the Old Testament feast. That day the church of Jesus Christ became the temple or dwelling place of the Holy Spirit on earth, testifying to all of Jesus Christ's ultimate victory over sin and death.

- *Read Leviticus 23:15–17.*

- *Read carefully Acts chapters 1 and 2.*

- *Remembering that Jesus was crucified at Passover and the Feast of the Unleavened Bread, read Acts 1:3–5 again and note the time frame. Do you think the time the disciples waited in the Upper Room for the coming of the promise of the Holy Spirit was a matter of days, or months?* _____

- *Read 1 Corinthians 15:3-6 and define the gospel in your own words.*

_____

_____

Notice how the first four feasts of Israel trace the Gospel as Paul outlines it in 1 Corinthians 15:3–6:

Christ died for our sins according to the scriptures	Passover
He was buried	Unleavened Bread
He rose again according to the scriptures	First Fruits
After that he was seen of [many witnesses]	Pentecost

The Feast of Trumpets—Second Coming

The first three feasts were all grouped together in the spring. Pentecost, or the feast of Weeks, came fifty days later. The final three feasts were similarly grouped together in the time of the fall harvest. The Hebrew calendar is lunar as compared to our solar calendar, making for no direct correspondence between the months mentioned in the Bible and the months of our calendar today. These final three feasts correspond to that period of the year marked by our late September and early October depending on the year.

Trumpets have played a prominent role throughout human history. For armies, they have been a vital means to communicate instructions in war or for ceremonial purposes at other times. For the general populace, trumpets also have been used both ceremoniously and practically. In the

Trumpets have played a prominent role throughout human history.

Old Testament law God used trumpets for various purposes in the nation of Israel.

- *Read Numbers 10:1–10. What are some of the ways you see in this passage that trumpets were used in Israel?*

_____

_____

God made trumpets central to one of the seven feasts of Israel. While English speakers call this the Feast of Trumpets after the language of the Old Testament, Jews call it *Rosh-Hashannah*, the beginning of the Jewish civil year; just as Passover begins the religious year. Jews also use the biblical language, *Yom Teruah*, the blowing of the *shofar*, ram's horn, or trumpet.

- *Read Leviticus 23:24–25.*

- *Read Psalms 81:3. To this day Jews use this verse on the Feast of Trumpets.*

- *Read Exodus 19:16–25 showing the preparation for Moses going up on Mount Sinai to receive the Ten Commandments. How would you describe the role and purpose of the trumpets?*

_____

_____

Just as the trumpets helped prepare Israel to receive God's presence and the Ten Commandments, this Feast of Trumpets plays a similar role each year in the nation of Israel. The Day of Atonement that we will study in just a moment followed immediately after the Feast of Trumpets. The Day of Atonement is the one day a year when the High Priest enters into the holiest place in the Tabernacle to present the blood sacrifice for the nation's sin. Just as the trumpets prepared Israel for the Ten Commandments, they prepared Israel for the day when God would deal with the consequences of their sin that would break the Ten Commandments.

The Old Testament prophets foresaw trumpets as associated with the coming of the Messiah.

- *Read Isaiah 18:3 and 27:13.*

- *Read Joel 2:1–3 and verse 21.*

- *At first glance do you think these passages announce Christ's first or second coming?*

_____

_____

To the New Testament believer the Feast of Trumpets casts a prophetic view toward Israel's return to God and the land. New Testament followers of Christ are also listening for the sound of a trumpet.

- *Read 1 Corinthians 15:50–54.*

- *Read 1 Thessalonians 4:13–19.*

Be careful not to confuse these trumpets that call out of the New Testament Church with the trumpets that herald the Messiah's return to his people Israel.

The Day of Atonement—Israel's Conversion

On this day the High Priest of Israel delivers up the sacrifice for the sin of the nation. Jews call this very sacred day *Yom Kippur*. The word atonement is used frequently in the Old Testament but only once in the New Testament in Romans 5:11. The meaning of the concept of atonement is to "cover." In the biblical sense, when the Hebrew people made the sacrifice on the Day of Atonement, they were asking God to cover their sin. Remember, sin would not be dealt with once and for all until Christ came as the Lamb of God. You can get an idea of the meaning of atonement by looking closely at the English word. Atonement is what we do to be "at one." On this day, Israel offered a sacrifice to atone for the sin of the nation and be at one with God.

- *Read Leviticus 23:26-32 and list what God required of Israel on the Day of Atonement:*

  _____

  _____

- *Read Romans 5:8–11. Is our atonement something we receive in the future or something we now possess?*

  _____

  _____

- *Are we required to keep the Feast of Atonement as the Jews did? Why or why not?*

  _____

  _____

- *Read Hebrews 9:1 through Hebrews 10:25. Does this passage support the answer you gave above?*

  _____

  _____

The prophetic meaning of this day is important for us to understand. It looks forward to the time when Israel will recognize the Messiah at

The meaning of the concept of atonement is to "cover."

his appearing, be converted, restored, and "at one" with their God as Christ's once and for all sacrifice for their sin will be applied to them.

The Feast of Tabernacles—The Kingdom Established on Earth

Finally, the Feast of Tabernacles commemorates those years Israel was in the desert wilderness dwelling in tents, booths or tabernacles. To this day many Jews celebrate this feast by setting up tents or other temporary dwellings in their yards or other places. From a very practical perspective, this feast reminds the Jewish people of the years their ancestors spent living in tents in the wilderness and makes them thankful for God's blessings. To remember where we have come from and how God has blessed us is always a good thing.

- *Read Leviticus 23:33–43. How long is this feast to last?* _____

- *Read another account of this feast in Deuteronomy 16:13–15. In addition to remembering how their ancestors lived in tents in the wilderness, what other purpose can you see in this passage?*

  _____

  _____

- *Read John 7:1–31. Based on what you have learned, what time of year did the events in this passage occur?*

  _____

  _____

- *Compare John 7:2 and 7:14. Approximately how many days pass between these two verses?*

  _____

  _____

- *Read 2 Corinthians 5:1–6 where Paul is speaking of our bodies. What is the figure Paul uses to speak of our physical bodies?*

  _____

  _____

- *That Paul would call our bodies "tabernacles" obviously points to their temporary status. Just as the other feasts have some application for our lives as New Testament believers, what type of application can you think of for the Feast of Tabernacles?*

  _____

  _____

- *Read John 1:1–14. When the "Word," Jesus Christ, became flesh, what did the Word do?*

_____

_____

When John says the *"Word was made flesh, and dwelt among us"* in verse 14, the Greek verb translated "dwelt" literally means "to tabernacle." Like the other feasts, the Feast of Tabernacles also has a future application pointing to that time when Christ will return to dwell (tabernacle) among men on this earth. This looks forward to the day when God's plan to set up his kingdom on earth will be reality at last.

Each of these feasts merits further study and has applications not only to future events but also to our daily living. Here, we looked briefly at these feasts simply to piece together one of the "borders" of the Bible's puzzle. Knowing a little about this series of seven feasts will help you understand the context as you encounter them in scripture. They outline the flow of God's plan not only for Israel but all mankind.

Other Feasts

As mentioned earlier, the Hebrew people observe other feasts and traditions in addition to the seven spelled out in Leviticus 23. Some have their origin in history and tradition; others come directly from scripture, such as the Feast of Purim taken directly from the events recorded in the Book of Esther, when the Jews were saved from their enemy.

Notice how the prophetic meaning of the first four was fulfilled in Christ's First Coming, while the final three await final fulfillment in Christ's Second Coming. Already you have seen several references to these feasts in the New Testament and understand them better than you did before.

Seven New Testament Mysteries

Taking the Mystery Out of Mysteries

The New Testament reveals some "mysteries" that make for some nice "edge pieces." The word "mystery" is applied to at least seven concepts or truths in the New Testament. Understanding these mysteries gives good structure for piecing together the other pieces of New Testament scripture.

Before going any further we need to understand the meaning of the word "mystery" in the context of the New Testament. The Greek word translated as "mystery" in our New Testament does not mean something unknowable, but rather something that was once concealed but now is fully revealed. We like to use the word "mystery" today to mean some-

Each of these feasts merits further study and has applications not only to future events but also to our daily living.

thing we do not know or understand. In the Bible, a mystery is something we can know and understand, though it was once hidden.

- *Read Ephesians 3:1–6 and describe the mystery Paul says was not known in previous ages.*

  _____

  _____

- *Can we understand this mystery today?*

  _____

  _____

In the Old Testament ages no one had any idea God would one day take Jew and Gentile to make one new creation in Christ. That Gentiles could come to God was never the issue. God's plan was always to take his truth to the peoples of the world through Israel. Today, Gentiles become followers of Christ directly, not through the Hebrew law of the Old Testament and converting to Judaism. Jews, too, come to Christ directly, not because of their Judaism.

- *Read Galatians 3:1–14. Is it possible to be justified, or saved from sin by keeping the Old Testament law? Explain your answer.*

  _____

  _____

- *Does Galatians 3:28 teach that being "in Christ Jesus" builds barriers between people, or breaks them down?*

  _____

  _____

- *Read Colossians 1:25-27. This is another example of the use of the word "mystery." What is the mystery Paul defines here?*

  _____

  _____

- *This passage in Colossians also shows the meaning of the word "mystery." Can we know and understand this mystery today?_*

- *Did anyone understand this mystery in Old Testament times?*

  _____

  _____

In the Bible, a mystery is something we can know and understand, though it was once hidden.

The essential elements are consistently the same. A mystery is something previously hidden, but now made known through divine revelation. As mentioned, there are no fewer than seven such mysteries uncovered or revealed in the New Testament. Understanding these mysteries is yet another way to help you organize the content of the New Testament. More than an aid to learning, we have a responsibility to understand and teach these mysteries just as the apostles and prophets passed them on to us.

- *Read 1 Corinthians 4:1–2 and tell what our responsibility toward the mysteries of God is.*

———————————————————————————

———————————————————————————

We have been using a puzzle analogy, beginning with the edge and corner pieces before fitting in the remaining pieces. That is a good analogy, but it is pretty one-dimensional. In recent years even jigsaw puzzles have gone multi-dimensional! Bible study has different dimensions as well. Rather than seeing dispensations, feasts, mysteries and the like as groupings along the single edge of a puzzle, think of them forming edges in different dimensions or layers.

For example, one dimension would be our book-by-book Bible survey in the previous chapter. Understanding the place, purpose and content of each book is one way to organize our thoughts in approaching the scriptures. In another dimension the feasts or New Testament mysteries form an edge that helps us organize our thoughts and study from a different perspective. I don't mean to confuse you, but firmly grasp that there is not just ONE WAY to study or understand the Bible. Biblical truth is absolute, not relative, yet has different dimensions.

Just as we did with dispensations and feasts, we will briefly examine the various mysteries revealed in the New Testament.

The New Testament Mysteries

The Mystery of God Manifested in the Flesh

- *Read 1 Timothy 3:16 and tell about this mystery.*

———————————————————————————

———————————————————————————

The Hebrew people always expected the Messiah. What they did not expect was the unique manner in which he arrived, born as a human baby in Bethlehem, yet still fully God! Some expected him to come as a political conqueror. Others thought he might appear as a religious leader or a combination of both. No one could have imagined he was to be born as a baby in a manger, God in human form. This was a mystery.

So much New Testament truth revolves around this wonderful mystery of God in the flesh. Jesus Christ is the God-Man. He is no less God than he was man, nor less man than he is God. This thread of truth runs through the entire New Testament from the Gospels to the Revelation.

The Mystery of the Church as One Body in Christ

- *Read Ephesians 3:1–6 and explain the mystery about Gentiles that Paul reveals.*

  _____

  _____

We have already discussed the mystery of God making both Jew and Gentile one new creation in Christ. Now, see how this thread runs through the entire New Testament. Even the apostles did not fully comprehend this mystery at first.

- *Read Acts 10. Do you think Peter understood the mystery Paul wrote about to the Ephesians?*

  _____

  _____

- *Read Acts 11:1–18. What was the impact of the events of Acts 10 on the apostles and other believers in Jerusalem when Peter shared with them what happened?*

  _____

  _____

- *Reflect on your understanding of the mystery Paul reveals in Ephesians. How should this affect your life and the way you relate to people who are not like you?*

  _____

  _____

The revelation of all people groups made one in Christ is one of Paul's greatest contributions to the Christian faith, and he dedicates much space in his epistles to the exposition and application of this great mystery.

Seven New Testament Mysteries

Mystery of God manifested in the flesh
–1 Timothy 3:16

Mystery of the Church as one in Christ
–Ephesians 3:1-6

Mystery of Christ indwelling the New Testament believer
–Colossians 1:27

Mystery of the restoration of Israel
–Romans 11:25-27

Mystery of the rapture of the Church
–1 Thessalonians 4:13-18

The Mystery of Christ Indwelling the New Testament Believer

- *Read Colossians 1 and pay close attention to verse 27 where Paul defines this mystery. What is it?*

_____

_____

The content of Colossians parallels that of Ephesians in many ways. Yet, there are significant differences. In Ephesians the emphasis is on the fact that we are all one in Christ. Repeatedly, we see the phrase "*in him,*" "*in the Lord,*" or something similar. Colossians gives the corresponding truth from a different perspective. Not only are we in Christ, he is in us—you and me! Imagine that! God lives inside the believer! No longer is God behind the veil in the holiest place in the temple. Now, his temple is in us. Much of the New Testament emphasizes our position in Christ, but the story is not complete without the equally important truth of Christ in us.

This is not to say that the perspectives of the mysteries revealed in Ephesians and Colossians are mutually exclusive. To the contrary! The two perspectives complement each other and the only difference is that of emphasis.

- *Read Ephesians 3:17. Does this agree with Colossians 1:27?*

_____

_____

- *In Romans 8:10 where is Christ said to be?*

_____

_____

- *In Galatians 4:19, what is Paul's desire for the Galatians?*

_____

_____

_____

- *Read Colossians 1:27–29 again. Do you see a common theme between Galatians 4:19 and what Paul says in Colossians 1:28? _____ What is it?*

_____

_____

The Mystery of the Restoration of Israel

- *Read Romans 11:25–27. Who has been blinded in part?*

  _____

  _____

- *What is the mystery Paul talks about here?*

  _____

  _____

On the surface one might not think of the restoration and future conversion of Israel as having much to do with New Testament Christianity. Yet this is vital for us to understand. God's grace that he extends to the church in this age does not mean he is finished with Israel. Israel is blinded only *in part* until the *fullness*, or salvation of the Gentiles is finished. God has made a wonderful new thing by bringing both Jews and Gentiles together in the church, the body of Christ. But, that does not mean God will not ultimately fulfill all the many promises he made to Israel.

Notice also the phrase "in part" leaves salvation in Christ open to any individual Jew, though the nation as a whole has still not turned to the Messiah. Paul was a Jew, of course, as were most followers of Christ for the first couple of decades of Christianity.

The early years of the Christian church were filled with conflict, division, and confusion between believers from a Jewish background and those who came to Christ from a Gentile background. We see some of those conflicts in Acts, and Paul's writings address this problem as well. These truths were mysteries. Old Testament Hebrews had no idea about these truths. Can you imagine the inner conflicts, confusion, and insecurity many of the early followers of Christ must have faced? Jewish believers struggled to think a Gentile could be a follower of Christ without becoming a Jew. Gentile believers just wanted to follow Christ, not convert to Judaism. Maybe now you can better understand better why it is important to be good stewards of these mysteries.

The Mystery of the Calling Out of the Church

- *Read 1 Corinthians 15:50–58 and describe the mystery Paul reveals here.*

  _____

  _____

  _____

- *Will the fulfillment of this mystery be gradual or immediate?*

  _____

  _____

- *When will this occur?*

  _____

  _____

- *Read 1 Thessalonians 4:13–18. What musical instrument does this passage have in common with the mystery of 1 Corinthians 15:50–58?*

  _____

  _____

- *When Christ comes where will those who are alive on earth at that time meet the Lord?*

  _____

  _____

The two passages above complement each other and speak of the same "mystery." Both scriptures teach what is commonly called the "rapture," or the calling away of the church of Jesus Christ shortly before his Second Coming. While one can find images and symbols of this future event in the Old Testament, as in the case of the "rapture" of Enoch shortly before the judgment of the flood (Genesis 5:24), this was clearly a mystery no one saw or understood in ages past.

The Mystery of Iniquity

- *Read 2 Thessalonians 2:7–9. Who will be revealed?*

  _____

  _____

The context of this passage deals with the coming of the infamous Antichrist during the worldwide tribulation leading to Christ's Second Coming. The Antichrist is "that Wicked" Paul mentions here to the Thessalonians.

- *Based on this same passage in Thessalonians, what is already working?*

  _____

  _____

- *Read 1 John 4:3. Do you think John might be talking about the same mystery Paul mentions to the Thessalonians?*

_____

_____

The theme of the coming Antichrist appears many times in the New Testament, and even many Old Testament prophets saw this culmination of evil in the time of the Messiah's coming. However, to those Old Testament prophets, the theme of the spirit of Antichrist being already at work was a "mystery." They did not understand the Messiah would come twice! No one did. Actually, had the Jews accepted the Messiah, all the prophecies could have been fulfilled at Christ's first coming. Tracing the working of the spirit of Antichrist through the Bible is another valuable "edge piece" of the puzzle.

The Mystery of Babylon the Great

- *Read Revelation 17:1–5. What is the full name of this mystery?*

_____

_____

The context here points to the coming empire of the Antichrist. Be careful to distinguish this from the preceding mystery. The mystery of iniquity points to the evil spirit of Antichrist. Here, we see the culmination of the spirit of Antichrist's work through the ages, unifying all religions except the Church of the New Testament under a single head, the very embodiment of evil. Both truths are closely related, of course, and they provide further doctrinal parameters for "framing" the New Testament.

The coming empire of Antichrist is a deep study and one even serious Bible students find difficult to understand completely or agree about among themselves. Here, a mystery is revealed to us even though its complete fulfillment is in the future. Though we struggle with many of the details, the theme of the coming empire of Antichrist runs throughout the Bible and provides still more edge pieces to the puzzle.

In this chapter we have seen different ways to divide up the Bible and trace common themes. We learned about dispensations, the feasts of Israel, and the New Testament mysteries. Above all, remember what I have stressed repeatedly: there is no "one way" to understand the Bible as long as you seek to understand it from God's perspective and not man's. God gives you many "handles" on the Bible to pick it up and learn his truth. We have compared this to finding edge pieces to a puzzle. Others may define the dispensations, feasts, or mysteries in slightly different ways. That's fine. The important thing is to realize that we are all trying to do the same thing, seeking to understand the Bible's absolute truth and ultimately to enhance our relationship with God. Just like measuring an absolute distance, we can do it with many different units of measure, but the distance does not change. What a comfort that is!

From our previous jigsaw puzzle analogy, we can return to the concept of the work of an effective investigator: A case can be analyzed and studied in a variety of ways—some more successful than others—but, the facts of the case never vary. What is required is the commitment to find the pieces of the puzzle, put them together and form a picture.

You can do that as well, as you prayerfully consider the investigative tools you now have and the various ways to organize biblical truth we have considered in this chapter. The truth of the Bible does not change, but there are many way to study, analyze, and apply that truth.

Notes

1. Kay Arthur is one who uses this illustration in her excellent book on Bible study. Kay Arthur, *How to Study Your Bible* (Eugene, OR: Harvest House Publishers, 1994), 22–23.

2. Do not confuse these with other feasts celebrated by Jews today. Here, we are speaking only of those seven feasts found directly in the Old Testament.

NOTES

What is required is the commitment to find the pieces of the puzzle, put them together and form a picture.

CHAPTER FOUR

That's Not Just Your Interpretation!

Have you ever had this experience? You have been discussing the Bible with another person. You have tried patiently not to be rude, pushy, obnoxious, holier-than-thou, or any other of those undesirable characteristics often associated with people discussing the Bible. Then, it happens. The person with whom you have been exchanging views looks up at you, and you already sense what is coming. "Well, that's just *your* interpretation." Sometimes, that is just another way to say, "End of discussion."

Equally difficult to deal with is the smug response that says, "Well, this is simply what the Bible says and that settles it! There is no interpreting to the Bible. We ought to just take the Bible literally for what it says and leave it at that." This statement usually means this person wants everyone else to share his or her understanding of what the Bible says. Anyone who sees something different is just plain wrong!

What can we say about interpreting the Bible? Is there any way to say whose interpretation is right or wrong? Honestly, we all interpret the Bible in light of our knowledge, understanding, culture and life experience. To say differently is just ignorance or arrogance.

Returning to our analogy between law enforcement investigation to find the truth at a crime scene and biblical investigation to find God's truth in the Bible, a tremendous amount of information can be gained by a traffic accident investigator who examines skid marks. By examining the skid marks a trained investigator can determine the type of car, speed it was traveling when the brakes were applied, amount of air pressure in the tires and what the surface of the street was like at the time of the accident. An untrained person just sees skid marks and may inaccurately interpret what they indicate about the accident. The skid marks stay the same, no matter how they are interpreted. The difference between the two interpretations is the amount of knowledge and experience, not the skid marks.

Yes, the Bible *is* absolute truth. We began with this premise. The problem is simply this: none of us has absolute understanding. We are all works in progress. And, sometimes we simply lack the necessary knowledge and experience to interpret it correctly.

Understanding the Bible is not a matter of *their* interpretation, *your* interpretation, or *my* interpretation. The only correct interpretation of scripture is that given by the author himself. The primary objective of

> **The only correct interpretation of scripture is that given by the author himself.**

Bible study is to discover God's intended, everlasting meaning when he inspired different individuals over the ages to write scripture under the inspiration of the Holy Spirit. The issue is what God means, not what we think. First, we need to be sure we understand what we mean by biblical interpretation.

What Does It Mean to Interpret the Bible?

Interpretation Is the Search for Meaning

Biblical scholar Paul Lee Tan defines interpretation as "to explain the original sense of a speaker or writer."[1] Interpreting the Bible is simply a matter of determining the meaning God intends for us to have in scripture. There is nothing mystical about this process. Interpretation is not seeking for some hidden or undiscovered meaning, but understanding as clearly as possible God's intent in the words of the Bible.

Understanding the Bible Is Not a Matter of Private Interpretation

In the first chapter we looked at 2 Peter 1:20–21 to appreciate how God spoke the words of scripture through human instrumentation. Let's revisit that passage with the objective of learning about interpretation.

* *Read 2 Peter 1:20–21 and describe what this verse says about private or personal interpretation.*

  _____

  _____

Peter's statement about scripture not being of "private interpretation" makes it clear that correct understanding of the Bible does not depend on anyone's individual interpretation. At issue is what God had in mind when he wrote the Bible, not what any person in particular thinks a certain scripture may mean. Sometimes, even the men God used to write scripture did not fully comprehend its significance.

* *Read 1 Peter 1:10–12 carefully. What was the conflict felt by these prophets of whom Peter speaks?*

  _____

  _____

* *What did God reveal to them as to the significance of their prophetic writings?*

  _____

  _____

The Christian's walk was never intended to be lived in isolation, but in celebration with other believers.

Again, the objective is to discover God's purpose in scripture. Our difficulty, of course, is that each one of us sees through the lens of our imperfect humanity. In 1 Corinthians 13:12 Paul expressed our struggle with this natural human condition by saying that now we see as though through a "glass darkly."

Every human being who reads the Bible is interpreting in one way or the other. We all tend to see the Bible through the eyes of our own language, culture, experience, prejudice and presuppositions. If our goal is to arrive at the meaning God intended, we must be honest with ourselves about this natural tendency we all share toward "private interpretation."

Until long after the invention of the printing press it was rare indeed for an individual Christian to have a personal copy of the Bible. Most people received their Bible knowledge when the Bible was read in public gatherings such as church services. While we would see this as very restrictive to our modern individuality, one benefit of this communal approach to the Bible was the protection afforded by the whole congregation coming together in one place at one time to discover God's intent in scripture. Solomon spoke of the wisdom available in the multitude of counselors (Proverbs 11:14; 15:22; and 24:6).

Conversely, this situation is potentially dangerous when a congregation has one leader claiming to be the only one who can correctly interpret scripture. That is simply another form of private interpretation, and it is infinitely more dangerous if the person with the private interpretation is an influential leader.

The point is to see the protection afforded by being in an environment where there is freedom to be honest and express one's opinion, yet all are able to come together and agree on the primary teachings of the Bible. The Christian's walk was never intended to be lived in isolation, but in celebration with other believers. None of us has perfect understanding, but together we are led by the Holy Spirit of God to arrive at biblical understanding that bears witness in the hearts of the overwhelming majority of believers.

The goal of this book is not to convince you to see my interpretation of the Bible, or for you to discover your own interpretation. Full disclosure demands that I tell you I have definite presuppositions as I approach the Bible. Everyone does. We all have perspectives that are a combination of many experiences and input from multiple sources. However, we need to honestly recognize the possibility that our understanding of the Bible is affected in some way by our prejudices and presuppositions. We can't help that we have certain predispositions. The mission of good Bible study, though, is to discern what God himself had in mind when he wrote it. We cannot do this without the help of the Holy Spirit.

- *Read 1 Corinthians 2:13–14 and describe what this verse says about man's wisdom, or personal interpretations.*

Aim at a Literal Interpretation of Scripture

Having put aside any search for hidden or personal meanings in the Bible, our goal is to simply observe what the Bible literally says. Some preachers express this sentiment by saying, "God said what he meant, and he meant what he said!" I've said that myself.

That statement certainly sounds good, but in reality there are several factors complicating our understanding. Interpreting the Bible is not quite as clean and simple as that sounds. In this chapter, we will learn some of the challenges of investigating the Bible and spend the rest of the book learning how to investigate the Bible to find God's interpretation and to understand correctly and literally what God said.

Paul Lee Tan again helps us understand what many have called "literal interpretation."

> **To interpret 'literally' means to explain the original sense of the speaker or writer according to the normal, customary, and proper usages of words and language. Literal interpretation of the Bible simply means to explain the original sense of the Bible according to the normal and customary usages of its language.**[2]

This literal interpretation of the Bible is sometimes called the Grammatical-Historical Method of interpretation. This simply emphasizes the need to consider the meaning of the words of scripture strictly within the historical context in which they were written and the normal and customary grammar of the language in which they were written.

Do Not Take Literally Too Literally!

To say we want to take the Bible literally does not mean we ignore normal and accepted figures of speech and the figurative use of words and phrases. For example, when Jesus said, "*I am the bread of life*" (John 6:35), he did not mean to say he was quite literally a loaf of bread! Any reasonable person understands this to be a figurative way to say that he is the very essence of life.

Every one of us uses figurative speech on a daily basis. We might say, "Love makes the world go 'round." We have no intention to mean that love literally is a fuel or machine that causes our planet to rotate in 24-hour cycles. When we speak of the sunrise or sunset, no one has to explain this is not to be taken literally. This is merely a figure of speech used even by scientists who clearly understand the sun does not "rise" and "set" in any literal sense. Yet, when we speak of the sunrise or sunset, no one tries to discern any hidden or secret meaning behind those figurative phrases used to literally describe the beginning and ending of our sunlight periods. The Bible uses figurative language, too.

Another point to understand is that a literal interpretation of scripture does not ignore the spiritual dimension of the Bible. The Bible is more than words on paper; it is a living book, God's book.

NOTES

The goal of this book is not to convince you to see "my" interpretation of the Bible, or for you to discover your own interpretation.... The mission of good Bible study, though, is to discern what God himself had in mind when he wrote it, and we cannot do this without the help of the Holy Spirit.

85

- *Read Hebrews 4:12–13. What is the figure that represents the Bible in these verses?*

  _____

  _____

- *What are the characteristics of the Bible mentioned in these verses?*

  _____

  _____

The Bible is more than just words on paper; it is a living book, God's book.

In the first chapter we said a potential error in Bible study is to see only the historical and grammatical aspect of the Bible and miss the spiritual depth of application. The opposite extreme that reads things into the Bible is just as fatal to good Bible study. The key to avoid reading our own thoughts into the Bible is to recognize that only the Holy Spirit, not our imagination, reveals that spiritual dimension of scripture (1 Corinthians 2:9–14). Furthermore, the Holy Spirit would never reveal any meaning outside the boundaries of the rest of the Bible or in contradiction to it.

The spiritual dimension of scripture revealed by the Holy Spirit is far different from a dangerous practice some call "spiritualizing" scripture. Spiritualizing scripture is taking verses and passages out of their natural context to give them some "spiritual" sense never intended by either the human author or the Holy Spirit.

Sometimes, a statement such as this precedes the practice of spiritualizing: "Well, this is what this scripture says to *me*," as though no one else might see the same thing. Yet, the person often goes on to give a meaning that has absolutely nothing to do with the context or God's original intention in having written the scripture. This is an example of "private interpretation." This approach to scripture gives rise to strange cults and strange groups that give faith a bad name.

However, let me clearly state that literal interpretation does not eliminate the possibility that a passage of scripture may have multiple applications of a single truth. An example of this is what David prayed in Psalm 51. This Psalm shows David dealing with the guilt and shame of the sin surrounding his affair with Bathsheba. David prays seeking forgiveness and restoration.

- *Read Psalm 51:11 and list the two requests David makes in this verse.*

  _____

  _____

This statement applies to David differently than it does to you and me. First, we must understand exactly what David says within the historical and grammatical context of those words. Here is a man broken by his sin and crying out to God for forgiveness. He quite naturally fears the consequences of what he has done. So, he prays God would not remove him from God's presence or take away the Holy Spirit, which was sometimes a sin consequence for the Old Testament Jew, but is not for the New Testament believer. That is what the scripture says, but the application for David is different than for the New Testament believer.

- *Read Hebrews 13:5 and Matthew 28:20. Will God ever leave us or forsake us?*

  _____

  _____

- *Read Ephesians 1:13–14. What is the seal of our salvation?*

  _____

  _____

- *If the Holy Spirit is the seal of our salvation, can the seal of our salvation be broken?*

  _____

  _____

- *Read Romans 8:9. Is it possible to belong to Christ and not have the Holy Spirit?*

  _____

  _____

- *Given what we have seen above, would the New Testament believer ever have reason to pray as David did that the Lord not take away his Spirit?*

  _____

  _____

It is impossible for New Testament followers of Christ to be separated from God's presence. While the conditions of David's prayer do not apply directly to our case today, we can learn much in this prayer about brokenness. Here's the point: Psalm 51:11 has only one meaning, but that meaning applies differently to David than to the New Testament believer.

The Reformer John Calvin is often quoted as saying, "The Word of God is inexhaustible and applicable at all times, but there is a difference between explanation and application, and application must be consistent with explanation." In other words, a verse or passage of the Bible has only one meaning, though that meaning may be applied in different applications as long as it does not conflict with the original intent of the passage. Our goal is to first determine the correct historical-grammatical meaning. Then, we can apply that meaning in different situations as long

It is impossible for New Testament followers of Christ to be separated from God's presence.

as we stay within the parameters of scripture. Remember the investigative principle: survey, then search.

Finally, a literal understanding of the Bible does not exclude the use of symbols, types, word pictures and certain figures of speech. Clearly, there are events, figures, objects and people in scripture having significance beyond the historical-grammatical surface. The story of the Passover in Exodus 12 details an actual, historical event of momentous importance in the history of Israel. But, this passage clearly has prophetic significance, foreshadowing Christ's sacrificial death for us as the Lamb of God.

- *Read 1 Corinthians 5:7 and write what Christ is called in this passage.*

We know the Passover is a picture, type or representation of the sacrificial death of Christ not because someone said so, but because the Bible itself says so. This is the difference between correct interpretation and private interpretation. This key to understanding all types, figures, and figurative language in the Bible is to allow the Bible to define them, not our imagination. We'll have much more to say about all this later.

Hermeneutics Is the Study of Correct Interpretation

Hermeneutics is not a disease even though it may sound like one. Chances are you've heard the word *hermeneutics* before in one context or another. This word appears frequently in relation to Bible study but also is used in a variety of professional and academic contexts. Broadly, hermeneutics is the science of interpretation or meaning. Biblically, hermeneutics is "the art and science by which one interprets the biblical text."[3]

The history of the word *hermeneutics* goes back to ancient mythology. The Romans called the god of science, writing, art and speech "Mercury," but earlier the Greeks called him "Hermes." In Greek mythology, Hermes was the messenger god. When the gods had communications for mankind, Hermes delivered the message. As this mythology permeated Greek culture, anyone who interpreted any material supposedly had received a portion of Hermes' mystical gifts. *Hermeneutics*, the name given to the science of interpreting the Bible is derived from Hermes.

With this understanding, let's look at a passage in Acts. Paul and Barnabas are beginning their first missionary journey and have come to the Galatian city of Lystra. Paul miraculously heals a man crippled from birth and the people are amazed.

- *Read Acts 14:8–12.*

- *What did the men of Lystra call Barnabas?*

_____

_____

_____

- *What did they call Paul?*

_____

_____

_____

Even the little bit of information above that we learned about Greek culture, helps us correctly interpret this passage. The people of Lystra thought these men must be gods and, since Paul was the messenger, he must be Mercury, or Hermes.

By New Testament times, the Greeks incorporated this into a verb, *hermeneuo*, which translates into English as "to interpret." A form of this word *hermeneuo* appears several times in the New Testament. Here are some examples from the first chapter of John. In each case the word hermeneuo is translated "interpreted" or "interpretation."

- *Read John 1:38. What does this scripture say is the interpretation of Rabbi?*

_____

_____

_____

- *Read John 1:41. What is the interpretation of "Messiah" according to this verse?*

_____

_____

_____

- *Read John 1:42. What does the Lord say is the interpretation for the name "Cephas?"*

_____

_____

_____

Hermeneutics is a science because it is based on certain principles and rules of understanding that we will begin to learn in the next chapter. Hermeneutics is also an art, because the application of those principles and rules can be rather complex and requires the development of skills gained only through time and experience.

Why Do We Need to Interpret the Bible?

If the objective is simply to read out of the Bible literally what it says, why do we need to bother with interpretation? That is a very good question. On the surface it sounds simple. In practice, though, understanding the Bible is sometimes not as clean and simple as we would wish. In the very first chapter we established that anyone can understand all they need to know about life, God, and forgiveness of sin simply by reading the Bible themselves. There are certain passages, though, where we need help. God has provided for help in understanding most of those difficult passages.

A story in Acts 8 is a good example. Philip was a gifted evangelist who was busy evangelizing Samaria when the Holy Spirit miraculously transported him to the desert to witness to a single Ethiopian eunuch. This eunuch was a high government official, a convert to Judaism who had come to Jerusalem seeking God through the truth of the scriptures. Returning home, he was still seeking and somewhat confused. Philip joins him in his chariot. Here is the exchange.

- *Read Acts 8:26–40.*

- *What did the eunuch tell Philip he needed to help him understand the scripture?*

    _____

    _____

The Ethiopian was an intelligent man who wanted to understand (interpret) the scriptures, yet he needed help. God provided Philip guide him.

- *Read Ephesians 4:11–12. In this passage Paul describes certain kinds of spiritually gifted men that God has given to the church. List those that Paul mentions:*

    _____

    _____

- *How does God use these individuals in the church?*

    _____

    _____

- *Read Romans 12:7 and 1 Corinthians 12:28. What kinds of ministries do you see in these two verses that are also mentioned in Ephesians 4:11?*

    _____

    _____

> **God has provided for help in understanding most of those difficult passages.**

- *If God has given teachers with the gift of teaching to the church, do you think there must be a need to help others understand (interpret) the scriptures?*

  _____

  _____

- *Read Luke 24:13–27, as the resurrected Christ appears to two disciples on the road to Emmaus. Overcome by the emotional events of the past days, they needed help to understand how all that happened was really the fulfillment of scripture. In Luke 24: 25–27, what does this passage say Jesus did with the scriptures?*

  _____

  _____

- *Read Luke 24:44–48 when the Lord appeared to others of his disciples. What does it say Jesus did with the scriptures?*

  _____

  _____

Even in the Old Testament we see the same principle of God using human instrumentation to help people understand scripture. A remnant of Jews had returned from captivity to rebuild the walls of Jerusalem. The people assembled in the streets of Jerusalem for Ezra to minister the Word of God to them.

- *Read Nehemiah 8:1–9. How did all the people understand the word of God?*

  _____

  _____

The Bible is enormous in scope, work, and infinitely deep. Struggling in places to understand its meaning does not imply a lack of intelligence or effort. At the same time, this does not mean we blindly accept what someone else teaches about the Bible. We maintain balance by remembering that the correct interpretation of scripture is not dependent on what anyone in particular thinks (private interpretation), but on the leadership of the Holy Spirit who lives in every genuine follower of Christ. God uses spiritually gifted, experienced leaders in the body of Christ to help others come to correct understanding of Bible passages.

Though there will always be disagreement about certain aspects of understanding the Bible, all genuine followers of Christ can agree on most of the essentials of God's truths, such as the inspiration and authority of scripture, the deity of Christ, salvation by grace and other fundamental truths. Stay away from anyone who gives the impression that he or she is one of the few people who truly understand the Bible, and everyone else is wrong.

The Bible is enormous in scope, work and infinitely deep.

Through the ages gifted teachers have passed down principles of biblical interpretation. Those principles are needed because of certain barriers that hinder understanding. This is why we need help. Before we learn some of the principles, let's consider some of those barriers.

The Language Barrier

The Bible was written in three ancient languages: Hebrew, Aramaic, and Greek. In the first chapter we discussed some of the challenges of literally translating from one language to another. We also considered the benefits of a formal translation such as the King James Version for serious Bible study, which allows you to focus on each scripture passage word for word, instead of a less specific paraphrase or version translated for equivalency of thought.

Adding to the difficulty of literally translating words, the whole meaning of words can change completely, depending on the culture and context. As I travel from one Spanish speaking country to another (or to other English speaking countries for that matter) I must be very careful with which words I use. A word that may be perfectly acceptable and accompanied by several good meanings in the dictionary may have a different or even vulgar meaning in a certain country. The difference is not what is written in the dictionary, but the use of that word in the context of a given culture.

Even a modern English translation can offer language problems due to cultural difference. For example, if the translation is done in England, a word may have a different meaning in the United States.

Furthermore, the meaning of words changes over time. While I have extolled the positive benefits of the KJV, it offers the disadvantage of some words whose meanings have changed radically over the years. The Bible student must be constantly aware of this possibility.

In any version of the Bible, the translators make choices that are not necessarily a matter of right or wrong translation, but between two or more real possibilities. For example, 1 Corinthians 16:22 in the KJV reads, "If any man love not the Lord Jesus Christ, let him be *Anathema Maranatha*." Those final two words are not translated! They are "transliterated," meaning that the original words are put into the manuscript without being translated. There is definitely a language barrier there! In this case a teacher who has studied Greek needs to explain that the word *anathema* means "accursed," and that an everyday Aramaic expression speaking of the Lord's coming in judgment was maranatha, "The Lord comes."

Issues of grammar, syntax and idioms, a style of speech peculiar to a certain language, are examples of other challenges that make gifted teachers such a blessing. But, the job of the teacher is not to act as an intermediary or a mediator between you and the Bible. A teacher is to be a facilitator, who equips you with the necessary rules, principles and information in order for you to understand the Bible for yourself.

The Culture Barrier

Having commented on the connection between language and culture, culture itself is a big obstacle for properly understanding scripture. Every group of people in the world forms a unique culture that is constantly evolving.

A beautiful example of the importance of cultural understanding is Jesus' encounter with the Samaritan woman at Jacob's well in John 4. This woman had been married five times and was living at that time with a man to whom she was not married. To avoid the stigma of her situation, she would come to the well in the midday heat when no other women were likely to be there. As she approached the well that day, a stranger was there—Jesus. To our ears today the Lord's first words sound very curt and almost rude. "Woman, give me to drink" (John 4:7). Doesn't it seem Jesus is being a little demanding of a stranger? He has not even exchanged any introductory pleasantries.

The average reader is not aware of the strong traditions, rituals and social contracts involving water in the Middle East of those days. An approach like Jesus used in that setting established a social contract of friendship for people who offer water to a stranger. We hear, "Woman, give me to drink." She heard, "I want to be your friend." You can imagine what a shock that must have been to her!

Basic understanding of culture can make a tremendous difference to proper interpretation of the Bible. No one can learn everything about the cultures in the Bible, but we can and will learn some basic tools and principles to assist us in proper, not private, interpretation of the Bible

The Literary Barrier

In addition to the meaning of individual words, the historical and grammatical contexts and cultural considerations, the particular literary genre of a passage of scripture also affects interpretation. Several categories of writing appear in the Bible – poetry, parables, proverbs, historical narrative and letters (epistles), some to a broad group of readers and some to specific persons or people in a certain city or region.

Reading the book of Romans is almost like reading a legal brief at times. The approach needed to understand Romans is far different than that required for Song of Solomon or Job. The parables of Jesus are totally different in nature than the Psalms. We will learn tools and principles to assist us in learning to understand these different types of biblical literature.

Why Can't Everyone Agree on the Same Interpretation?

This is another good question. If there is only one correct interpretation of scripture and interpreting the Bible is simply a matter of the Holy Spirit leading us to apply a given set of principles, rules and tools to understand God's original intent in scripture, why is there so much disagreement?

Any number of reasons could explain why people do not understand the same meaning in a given passage of scripture. Before examining some of those reasons, we must remember this fundamental truth: there is only one meaning of any passage of scripture and it is never a matter of private interpretation.

Another way to express this fundamental truth is to say Biblical interpretation is objective, not subjective. The Bible is God's inspired revelation to mankind. The Bible's meaning does not depend on what we think or imagine. Our job is to learn exactly what God meant to say. God doesn't change and his truth doesn't change. Therefore, Biblical interpretation is not subjective or relative, but objective.

We approach scripture, then, with this presupposition: the correct meaning is given to us by the Holy Spirit as we read OUT OF the Biblical text exactly what it says, not what we may READ INTO the text, influenced by our preconceived ideas and opinions.

Seminary professor Howard Hendricks illustrates the objective nature of God's truth and the subjective nature of our experience by revealing he is color-blind.[4] He especially has difficulty distinguishing between blues and greens. If a student comes to his class wearing a green sweater and Dr. Hendricks might compliment that student for the beautiful blue sweater, but the sweater is still green no matter what Dr. Hendricks' perception may be.

That example is similar to what happens when different believers have differing opinions about the meaning of a passage of scripture. The one divinely intended meaning of scripture does not change, even though several people have differing perspectives of that same passage. The truth of scripture is absolute. Our understanding is limited by our human condition and other factors. Let's consider some examples of why different people can hold different views of the same scripture.

Some Do Not Pay Attention to Every Word

How many times do we hear someone say, "Money is the root of all evil?" This is one of those expressions repeated almost universally in a host of settings, not just in church. However, check out what the Bible really says.

> *Biblical interpretation is objective, not subjective. The Bible is God's inspired revelation to mankind. The Bible's meaning does not depend on what we think or imagine. Our job is to learn exactly what God meant to say. God doesn't change and His truth doesn't change. Therefore, Biblical interpretation is not subjective or relative, but objective.*

- *Read 1 Timothy 6:10.*

- *What does the Bible actually say is the root of all evil?*

  _____

  _____

The above example is classic, but clearly illustrates why different people could have differing ideas about the meaning of a passage of scripture. The message of the Bible does not change, only the perspective of people who read it. Not paying attention to every word yields a good chance of distorted or incorrect interpretation.

Some Twist Scripture to Fit Their Own Ideas, Opinions, and Traditions

- *Read 2 Peter 3:15–16. What were some people doing to Paul's writings and the other scriptures?*

  _____

  _____

- *What are the characteristics of people who would do this according to Peter?*

  _____

  _____

To "wrest," means to wrestle, twist, or distort. Even in the first century there were people taking Paul's words out of context and twisting them even before the New Testament was completed. We should not be surprised to see the same practice continue to this day. Some twist the meaning of scripture purposefully and maliciously to justify their sin, their religious tradition, or to manipulate others. If we are honest, we must admit that it is easy for any of us to view scripture through our preconceived ideas. We don't even have to try; it just happens.

Scripture twisting has been going on since the Garden of Eden. God's instructions to Adam and Eve were clear.

- *Read Genesis 2:16–17.*

- *What freedom did God give to Adam?*

  _____

  _____

- *One tree was the exception. Which was it?*

  _____

  _____

- *Specifically, what was Adam prohibited from doing with that tree?*

  _____

  _____

- *What was the consequence of disobedience?*

  _____

  _____

- *Read Genesis 3:1–6 and observe how God's words were quoted.*

  _____

  _____

When the serpent appears, his first words cast doubt on what God really said. "*Yeah, hath God said…*"? (Genesis 3:1 KJV) is equivalent to how one might say today, "Is that what God really said?"

- *Read again Eve's response in Genesis 3:2–3. Do you see any difference between what God said in Genesis 2:16–17 and what Eve quoted in Genesis 3:2–3?*

  _____

  _____

Eve responded by quoting God, a very good response. But, she left out the word "freely" and revealed her focus was on the single prohibition, not God's abundant provision. Poor Eve! She had only two verses in her "Bible," but she failed to memorize them or interpret them correctly. The serpent aggressively moved in for the kill.

- *Read what Satan says in Genesis 3:1. Carefully compare that passage once more with God's words in Genesis 2:16–17. Do you find any differences between what Satan says and what God actually said?*

  _____

  _____

Instead of leaving out words of scripture, Eve added a phrase that God didn't say. God said, "*thou shalt surely die*" (Genesis 2:17), a certainty. But Eve said, "*…lest ye die*" (Genesis 3:3), a possibility. Eve didn't flinch at this private interpretation. She wasn't paying attention to every word.

- *Read Satan's words in Genesis 3:4. How does this match up with what God said?*

  _____

  _____

The Bible is infinitely deep; we are not.

Once bad interpretation controlled the conversation, the serpent was able to openly deny the truth of scripture. Ye shall not surely die (Genesis 3:4). Sin followed immediately as Eve ate of the forbidden fruit and gave it to her husband. Twisting scripture is dangerous and the result can be catastrophic.

Scripture Is Infinitely Deep

The Bible is infinitely deep; we are not. This is another reason people often disagree as to the truth of scripture. Even if all of us were equally skilled in Bible study, there would still be parts of the Bible that we could not fully understand. If we could understand absolutely everything, we would be equal to God. That is not going to happen. While accessible to all, the Bible will always have those deep passages we'll never fully understand.

To borrow Howard Hendricks' illustration again, there will always be areas of the Bible where we are all a little "colorblind." So, don't let it affect you to see sincere believers differ in interpretation of portions of scripture. There is only one meaning of scripture, and it does not change. With our imperfect human nature we struggle to arrive at that meaning. But God makes the most important things clear to any Bible student who follows the proven steps to investigate the Bible.

Remember that in the New Testament, Christians are repeatedly called "children" as in 1 John 5:2. *"By this we know that we are the children of God…"* As we noted earlier, the God who gave us salvation as a gift (Ephesians 2:9) wants his children to obey his commandments. Why would God save us, instruct us to obey his commandments, then state them in words his children can't understand? God commands in plain talk!

Example of Private Interpretation

Allegorical Interpretation

In the first chapter we met Origin of Alexandria who popularized the allegorical method of interpreting the Bible. This is the approach that "sees" hidden meanings in scripture that simply are not there. Proponents of this approach view the plain meaning of scripture as almost a side issue. They invent meanings that come from their imagination and personal agendas and that have nothing to do with God's intent.

During the Middle Ages the allegorical approach flourished and became increasingly mystical. It involved the belief that a person can have direct, subjective communion with God, based on feelings instead of being based on properly interpreted scripture. Some theologians list what they term the "mystical approach" as a different category than the allegorical method, though all agree they are closely related.

NOTES

Let's say someone in Kansas City is praying about whether to take a new job in Chicago, many miles to the north. One day, Deuteronomy 2:3 catches their eye. "Ye have compassed this mountain long enough: turn ye northward." Completely ignoring the context, they take the words "turn ye northward" as God's special revelation to them to move north to Chicago. While not wanting to question anyone's sincerity, this is an obvious case of "private interpretation," having nothing to do with the message of the scripture.

The fact that these "hidden meanings" come from the mind of the interpreter is what categorizes them as private interpretation. Our goal in interpreting the Bible is to discover the clear meaning of scripture God intended it to have.

Devotional Application

This approach takes words, phrases and whole passages from the Bible and applies them to personal life with no thought for their context and God's intended meaning. People who use this method simply apply scripture to life situations however they seem to fit, whether they fit God's clear meaning or not.

For example, some preachers and teachers have taken Matthew 10: 19 as an excuse not to prepare or study. *But when they deliver you up, take no thought how or what ye shall speak: for it shall be given you in that same hour what ye shall speak* (Matthew 10:19). Even a casual reading of this passage in its context reveals Jesus had nothing of the sort in mind when he spoke these words to his apostles when he sent them to announce the arrival of the Kingdom to the nation of Israel.

Some people read their Bibles expecting God to speak to them in some specific way. They take words out of context and apply them to life situations with no thought for the intended meaning and context. Yes, God *does* speak to us as we read scripture, but he speaks within the natural and normal context of the Bible.

Humanistic or Rationalistic Interpretation

Some approaches to scripture begin with the assumption the Bible is NOT divinely inspired and must be considered no differently from any other book. This approach seeks to explain away supernatural elements of the Bible through humanistic or rationalistic theories.

- *Read John 11. What happens when Jesus commands the tomb of his friend Lazarus to be opened?*

_____

_____

Those who see the Bible from a purely humanistic or rationalist point of view would suggest, for example, that Lazarus had been in a coma when Jesus came to him. Lazarus must have revived, and in ignorance the disciples attributed this to Jesus having raised him from the dead. This humanistic predisposition prompts then to offer a rational explanation instead of accepting that a miracle occurred. Accepting that a miracle occurred does not fit into the preconceived ideas.

Humanism and rationalism are no respecters of persons or miracles. Proponents of these views must even explain away the resurrection of Christ. Each Easter many newspapers carry articles by religious liberals or modernists who suggest Christ did not really die on the cross, but merely passed out. Later, having been placed in a cool cave-like tomb, he revived, and it was commonly reported he rose from the dead.

This also is private interpretation, seeking personal explanations for scriptures that do not fit one's presuppositions. This workbook is based on a set of presuppositions, too, believing that Jesus is the Christ, the Son of God, and that the Bible is different than any other book because it is the divinely inspired word of God without error. Rather than change scripture, we are committed to allow scripture to change our lives by adjusting to God's truth. Our goal is to read OUT OF the Bible what is really there and not read INTO the Bible things that proceed from our imaginations or prejudices.

Preparing for the Process of Interpretation

This chapter concludes our foundational work of assimilating the "big picture" of scripture. Let me summarize four simple commitments you must have before going any farther in learning the specific tools and principles of Bible study.

Make Sure You Know God as Both Savior and Lord

To understand the Bible, you must know the author of scripture and relate to him on the basis of his grace. Be certain of your salvation. If you are already a follower of Christ and have the assurance of eternal life, make sure your relationship with God is solid so as to facilitate the Holy Spirit's ministry of leading you into all truth.

Assume the Bible Is the Word of God

Though you do not understand everything you read in the Bible, commit to obey what you *do* understand because it is God's Word. Do not change the Bible to fit your understanding, but change your understanding and actions to fit the truth of God's Word.

Pray for Understanding

Interpreting the Bible is a spiritual discipline. The Psalmist gives us a good model to follow each time we approach the Word.

- *Read Psalm 119:34.*

- *Write this brief verse out in your own hand.*

_____

_____

- *What is David's request?*

  _____

  _____

- *What two things does David promise to do in return?*

  _____

  _____

- *Read James 4:2. Why do we not have the things we desire?*

  _____

  _____

- *How should you connect the example of Psalms 119:34 with the truth of James 4:2 as you prepare to study the Bible?*

  _____

  _____

Hebrew scribes had elaborate rituals to follow as they made copies of the scriptures. Before writing the name of God, for example, they would get up and ceremoniously cleanse themselves. If they went to that effort to ensure future generations would receive the precise, exact words of God, can't we be disciplined enough to initiate our Bible study with an attitude of prayer?

Commit to Learn Principles and Tools of Bible Study

Just as you committed to set aside a daily time to be with God in his word, commit just as seriously to set aside time and effort to improve your Bible study skills. The next section of this workbook will teach you several basic principles of Bible study.

Notes

1. Paul Lee Tan, *The Interpretation of Prophecy* (Winona Lake, IN: Assurance Publishers, 1974), 29.

2. Ibid., p. 29

3. Mal Couch, gen. ed., *An Introduction to Classical Evangelical Hermeneutics: A Guide to the History and Practice of Biblical Interpretation* (Grand Rapids: Kregel Publications, 2000), 32.

4. Howard Hendricks

CHAPTER FIVE

Learn to Ask the Right Questions

Comparing Bible study to detective work, the first four chapters concentrated on seeing the big picture just as a detective might do coming upon a crime scene. Now, we move on to another phase of our investigative work. Having surveyed the big picture, the detective begins the questioning process. There will be questions for the victim (if the victim is alive and able to talk), witnesses and any potential suspects. There are also many questions the detective must ask himself or herself, contemplating how various pieces of evidence, eyewitness testimony, and other factors fit together. Learning investigative principles of Bible study also requires skill in asking questions.

I've discussed this similarity between Bible study and detective work with several friends in law enforcement. All agree that asking the right questions is an essential skill in solving a crime. One police officer added that the best detectives make it a point to ask only those questions for which they already know the potential answers. In other words, a good detective doesn't just ask questions haphazardly. Asking the right questions involves purposeful strategy and thoughtful analysis.

As Bible students we must not only learn to find and ask the right questions, but we must consider the potential answers. In this chapter, we will begin to lay the foundation for such a strategy by learning three basic questions essential to any good investigative Bible study strategy. In the next two chapters, I will give you three pivotal questions each, for a total of nine. These are not the only questions you could ask, of course, but they will form a good foundation for further study.

These first three questions should be part of our natural approach to book, chapter or verse in the Bible. We need to ask these questions every time we come to a passage of scripture—no exceptions. The other questions we will learn are also important, but these first three are essential to proper Bible interpretation. The three are related, and all contribute to a better understanding of the context of a specific passage of the Bible.

Becoming a Good Invesigator of the Bible

Part One: Getting the Big Picture

Part Two: Developing Investigative Skills

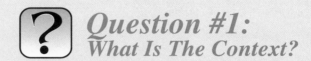

Question #1:
What Is The Context?

No principle of Bible study is more important than context. I mention this so often in preaching, that the people in our church respond in unison when I ask the question, "What's the first rule of Bible study?"

"Context!"

As a pastor, I believe an important function of my ministry is to embed good principles of Bible study deep within the hearts of the members of our church. I constantly point out how sound principles of Bible study lead us to proper interpretation of God's truth.

My job is to equip them to understand the Bible for themselves. Good teachers are needed in the body of Christ, yet individual Christians should have the confidence skill to study the Bible to discover God's truth and application for their lives, even when a gifted teacher is not around.

Context Is a Matter of Common Sense and Courtesy

Sometimes people ask me where these rules and principles of Bible study come from. Some of them come directly out of the Bible. Others result from observation of many Bible students over the centuries. This principle of first examining the context of a passage of scripture is rooted in common sense and courtesy.

How many times do we hear celebrities and politicians quoted out of context? It happens all the time, doesn't it? Have you ever been involved in an unpleasant situation at work, school or at home because of something others thought you said, but your words were totally taken out of context? This has happened to just about everyone at one time or another.

We do not like it when our words are taken out of context and twisted to give a different meaning, or opposite of what we meant to say. Why should we treat God with any less respect and courtesy than we would expect for ourselves? Much bad teaching is the result of people taking words and passages from the Bible out of context[1].

Here's a simple example of how this works. I have never known anyone to suggest this seriously because the example is obviously absurd, but one could claim accurately that the Bible says there is no God. That's right! The Bible clearly says there is no God.

- *Read Psalm 14. Notice the clear statement in verse 1, "there is no God."*

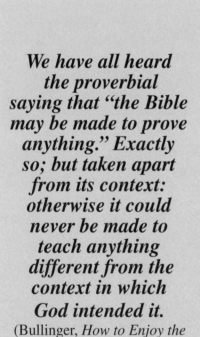

We have all heard the proverbial saying that "the Bible may be made to prove anything." Exactly so; but taken apart from its context: otherwise it could never be made to teach anything different from the context in which God intended it.
(Bullinger, *How to Enjoy the Bible*, 264–265)

- *What is the context of those remarks?*

_____

_____

The Bible contains thousands upon thousands of words! By the sheer volume of material and scope of content, one could prove almost anything by taking words of the Bible out of their proper context. This is not just a theory. It happens all the time!

Kay Arthur correctly points to the origin of the word "context. "The word *context* means 'that which goes with the text.' In general, then, context is the environment in which something dwells, the setting in which something exists or occurs."[2] Arthur illustrates the importance of context by the word "trunk." What is meant? A car trunk? An elephant's trunk? A tree trunk? Someone's swimming trunks? A large piece of luggage? The only way to answer that question is to know the context.

In the Bible "faith" is a very common word. Sometimes faith means the act of believing, as in "having faith in God." Other times, the same word means the content of what we believe, as in our need to "defend the faith." "Faith" is used in both senses in the Bible, and only the context guides us to determine which of these two meanings is intended.

- *Read Ephesians 2:8. In this context does the word "faith" mean the act of believing, or the content of what we believe?*

_____

_____

- *Read Jude 1:3. In this context does the word "faith" mean the act of believing or the content of what we believe?*

_____

_____

Every Part of the Bible Has a Context

Whether we look at a single word, a verse or a whole chapter, we must always be aware of the larger context. Even the individual books of the Bible fall into a larger, "big picture" context as we saw in chapter two.

Context is so important because it can totally alter the meaning of words, phrases and sentences. In interpreting the Bible, nothing is more critical than context. Bad doctrine or heresy more often than not is simply truth out of context.

If someone suggested to you that we should worship pink worms with green polka dots that control the universe from their nest miles beneath the surface of the earth, I would hope you would not pay much attention! But, if someone came to you generously quoting scripture and laying out logical arguments, the appeal would be infinitely greater. The greater the appearance of truth, the more dangerous is the heresy. A

Context is so important because it can totally alter the meaning of words, phrases, and sentences. In Biblical interpretation nothing could be more critical than context. Bad doctrine or heresy, is more often than not simply truth out of context.

heretic can speak 95% truth. A 5% portion of truth taken out of context, though, can have eternal consequences.

Learning to pay attention to the context can begin with something as simple as examining the first verse of a Bible book. Consider the book of Obadiah.

- *Read Obadiah 1:1. According to this verse Obadiah's prophecy concerns what group of people?*

_____

_____

This little one chapter book informs us in the very first verse that the subject of Obadiah's prophecy is God's coming judgment on the nation of Edom, not Israel. Most of the Old Testament prophets ministered to the Hebrew people, either the northern tribes of Israel, or the southern kingdom of Judah. As we learn in Obadiah some prophets received messages for the nations surrounding Israel. Before starting a verse by verse analysis of a passage, the observant Bible student takes into account the correct context.

James provides a New Testament example of how important it is to ask the right questions concerning context.

- *Read James 1:1. Who are the intended readers of James' letter?*

_____

_____

A singular fact leaps off the page! James is writing to Jews. Specifically, he writes to "*the twelve tribes*" that had been scattered throughout the world during centuries of persecution.

Does this mean the book of James has no message to Christians? Of course not! Remember that in the early years of the church almost all followers of Christ were from a Jewish background. Not until Acts 10, several years after the events in Acts 2, did the first Gentile come to Christ without first converting to Judaism: Cornelius, a Roman centurion. Only after the events in Acts 11 about the church in Antioch of Syria did Gentiles begin to convert openly to Christ in large numbers without first becoming converts to Judaism.

The opening words of the book of James instantly give us important information to understand the context. That the book is specifically addressed to Jewish Christians strongly suggests James was written in the early years of Christianity before Gentiles became the majority in the church. In James' mind he presupposes that his readers are familiar with the Old Testament. James himself was a Jew, so he writes from the perspective of understanding Jewish culture.

Does the fact this letter is addressed to the twelve tribes mean there is no application to New Testament Christians today? Again, the answer is a resounding no!

- *Read 2 Timothy 3:16. What portion of scripture is divinely inspired and profitable to the New Testament believer?*

_____

_____

"*All scripture*" includes James. Asking the question of context protects us from incorrect assumptions as we study James. The recipients of James' letter were "Christians;" they just didn't know it yet! Believers were not called "Christians" until Acts 11:26 mentions the church in Antioch. It took some time before the name was commonly used.

When the word "Christian" was first used, Paul had not written a single word of scripture. And, Paul was the one who gave us the revelation of the mystery that Jew and Gentile are one in Christ. Several decades passed before all believers began to fully comprehend the radical new nature of New Testament Christianity.

Before mindlessly lifting verses out of James to apply to our lives today, we must be sure we correctly understand what those verses really say and mean. That requires properly understanding the context, and taking into account the Jewish background against which James wrote these words.

Hebrews, the book immediately before James, has a similar Jewish context. In this case one doesn't even have to read the first verse. The name of the book, Hebrews, makes that clear. The same things we learned about the context of James apply to Hebrews. Both these books have passages that are controversial and attract strange interpretations. While difficult passages exist in both books, much of the misunderstanding can be clarified by taking into account the Jewish context.

Later in this book, we will see some examples of how this Jewish context plays an important role in learning to use investigative principles of Bible study. Right now, observe that most of what is needed to understand context is to simply pay attention and use our common sense.

Also, notice the importance of that "big picture" which is so important in any investigation to understand context. Often, when emphasizing context, we tend to pay attention only to the immediate context of the words of scripture. Though immediate context should always be of utmost concern, complete understanding must take the larger context into account.

The Gospels Illustrate the Importance of Context

This is yet another example of how important it is to see how the whole Bible fits together. As followers of Jesus Christ, we love the Gospels because they tell about the life and ministry of our Lord. The Gospels have a proper context, too. A very important statement in Hebrews sets our parameters.

Right now, observe that most of what is needed to understand context is to simply pay attention and use your common sense.

- *Read Hebrews 9:17. According to this verse what makes a testament validated or in force?*

  _____

  _____

Think about what this verse says. If your rich uncle included you in his last will and testament, your inheritance does not become effective until his death. I realize that today we have all sorts of financial vehicles, such as "living trusts" and the like, but traditionally, someone's last will and testament only becomes effective upon their death.

In the immediate context of Hebrews 9:17, the author speaks of how Christ's death makes the New Testament effective and grants us free access to God and forgiveness of sin. Properly speaking, the "new testament" does not begin until Christ's sacrificial death. The new testament we are speaking of here does not refer to the collection of 27 books that make up the second major division of your Bible: it refers to the new agreement, covenant, promise, or testament God offers to us in place of the old testament of the law.

Seeing the four Gospels as a transition from the Old to the New Testament has profound impact for correctly interpreting the Bible. Even though the Gospels tell us the story of the life and ministry of Jesus Christ, we should view the bulk of the four Gospels as transitional. That means we should not go to the Gospels and blindly take verses out of context to make direct application to the New Testament church. Matthew 10 illustrates what I am saying.

- *Read Matthew 10. According to verses 5–7 to whom is Jesus talking?*

  _____

  _____

- *To whom is Matthew 10:8 written?* _____

- *To whom is Matthew 10:19–20 written?* _____

- *To whom is Matthew 10:34 written?* _____

In this chapter, Christ selects and sends out his 12 apostles to announce the coming of the kingdom to Israel. This is the official offer of the Kingdom of Heaven to Israel. Some churches would love to lift verse eight out of context and use it as a pattern for their worship services. As noted in the last chapter, some preachers love to claim verses 19 and 20 as an excuse not to study and prepare. People with certain political agendas could use verse 34 with dangerous consequences. However, verses five through seven put things in the proper perspective of Jesus giving the 12 apostles their marching orders.

This passage makes perfect sense when we understand the Lord is not sending out New Testament missionaries, but Jewish apostles to the nation of Israel to extend to the Jews an official and legitimate invitation to receive the King and his Kingdom. It was due to their rejection of Him, recorded in chapters 11 and 12, that the Gospel was extended to the gentiles as we are familiar today.

None of this means these passages such as Matthew 10 have no application for us today. Certainly they do! As we saw in 2 Timothy 3: 16, all scripture is inspired and applicable to all believers. But, we must learn to interpret and make those applications properly. We'll learn more about making proper applications later. For now, the important thing is to be very careful that we understand the big picture.

Learn to Use This "Context" Principle by Good Technique and Practice

Good Bible study must be rooted in proper understanding of the context, both the immediate context and the larger context of scripture. Below is a checklist of the context questions to ask ourselves as we approach the study of any portion of scripture.

1. ***The context of the book:*** Where does this particular book of the Bible fit into the "big picture" of scripture?
2. ***The context of the chapter:*** Where does this particular chapter fit in relationship to the rest of the book and to God's purpose for including it in the Bible?
3. ***The context of the passage or verse:*** Where does this verse or these verses fit in relationship to the thrust, theme and context of the chapter?
4. ***The context of the words:*** What do the individual words mean according to the history, grammar, literary usage, and context of the larger context?

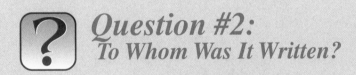

Question #2:
To Whom Was It Written?

This is the second of the three fundamental questions we ask in our approach to any scripture. First, what is the context? Then, to whom was this passage written?

Do you remember the comment from the police officer about the wisdom of asking questions with known answers? "To whom was it written" illustrates this principle. Asking to whom a passage of scripture is written only allows for a limited number of answers.

The Bible Addresses Three Basic Groups of People

Many different ethnic groups make up our world. To keep things simple, though, we can see the Bible as addressing three basic groups of people. Determining which of these three basic groups a passage addresses puts us on a solid footing to understand the proper context of a biblical passage. Paul mentions all three of these groups in a single verse in 1Corinthians.

- *Read 1 Corinthians 10:32. What are the three groups of people we are told not to offend here?*

_____

_____

The Hebrew people, or Jews as they are commonly called today, are the physical descendants of Abraham, Isaac and Jacob. In the Bible, Gentiles are everyone else who is not Jewish. Following the death, burial and resurrection of Jesus Christ, a new group of people came into existence—the church. God revealed to Paul that in the church there is no Jew or Gentile, but an entirely new classification made up of the followers of Christ.

When we ask to whom was a passage written, we know the answer will be to Jews, Gentiles, the church, a combination of two of them, or all three.

Be careful here! Don't think for a minute those passages of scripture not addressed directly to you as a New Testament Christian have no value for your life. **ALL** scripture is profitable according to 2 Timothy 3:16. Determining to whom a passage is addressed simply assists you in more complete understanding of the context and how to correctly apply the biblical truth to your life.

All Scripture Is FOR Us; Some Scripture Is Written TO Us

We have repeatedly seen in 2 Timothy 3:16 that all scripture can be profitably applied to our lives. The issue is whether a portion of scripture applies to us directly or indirectly. Let me illustrate.

Let's say my grandfather left a valuable piece of waterfront property to me in his will. Not long after his funeral, I am sitting in his attorney's office for the reading of his will. Aside from the normal legal language that confirms the transfer of that beautiful property to my name, I discover my grandfather had instructed his lawyer to read a letter to me he had written before his death. In the letter, Granddad offered me a wealth of wisdom and insight. He discussed his joy at being able to leave me a piece of property that would ensure my financial security, but also gave me wonderful counsel to deal with both the privileges and responsibilities of that inheritance. He shared some of his own experiences and lovingly made application to my life.

Now, that did not really happen. I can assure you I have no supervaluable property anywhere! But, were such a thing true, you might imagine I would be overwhelmed at my grandfather's love toward me.

When we ask to whom was a passage written, we know the answer will be one of those three groups of people or a combination of these groups: Jew, Gentile, or Church.

I had a wonderful relationship with my real grandfather, and I can tell you I would have valued a letter like that more than the property itself. What if I decided the letter was so valuable I wanted to share it with others? I could make copies of that beautiful, insightful letter to give to friends or others I felt would benefit from Granddad's wisdom.

Suppose someone read the letter, appreciated the wisdom, could directly apply it to his life, then showed up at the county courthouse to try and claim the deed to the property? Of course, they couldn't! The property was given only to me, even if every word of the letter had meaning and application to others, as well.

This is exactly the point in distinguishing between these three groups of people in the Bible. God gave Abraham and his descendants a beautiful piece of property as described in detail in the Old Testament. I can learn and benefit from every word in the Old Testament, but the land of Israel still belongs to the children of Abraham, not to me! We can all benefit spiritually from God's words to Abraham, yet we don't receive the rights to the material benefits.

Do you see how this works? All scripture has application *for* my life, but not all scripture is addressed *to* me. This greatly affects *how* I apply it to my life, but not *whether* I can apply it to my life. All of this has to do with the proper context, of course.

Learn How To Use This principle

Have you ever been involved in a discussion with someone who insisted you could lose your salvation? Often, these discussions involve both parties dueling with scripture verses to prove their point. Once again, the main issue is to understand the Bible within its proper context. Let's look at an example of a passage someone might use to claim that we can lose our salvation if we don't work at it.

- *Read Matthew 24:13. Who does this verse say shall be saved?*

  _____

  _____

Is this a contradiction with the many Bible passages that teach salvation is by grace through faith alone? Here's one example of many that could be offered.

- *Read Ephesians 2:8–9. Do you think this verse contradicts Matthew 24:13?*

  _____

  _____

Let's take this apparent conflict and learn to apply some of the lessons about discerning the context of a passage of scripture.

All scripture has application for my life, but not all scripture is directly addressed to me. This greatly affects HOW I apply it to my life, but not WHETHER I can apply it to my life.

• *What is the context of Matthew's Gospel? Do you remember? Go back to our brief survey of the Bible in chapter two if you need to, then give a brief answer.*

_____

_____

Matthew, more than any of the other Gospels is aimed squarely at the Hebrew people (the Jews), pointing to Jesus Christ as the promised Messiah who is the fulfillment of what the Old Testament prophets had predicted. Matthew gives us the official offer of the Kingdom to Israel and the official rejection by the Jewish leaders.

Having established the Jewish focus of Matthew's Gospel, let's work to understand the context of Matthew 24 where this difficult verse appears.

• *Read Matthew 23. Does anyone besides Jesus speak in this chapter? Yes or no.*

_____

_____

• *Jesus has some very hard things to say in this chapter. Who is Jesus talking about with these hard sayings?*

_____

_____

The scribes and Pharisees were fundamentalist religious leaders among the Jews. They were constant critics of Jesus and actively worked to minimize or eliminate his influence on the people.

• *Look again at Matthew 23:34–39. Summarize the warning Christ gives in this passage.*

_____

_____

Matthew 24 begins against the background of this context. You can be assured that Jesus' disciples listened in wide-eyed amazement, hearing perhaps the harshest words they had ever heard him say.

• *Read Matthew 24:1. What did the disciples of Jesus do?*

_____

_____

As they walked away from that intense confrontation, his disciples were pointing out to Him the Temple complex. Remodeled by Herod to gain favor of the Jews, the Temple was truly magnificent, literally gleaming in the bright, Middle Eastern sun. Yet, their mouths must have dropped open when Jesus spoke his next words.

- *Read Matthew 24:2. What did Jesus say was going to happen?*

  _____

  _____

This would have been much like telling a native New Yorker before September 11, 2001 that the twin towers of the World Trade Center were going to come crashing down. We must not underestimate the impression this statement of Jesus would have made upon anyone who heard him.

Heading east across the Kidron Valley, Jesus and his disciples made their way up the slope of the hill known as the "Mount of Olives," where Jesus then sat down. This was not far, and the Temple was still clearly visible in front of them as they gathered around the Lord.

- *Read Matthew 24:3.*

- *What two questions do Jesus' disciples ask him?*

  _____

  _____

What do we see here? The Jewish Messiah has just landed a stinging rebuke upon the Jewish leaders who earlier rejected the offer of the kingdom. He has announced that their sacred and beloved temple would be totally destroyed. The Jewish disciples of the Jewish Messiah want to know two things. First, when is this going to happen? Second, assuming such a catastrophe would be the end of the world and the coming of Messiah in glory, they ask what signs they should look for leading up to this cataclysmic event.

- *Now read Matthew 24:4–31 and briefly summarize to the best of your ability how Jesus answers the disciples' two questions.*

  _____

  _____

Now your summary of Jesus' words with mine and see how they match up: Jesus begins to speak with them about the signs leading up to a time of tribulation like none before or after and refers to a time predicted by the prophet Daniel as "*the abomination of desolation*" (Matthew 24:15). He tells them of other events leading up to his second coming to establish his kingdom and rule the earth (Matthew 24:29–31).

- *Having read this passage in context, do you think the primary thrust of Jesus' words is to explain how a New Testament believer can gain or keep eternal life?*

  _____

  _____

Most reasonable people would agree that the primary context of Jesus' words has to do with a future time of tribulation to come upon Israel as predicted by the prophet Daniel in the Old Testament.

- *Read Matthew 24:14, then 24:29. Now, read 24:13. Do you think "the end" mentioned in Matthew 24:13 is more likely to be the end of an individual's life, or the end of this future time of horrible tribulation that dominates the context?*

_____

_____

Understanding the context requires some reading and studied observation, but in the above analysis, we have done nothing here that you can't do.

This prophetic chapter about future events offers some challenges to understanding, but most people would conclude that Jesus' remark in Mathew 24:13 about enduring to the end has to do with events concerning the future of Israel and not the eternal salvation of a New Testament believer today.

- *To confirm this look once more at Matthew 24:14. When does this verse say the end shall come?*

_____

_____

- *Do you think the Gospel of the kingdom has been preached to all the world?*

_____

_____

Actually, statistics confirm that a sizeable percentage of the world's population still has never heard enough information about the gospel to either accept or reject Christ as Lord and Savior. We can conclude, then, the "end" Jesus speaks of is the end of the period of tribulation leading up to his return, not the end of an individual Christian's life.

There is more to do in Matthew 24 to illustrate the investigative principles we are learning. We have asked, "What is the context?" We also should ask the second question, "To whom is the passage written?" To practice this principle, let's look a little further. In Matthew 24:15, Jesus mentions Daniel's prophesy of the *"abomination of desolation."* This section of Daniel is not easy to understand, but you can see the context of Jesus' remarks by reading Daniel 8:13–14; 9:27; and 11:31.

- *Read Matthew 24:16. Remembering our three basic categories of people, Jew, gentile, and the church of God, to whom is Jesus speaking to in this passage?*

_____

_____

- *Do you live in Judea?*

_____

_____

- *Read Matthew 24:20. Are New Testament Christians commanded to keep the Sabbath?*

_____

_____

- *When Jesus says they should pray that they would not have to flee on the Sabbath, to whom would he be speaking? Jew, gentile, or church of God?*

_____

_____

Matthew 24 is a long, detailed, and challenging chapter. We could go on and on with questions and analysis. However, we have enough evidence to answer our basic question. To whom was this passage directly addressed? To gentiles? To the church? No, of course not! Jesus is speaking to Jews of a time yet to come. Understanding the context and to whom these words are addressed, we can then appreciate that this passage has nothing to do with the loss or gain of salvation by a New Testament believer.

Question #3:
When Was It Written?

This is the third of the trio of questions that need to be part of our automatic response each time we approach the Bible. Along with seeking to determine the biblical, historical, literary and grammatical context and to whom it was written, the careful Bible student wants to know when the passage was originally written. This question also has to do with the overall context of a passage of scripture.

A dispensation is a time period during which God is dispensing His grace in a certain way.

The Bible Is Divided into Different Dispensations

In chapter three we learned a little about the biblical concept of dispensations and the progressive nature of God's revelation to and relationship with man. We remarked how different people use different measures to divide the timeline of biblical history, much like using either kilometers or miles to measure a distance. The distance does not change, only the unit of measure. We defined a dispensation as a time period during which God is dispensing his grace in a certain way. The principle of Bible investigation we are considering now helps us determine where a passage of scripture belongs on that time line, no matter what unit of measure we use.

When I first became a believer in the 1960's, one of the hot issues in some churches was whether women should wear slacks. The idea was that men wear pants, not women. Yes, I know! Some readers are saying, "What?!" Now, I don't want to belittle or criticize any woman who for any reason chooses not to wear slacks. That is strictly a matter of personal preference. I raise this issue to illustrate once again the importance of context and the danger of supporting beliefs with Bible verses taken out of context.

The issue was not a church dress code, but the reliance on passages like Deuteronomy 22:5 for biblical support. Many an impassioned preacher thunderously quoted this verse pleading for women to wear only skirts and dresses and not slacks. Let's examine this issue by asking the right questions about the context of this passage from Deuteronomy.

- *Read Deuteronomy 22.*

- *Remembering or reviewing your notes from chapter two, what is Deuteronomy about?*

_____

_____

Obviously, this is an Old Testament passage, the second of three major discourses by Moses in Deuteronomy. In this discourse, Moses is reiterating the Ten Commandments and the rest of the law. Though there is wisdom in the law, the New Testament clearly teaches we are no longer bound to live by the law (Galatians 3–4, for example).

- *To whom was this passage in Deuteronomy 22 written? To the Jews, Gentiles, or to the church of God?*

_____

_____

The answer is clear in this case. As part of the law, this passage is directed at the Hebrew people, not New Testament believers or Gentiles.

- *When was this passage written?*

_____

_____

The very name of the book, Deuteronomy, means "second law." This passage belongs to the dispensation of the law and was written by Moses during his lifetime.

Let's explore the immediate context a little further.

- *Read Deuteronomy 22:11. What does this passage say about wearing wool and linen together?*

_____

_____

In the simplest terms this verse means one should not wear clothing of mixed cloth, such as cotton and polyester blends. In their effort to convince women not to wear pants, I wonder how many preachers have passionately quoted Deuteronomy 22:5 while wearing a 55/45% cotton/polyester blend shirt. See how important context is?

- *Read Deuteronomy 22:8. What do you think this verse is talking about?*

_____

_____

This verse teaches that when building a new home one should put a "battlement" or railing around the roof. In the semi-tropical climate of the Middle East, roofs are normally flat and often used as an outdoor "living room" in the evening to catch the breezes. There is wisdom in warning the Israelite to put a railing around that roof to ensure no one accidentally falls off and gets hurt. If we insist on a direct application of verse 5, why not a direct application of these other verses, too?

Speaking of the historical context, what about the culture of those times? One would not have to do much research regarding Deuteronomy 22:5 to discover that neither men nor women wore what we would consider "pants" today. So, if this verse should be applied directly today, what about those cultures even today where both men and women wear long robes?

Now that you have a better grasp of the historical application of this passage, ask yourself why does God include Deuteronomy 22:5 in the Bible? A basic and applicable truth emerges from this verse. A man should look like a man, and a woman should look like a woman. While culture and styles are in a state of continual flux, a man should not attempt to pass himself off as a woman, and that same holds true for the both genders. This is not too complicated if we just consider the context and ask the right questions.

*Our goal
in Bible
investigation
is to become
so accustomed
to asking these
questions we
don't have to
go though a
conscious
"check list."*

Putting It All Together

Three basic questions are foundational for proper interpretation of the Bible: What is the context? To whom was it written? When was it written? Answering these questions often involves areas of overlap. Taken together they guide the Bible student toward understanding the Bible in its proper context, and they should form part of our habitual approach to the Bible

Our goal in Bible investigation is to become so accustomed to asking these questions we don't have to go though a conscious "check list." These basic questions, and others we will learn, will become part of our normal and natural approach to Bible study.

Psychologists and educators often speak of what is commonly called the *Competency Model*, a process of five stages from total ignorance to a stage where one is so comfortable with a certain skill or competency they are not even consciously aware of what they are doing. There is debate as to who actually originated this model many years ago, but it is often quoted.

The first stage is *unconsciously incompetent*, not even being aware that you are completely incompetent in some area. Before you were even aware of the value of God's word, you could be considered unconsciously incompetent in Bible study.

Next, is the stage called *conscious incompetence*. At this point one is still incompetent, but aware of that incompetence. Perhaps you picked up this book on biblical investigation because you became aware one day of your lack of ability in Bible study and wanted to do something about it.

Conscious competence is that stage where you begin to learn skills and competencies, yet you very consciously have to work to use them. My prayer is that as you continue working your way through this book, you will learn to think about and carefully apply these principles of investigative Bible study and, as a result, come to appreciate them as indispensable keys to understand whatever scripture you study.

As you continue to grow and practice these skills, you progress to the stage of *unconscious competence*. You will become so comfortable using these investigative principles of Bible study you will tend to forget that others don't use them as easily as you do. They will become natural to you, and you will use them without consciously going through some mental checklist.

The final stage is called *conscious unconscious competence*. Confused? That means you are aware of how far you have come in your learning. You can remember how little you knew at the beginning and appreciate how much you have gained since then. Some who achieve that level decide they know so much that they can stop studying and testing themselves. Others realize their competency is not the end of learning, but rather an opportunity to move to higher levels of knowledge, wisdom and understanding.

My hope for you is that you put these principles into practice daily, until you are so comfortable with them you won't have to think about going through a checklist. Instead, you will feel confident about moving to even higher levels in the study of God's word and its meaning in your life.

Notes

1. A Bible teacher from generations ago said, "We have all heard the proverbial saying that 'the Bible may be made to prove anything.' Exactly so; but taken apart from its context: otherwise it could never be made to teach anything different from the context in which God intended it." (Bullinger, *How to Enjoy the Bible*, 264–265.)

2. Arthur, *How To Study Your Bible*, 20.

CHAPTER SIX

Learning to Listen Carefully

As a result of comparing Bible study to good detective work, we are learning to ask the right questions. Now, we must simultaneously develop another skill—learning to be good listeners. Good listening skills are the flip side of the same coin with good questioning skills. The two go together. If you aren't listening, why ask?

We began with three basic questions that ought to be a natural part of our thought process every time we approach scripture. Many questions can help us in our study of the Bible, but the three we learned are part of a strong foundation: What is the context? To whom was it written? When was it written?

Learning to listen as we ask these investigative questions completes a strong foundation. Although many voices clamor for our attention, a good Bible student learns to listen to three voices: the literal sense of scripture, the Holy Spirit, and each and every word of scripture.

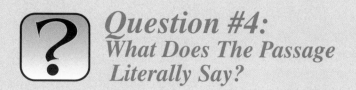

Question #4:
What Does The Passage Literally Say?

The Primary Sense of the Bible Is Literal

We dedicated time in both the first and fourth chapters to understanding what it means to interpret the Bible literally. We learned that a literal interpretation does not imply we are to take everything we read in the Bible in a purely wooden manner. Like most literature, the Bible employs figures of speech, including symbols and word pictures, spread throughout the varied literary styles of its 66 books.

However, the primary sense of the Bible is literal. The goal of Bible study is to learn what the scripture says in the natural, normal sense of the words in their grammatical, literary and historical context, not to look for some hidden meaning.

Some people imagine the Bible is filled with all sorts of complicated symbolism. Symbolism in the Bible certainly exists, but it doesn't occur nearly as often as you might think. Furthermore, when symbolism does appear in the Bible, it is usually seen clearly and the Bible itself tells you what the symbol means. The same is true of the symbols in the parables Jesus told.

A good Bible student learns to listen to three voices:

1. **The literal sense of Scripture**
2. **The Holy Spirit**
3. **Each word of the Scripture.**

When we speak of Democrats as donkeys and Republicans as elephants, we are using symbolism. Those commonly understood symbols are not "hidden." They are easily understood in their normal usage in the correct political context. Biblical symbolism is not too different. The symbols, word pictures, and other literary devices of scripture are either defined directly in the context of scripture or easily discovered by comparing scripture with scripture and by seeing the consistent usage of a particular symbol throughout the Bible.

The First Objective Is to Understand a Passage's Literal Meaning

This is where we must always begin to interpret the Bible. Even if a passage does have some elements of symbolism, we begin by understanding the literal, normal meaning of the words. This literal understanding is always the foundation for any other application of the passage. This protects us from reading our own ideas into the Bible. Our objective is simply to read what the literal words say, not what you think you see by "reading between the lines."

The questions we have asked so far are really a biblical application of the basic "5 W's and an H" we all learned from childhood: When, Where, Who, What, Why, and How? Our task is to carefully and prayerfully approach the biblical text to answer these questions without reading something into the text that is not really there.

I want to emphasize again that this does **not** mean we are to take everything the Bible says in an absolutely literal and inflexible sense. The context and intent of the words of scripture are all important. However, we cannot correctly understand the words in their proper context until we correctly understand what words are really there!

Here is a simple example of understanding the literal words of scripture without taking them in an uncritical, literal sense. Four times Paul commands us to greet the brethren with a "holy kiss" (Romans 16:16; 1 Corinthians 16:20; 2 Corinthians 13:12; and 1 Thessalonians 5:26). Now, that is literally what the Bible says. During flu season each year I'm thankful I understand enough about the Bible to not have to take those words in an unthinking, literal sense!

So, what **does** Paul mean? The first step is to observe literally what is said, yet to take the words in the proper historical and cultural context. Only then can we properly understand and apply Paul's intent when he wrote those words.

I lived many years in Latin America where a kiss on the cheek during greeting and goodbye is still practiced in many settings, so I can understand what Paul is trying to say. I have learned to apply the same intent to whatever culture and situation in which I find myself. Paul is simply instructing us to be careful to greet other believers in a special and warm way. That type of warm greeting can take place with or without physical contact and within the confines of any particular human culture.

The symbols, word pictures and other literary devices of scripture are either defined directly in the context of scripture or easily discovered by comparing scripture with scripture and seeing the consistent usage of a particular symbol throughout the Bible.

Biblical Symbolism Is Marked and Defined in the Bible Itself

Earlier I remarked that when symbolism is used in the Bible, it is usually marked and readily accessible. Here are a couple of examples to help so you can capture the idea.

The Parable of the Sower

This familiar passage in Matthew 13 contains a series of seven parables Jesus told, all having to do with the kingdom of heaven.

• *Read Matthew 13:1–9. According to verse 3 what type of story is this?*

_____

_____

A well-respected Bible encyclopedia defines a parable as:

… a placing of two or more objects together, usually for the purpose of a comparison…. In the more usual and technical sense of the word, "parable" ordinarily signifies an imaginary story, yet one that in its details could have actually transpired, the purpose of the story being to illustrate and inculcate some higher spiritual truth.[1]

By observing that this story in Matthew 13 is a parable, we know that the seed, fowls, stony places, thorns and other items Jesus speaks of are symbols to illustrate some higher spiritual truth. We did not dream this up; the Bible clearly says Jesus is speaking in parables. Nor will we have to dream up meanings for the symbols if we apply some of the principles we have been learning.

Remembering the "big picture" of the New Testament, we recall that Matthew has the most decidedly Jewish focus of the four Gospels. As a Gospel, Matthew occupies a position of transition between law and grace, Old and New Testaments, Israel and the church.

In the context of Matthew, where does chapter 13 fit? This is not the time or place for a detailed analysis of the book of Matthew. A little understanding of the context, though, will help us understand the meaning of this parable.

We know that Matthew is very concerned to show Jesus as the promised Hebrew Messiah and often quotes from the Old Testament prophets to show how Jesus was the fulfillment of many of their predictions. A significant point in Matthew comes in chapter 10 as Jesus selects 12 apostles from among his disciples and sends them on a special mission.[2]

- *Read Matthew 10:1–7. To whom did Jesus send these twelve (verse 6)?*

  _____

  _____

- *What were they to announce (verse 7)?*

  _____

  _____

From what we have just seen, this is clearly a passage with direct application to Israel, not the New Testament church. In chapters 11 and 12, the Jewish leaders in Jerusalem reject the Messiah and his offer of the kingdom. (If you are not familiar with the book of Matthew, you might want to read these two chapters before going further.)

- *Read Matthew 13:1–2. Jesus went out of what?*

  _____

  _____

- *Where did Jesus sit down?*

  _____

  _____

Everything Jesus did and said had significance. The "house of Israel" (Matthew 10:6) had just rejected him and his kingdom. From this point, Jesus' ministry begins to take on a broader scope as he sits down by the sea. In the Bible, the "sea" often represents the peoples of the world (Revelation 17:15 is an example). Quite possibly, this definite action of Jesus is meant to set the stage for the seven parables of Matthew 13, each one describing some aspect of the mystery form the kingdom will take in this present age due to the rejection of Christ's rule by the Jewish leaders. We saw previously that God revealed to Paul that upon the rejection of a literal, earthly kingdom, the kingdom of God would exist in mystery form in the hearts of believers. These seven parables of Matthew 13 describe the mystery form of the kingdom.

- *Read Matthew 13:10. What question did the disciples ask Jesus here?*

  _____

  _____

Notice the surprise of the disciples. Matthew has recorded no parables by Jesus to this point in his ministry, and from the reaction of the disciples it would appear this was not the way Jesus normally taught.

- *Read Matthew 13:11–17. Why does Jesus say he is speaking in parables?*

_____

_____

Though he withheld truth from those who had rejected him in unbelief, Jesus immediately explained the symbolism of the parable to his disciples.

- *Read Matthew 13:18–23. Comparing this explanation given by Jesus with the parable itself in Matthew 13:1–9, the following exercises will help you determine what the key elements of the parable represent. First, read the explanation of the same parable found in Luke 8:11–15, where the meaning is even more direct.*

- *What is the seed that is sown? (Compare 13:3–4 with 13:19 and Luke 8:11)*

_____

_____

- *What is represented by the fowls (birds) that eat the seed that fell by the wayside? (Compare Matthew 13:4 with 13:19 and Luke 8:12)*

_____

_____

- *What is represented by the seed that falls on stony places? (Compare Matthew 13:5–6 with 13:20-21and Luke 8:13)*

_____

_____

- *What is represented by the thorns that choked the seed? (Compare Matthew 13:7 with 13:22 and Luke 8:14)*

_____

_____

- *What is represented by the good ground? (Compare Matthew 13: 8 with 13:23 and Luke 8:15) What have we learned here? While we began by looking at the literal, normal and obvious meaning of the words of scripture and not some hidden meaning, the symbolism of the parable was explained in the very passage.*

_____

_____

There are six other parables in the chapter and, while Jesus doesn't give the detailed explanation for each one, their meaning can be discerned by what we have already learned and by comparing scripture with scripture, not by inventing a meaning God never intended.

The Image of Christ in the First Chapter of the Revelation

Another example of how the Bible deals with symbolism is found in the first chapter of Revelation. Old and exiled to the Isle of Patmos, the Apostle John sees a vision of the resurrected Christ. Listen to John's description.

- *Read Revelation 1:10–16.*

John's description of Christ with candlesticks, flaming eyes, burning brass feet, seven stars and a two-edged sword is filled with enough symbolism to discourage some Bible readers. If one just continues reading, though, the main elements of the symbolism are explained just a few verses later.

- *Read Revelation 1:20.*
- *What does John say the seven stars represent?*

  _____

  _____

- *What do the seven candlesticks represent?*

  _____

  _____

Though the candlesticks and stars are defined here, the elements related to the appearance of the resurrected Christ are not. Yet even those elements can be discerned by comparing scripture with scripture.

- *Read Hebrews 4:12 and Ephesians 6:17. Compare with Revelation 1:16 what you have just read. By comparing scripture to scripture, what do you think is symbolized by the two-edged sword coming out of Christ's mouth in Revelation?*

  _____

  _____

The careful Bible student can locate other symbolic elements of Christ's appearance elsewhere in the Bible. It is important to see how the elements of the symbolism are clearly defined in their context or by comparing scripture with scripture. In no case does the reader have to guess or invent meaning for biblical symbolism. When the symbolic meaning of a passage is not easily seen by applying these principles, it is far better to just admit we don't understand than to try to force some meaning or opinion upon the passage.

In no case does one have to guess or invent meaning for biblical symbolism. When the symbolic meaning of a passage is not easily seen by applying these principles, it is far better to just admit we don't understand than to try to force some meaning or opinion upon the passage.

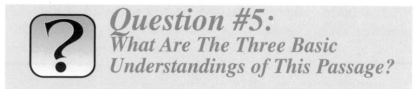

The Holy Spirit reveals God's truth to us as we compare scripture with scripture in the proper context.

Interpretation of Scripture Always Begins with the Holy Spirit

In 1 Corinthians 2:9–16 we learned that we can't understand scripture without the Holy Spirit. This doesn't mean we dream up our own private interpretation and blame it on the Holy Spirit by saying, "The Holy Spirit gave me this interpretation." Instead, we have learned that the Holy Spirit reveals God's truth to us as we compare scripture with scripture in the proper context.

This ability to interpret the Bible within its proper historical, grammatical and literary context and by comparing scripture with scripture is a wonderful safeguard against false interpretation and bad teaching. A scientist must do research in ways that can be repeated by others. If someone markets a cure for cancer but has no scientific research to back it up, the cure is rightfully dismissed as nothing more than snake oil. True scientific research is openly shared with colleagues who can independently repeat the same procedures to verify the results. In the same way, interpreting the Bible is based on context and comparison of cross-references of scripture and can be independently verified by anyone else who chooses to do so. This does not, of course, guarantee everyone is going to agree on everything. But, at least our disagreements can revolve around discussions of seeking the true sense of scripture instead of feelings, impressions and opinions.

All Scripture Has Three Primary Levels of Understanding

We have already emphasized the danger of looking for secret or hidden meanings, rather than only looking for the clear meaning of scripture, according to the normal and common usage of words within their proper context. The Bible does, though, have a depth of meaning beyond what is clearly apparent on the surface. We just saw again in 1 Corinthians 2:14 Paul's words to the Corinthians describing the need to spiritually discern the Bible. How can we reconcile these two extremes of only seeing what's on the surface, or of inventing our own personal interpretations that have no support in scripture?

A concept that has greatly helped my personal Bible study is to see each passage of scripture as having three basic levels of interpretation: historical, doctrinal and personal. Though this statement stands alone on its own merit, we will learn later in this workbook that learning how to properly apply these three basic levels of understanding that is the heart of what is called inductive Bible study. Let me explain by briefly introducing you to these three levels of understanding found in all scripture.

Historical Understanding

Historical understanding (or interpretation) is the single, obvious, meaning that is rooted in the historical, grammatical and literary usage of the words. All Bible study must begin here! As we have emphasized repeatedly, determining this historical and literal sense of scripture is our first goal every time we approach the Bible.

The Bible is unique among the world's religious literature in that it is primarily an accurate historical document about the lives of real people. Even the proverbs, parables and other literary forms in the Bible are inseparable from the lives of these historical people who received them from the Holy Spirit of God and committed them to writing. This historical understanding is essential. If we miss that fact, everything else will be twisted. No matter what, we must never violate the obvious, literal meaning of scripture.

Doctrinal Understanding

This is the second level of meaning of scripture. In Paul's second letter to Timothy, he said all scripture was profitable for doctrine (2 Timothy 3:16). Doctrine simply means "teaching." In other words, God never intended the Bible to be just a history book, but a book to teach us his truth. God teaches us HIS Truth through HIS interaction with HIS creation in HIStory.

Once we determine the historical setting of a passage of scripture, our task in this second level of understanding is to discover what truth or principle God wants to teach us. Sometimes, a historical event in the lives of real people teaches us a great spiritual lesson. Sometimes, a historical event or person predicts a future an event or events. At times, God uses a passage to both teach a principle and point to events in the future events. Shortly, we will look at some examples.

Personal Understanding

Armed with an understanding of the context and the historical setting of a passage, and an understanding of the truths and principles it teaches, the third level of understanding is to apply God's truth to our daily lives. After Paul told Timothy that all scripture was divinely inspired and given to teach us, he listed other purposes.

- *Read 2 Timothy 3:16. After stating that all scripture is profitable for doctrine, Paul gives three other purposes. What are they?*

_____

_____

Once we discover the historical meaning of a passage and the truth or principle it teaches, the third level of application is to learn how that truth should influence our lives.

In other words, scripture not only teaches us information, it also points out the areas of our lives that don't yet line up with God's truth and corrects or rebukes us. Scripture also shows us how to fix the problem and instructs us in righteousness as God sees it so we don't commit the same sin in the future. We are to take the biblical truth revealed in the context of history and learn how God would have us apply it to our lives.

Bible study is about looking at three layers of truth: 1) what is said; 2) what is meant by what is said; and 3) what should I do about what is said?[3] These layers of understanding are taught several places in the Bible.

- *Read 1 Corinthians 10:1–13, where Paul speaks of a historical event from Israel's history. What event or time period is seen in this passage?*

  _____

  _____

- *From 1 Corinthians 10:11, what is God's purpose in recording this story in the Old Testament?*

  _____

  _____

- *Looking at 1 Corinthians 10:12-13 in this context, do you think the trials in your life are unique?*

  _____

  _____

- *Summarize how you see the connection between the Exodus and your life today.*

  _____

  _____

- *In 1 Corinthians 10:13 God promises a way to escape from all of life's temptations. From this context where do you think we might find that way of escape?*

  _____

  _____

We have learned that God uses the lives and experiences of people who lived hundreds of years ago to show us how to face our challenges today. Searching the scriptures, we learn how God worked in the lives of others as an example of how he wants to work in our lives, too. In thinking through this passage in Corinthians, we examined the history, discovered God's purposes, and considered how to apply them to our lives today.

- *Read Romans 15:4. Many people today are looking for hope. Where is one place we can find hope according to this verse?*

_____

_____

- *Read Ecclesiastes 1:9 and 3:15. From these verses, is there reason to believe the Bible is relevant for your life today? Why?*

_____

_____

Examples

Let's practice seeing these three layers of understanding by looking at some examples.

- *Read Isaiah 7.*

God sent the prophet Isaiah and his son to rebuke Judah's King Ahaz for trusting Assyrian mercenaries to protect him from the immediate threat of neighboring Syria. Isaiah challenged Ahaz to ask God for a sign that the nation could trust in God rather than men. Ahaz refused to ask for a sign, saying very piously that he did not want to tempt God. The real reason, of course, is that Ahaz had already paid the Assyrians to send mercenaries. Isaiah called his bluff saying that even if he did not want to ask God for a sign, God would give him one anyway!

- *In your own hand write out the words of Isaiah 7:14.*

_____

_____

Much has been written about this very famous verse. Some think the "virgin" spoken of here is a reference to Isaiah's own wife. Even though she was not literally a "virgin," it was not uncommon to refer to one's wife as such in the same way a husband may refer to his wife of many years as his "bride." Others think this sign points to a son to be born to Ahaz. Still others say we should not understand this prediction to refer to any virgin in particular. Regardless of any specific "virgin" in the author's mind, the historical application of this sign is not hard to understand if we continue reading the context.

Within the time frame of a normal nine-month gestation period and before the newborn had grown to be able to tell the difference between right and wrong, the nation of Syria that Ahaz feared would cease to be a threat. The real threat would be the very Assyrians that Ahaz had hired for protection.

From a purely historical perspective it was not unusual for a Hebrew mother to name her child some compound name that included the name of God, such as Immanuel, meaning "God with us." There is more here than what is on the surface.

- *Read Matthew 1:20–23. In your own words explain the prophetic or future teaching of Isaiah 7:14 and how this prophecy was ultimately fulfilled.*

_____

_____

Matthew 1:20–23 clearly tells us this passage was fulfilled in Christ's birth. Yet, an examination of the context of Isaiah 7, reveals a real historical situation and fulfillment of the prophecy in Isaiah's lifetime. We have seen the historical application as well as prophecy that came to pass in Isaiah's lifetime, and also the lesson to Ahaz that God wanted him to learn. The next question is what God wants this passage to teach us today.

- *What can you learn to apply to your own life from the passage we have studied in Isaiah 7:14?*

_____

_____

There is no one correct answer to the above question. One possibility is that in whatever trial or temptation, you could learn you can trust in the God who is with you always (Immanuel), rather than put your trust in human efforts and resources. We might also learn that God wants to reveal and confirm his plan to us, even when we don't want to hear it.

Before moving on, let's take one more example of how we constantly look for these three levels of understanding: historical, doctrinal, and personal.

- *Read Joshua 1.*

- *According to Joshua 1:1–2 what major event has just happened?*

_____

_____

You can probably imagine how catastrophic this event would see, to the Hebrews. After leading Israel for more than 40, years Moses has died. This whole generation of Israel has known no other leader than Moses, who brought down God's law from Mount Sinai. Now, the nation is at last poised to cross the Jordan River into the Promised Land. People must have been wondering how Moses' death would affect their future.

- *After reading Joshua 1, briefly list and describe the key elements of this chapter. What is happening in the purest sense of the history described here?*

_____

_____

Now that you have grasped the historical meaning of this passage, let me tell you why God may have put this story in the Bible. Moses was the lawgiver. The nation stood ready to pass over into the Promised Land to establish the kingdom God had promised. Joshua, not Moses, would lead Israel to victory and set up the kingdom.

Joshua is the Hebrew form of the Greek name "Jesus". Jesus and Joshua are the same name.[4] There is a great truth in this book of Joshua you need to understand: Only Jesus can lead us to victory. The law can never fulfill God's promises to us.

- *Read John 1:14–17 and answer the following questions.*

- *What came through Moses?*

  _____

  _____

- *What came through Jesus?*

  _____

  _____

In a future sense, Joshua is a prophetic picture of the victory of Christ's Second Coming. God's kingdom on earth can become a reality only when Jesus (our Joshua) returns to earth.

Again we see layers of meaning. We considered the historical death of Moses' and the victorious entrance to the Promised Land led by Joshua. We saw the great truth of the contrast between the law on one hand and grace and truth on the other. Victory is through grace and truth, represented by Joshua, and not by the law. We also saw teaching for the future, in that only Jesus himself can set up the kingdom of God on earth. Now, let's explore this passage a little further to search for its personal application to life today.

- *Read Galatians 2:16–21 and Galatians 3. Does our righteousness come from keeping the law?*

  _____

  _____

Only Joshua could set up the kingdom in the Promised Land, and only Jesus can set up a literal kingdom of God on earth when he comes again. Likewise only Jesus Christ can conquer sin and death and set up the rule of the kingdom of God in our individual hearts today. This is a major personal application we can learn here.

- *Read Romans 14:17 and 1 Corinthians 4:20. What is the Kingdom of God like in this present time?*

  _____

  _____

> *In a future sense, Joshua is a prophetic picture of the victory of Christ's Second Coming.*

There is much more we could learn in Joshua. This brief exercise should help us remember to look for these three levels of understanding: What really happened in this story? What truth did God mean to teach by putting this passage in the Bible? How can I apply this truth to my personal life?

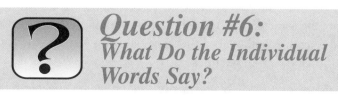

Question #6:
What Do the Individual Words Say?

Individual Words Are the Key to Meaning

A good detective pays attention to every word a witness or suspect says, and even pays attention to what is not said. A good detective also pays careful attention to every word in its proper context. Crime cases have been solved by a detective noticing a single word or phrase that led to putting many individual pieces together. There is a saying among investigators that a suspect will always tell you the truth—you just have to listen close enough and long enough to hear it. What they mean is that by listening to the precise words, writing them down and studying them, even people who are good liars will say something that betrays the truth, and those who are truthful will reinforce their truthfulness. It might not be enough to take to court, but it points the investigator in the right direction.

Every word and phrase of scripture has a specific purpose and meaning. God chooses his words with great care.

- *Read John 20:30–31. Is the Gospel of John intended to be a complete record of everything Jesus said or did?*

  _____

  _____

  _____

- *From this same passage, why did John choose the specific events of Jesus' life in his gospel?*

  _____

  _____

  _____

- *Read John 21:24–25. Does this passage confirm what we saw in John 20:30–31 about this book not being a complete record?*

  _____

  _____

  _____

- *If there is such a huge amount of information about all Jesus did and said, do you think the words actually recorded must be considered to be very important?*

_____

_____

The above two passages in John help us understand that there is no "filler" or "fluff" in the Bible. Had the Gospel of John (or any other biblical book) been intended merely as a complete historical record, much more could have been written. The words recorded in the Bible are there because they have significance that goes beyond the history.

- *Read Proverbs 30:5–6. Which of God's words are pure?*

_____

_____

- *According to verse six what should we never do to God's words?*

_____

_____

- *Read Revelation 22:18–19. What two things do we learn here that we should never do to the words of God?*

_____

_____

- *Read Psalm 12:6–7. How are God's words described here?*

_____

_____

God's words are the key to understanding the Bible, not merely his thoughts. When we change the words, we change the thoughts. Correct understanding demands we pay attention to every single word.

When we say the Bible merely "contains" the words of God we are in a dangerous position. As we discussed previously, if we do not have specific words to fall back on as our authority, we are tempted to stray from the specific meaning God intended. Not only that, who is in the precarious position of deciding which words in the Bible are God's and which are not? Words are important.

- *Read Matthew 5:17-18. When Jews of Jesus' days spoke of what we would call the "Old Testament," they often said simply, "the law." What did Jesus say here about the jots and tittles of the law?*

_____

_____

God's words, not merely his thoughts, are the key to understanding the Bible. When we change the words, we change the thoughts. We must pay attention to every single word.

"What's a *jot* and what's a *tittle*? To answer this question, turn to Psalm 119, the longest chapter in the Bible. This is what is called an acrostic psalm with 22 stanzas of eight verses each. Each stanza starts with one of the 22 letters of the Hebrew alphabet. In most Bibles the name of the corresponding Hebrew letter appears above the stanza, and each verse of that stanza begins with that letter of the alphabet. In some Bibles the actual Hebrew letter appears beside the letter written out in English.

For example, above the first verse of Psalm 119 is the word *aleph* or א the first letter in the Hebrew alphabet. Each one of the eight verses of this first stanza begins with the letter *aleph*. The same pattern is followed for each of the 22 stanzas of eight verses in Psalm 119.

Now, look at Psalm 119:73. Above this verse is *jod* or י, the smallest letter of the Hebrew alphabet, which is called "*jot*" in the translation from Greek in Matthew 5:18. Look at Psalm 119:25 and observe carefully the *daleth* or ד. Then, compare this *daleth* to Psalm 119:153 and the letter *resh* or ר. Look closely! The trained eye can perceive the slight curve on the corner angle of the *resh* and slightly longer stem of the daleth that differentiates it from the *resh*. This slight pen stroke is the difference between these two letters. This difference is called a *tittle*.

So, when Jesus says every jot and tittle of the law will be preserved, he is speaking not only of individual words, but the smallest letter and the slightest difference between letters! Clearly, words are important to God. By the same divine power that God used to inspire the words of scripture, he is able to preserve them in any of the world's languages to this day.

God's Favorite Words and Phrases

We all have favorite words and expressions that distinguish our personalities. These words and expressions either endear us to friends and family or drive them crazy. Maybe both! They **do** identify us and cause others to say, "That sounds just like Homer." Or, "That's just what Lois always says." This is why some people are good at mimicking or impersonating others. They pay attention to the little details like words, phrases, and shades of tone that identify us to others.

God also has favorite words and phrases that appear throughout the Bible. This is amazing. considering that God used over 40 human authors on three continents over a period of centuries! While preserving their distinct human personalities, God used these human authors to record his words just as he wanted them. And, in the scriptures there are key words and phrases that surface from time to time and "sound just like God."

These key words and phrases provide clues to compare scripture with scripture. Here are some examples I have observed from studying the Bible. This is not an exhaustive list but merely some examples to demonstrate how to listen for key words and phrases.

> **God also has favorite words and phrases that appear throughout the Bible.**

"The Day of the Lord" or "That Day"

The phrase "the day of the Lord" or simply "that day" often is used to speak of the Messiah coming in judgment and to establish his literal kingdom on earth. When Israel rejected Christ at his first coming, the Old Testament prophesies about the Messiah that weren't fulfilled in the First Coming will be fulfilled in Christ's Second Coming. Therefore, these phrases frequently help identify a passage as having something to do with the time frame of the Second Coming. This is not always the case, but you will be amazed how often it occurs.

- *Read Zechariah 12–14. How many times can you count the phrase "that day" or "the day of the Lord" in these three chapters?*

  _____

  _____

- *How would you summarize the content or basic theme of these chapters?*

  _____

  _____

- *Read Isaiah 2. How many times do you find the phrase "that day" or "the day of the Lord?"*

  _____

  _____

- *Summarize the theme and content of this chapter of Isaiah.*

  _____

  _____

As you read through the Bible, you will find "the day of the Lord" or "that day" many times. When you see it, look to see if the context has to do with the Second Coming. It won't always be prophetic, but many times it will, especially in the Old Testament books of the prophets. You will also see these phrases in the New Testament. Here's an example.

- *Read 1 Thessalonians 5:1–5. Tell where you see one or both of these phrases appear.*

  _____

  _____

- *What can you learn from these verses about things to come?*

  _____

  _____

"Those Days"

This very specific phrase often appears in the context of the time of tribulation immediately preceding the Second Coming of Christ. Do not be surprised to see some overlap between the time of tribulation and "that day" or "the day of the Lord," since the coming tribulation is technically part of the overall scene of "that day." Specifically, though, "those days" normally is associated with the terrible tribulation forecast to occur immediately before the coming of Christ.

- *Read Matthew 24. List the verses in this chapter where you find the phrase "those days."*

  _____

  _____

- *Describe "those days" Jesus is talking about in your own words.*

  _____

  _____

- *Read Joel 2–3. In which verses do you find the phrase "those days?"*

  _____

  _____

- *What similarities do you see between what Joel sees and what Jesus spoke of in Matthew 24?*

  _____

  _____

- *Read Jeremiah 31:31–34 that speaks of a day when God will make a new covenant with Israel and the nation will experience a genuine conversion when God writes his law upon the hearts of the Jews. Do you think this has already happened?*

  _____

  _____

- *From what you see in Jeremiah 31 when will this conversion of Israel happen?*

  _____

  _____

- *Read Jeremiah 33:15–18. When will these events happen?*

  _____

  _____

- *Read Jeremiah 50:4 and 50:19–20. When will Israel as a nation seek God and be pardoned?*

  _____

  _____

NOTES

Sometimes the phrase "those days" points indirectly to the coming time of trial and tribulation. This phrase occurs in several key places in the Book of Judges, a dark book about Israel spiraling into sin and apostasy in the generations after the victories of Joshua.

Judges easily breaks down into three parts describing the apathy, apostasy, and anarchy in the nation of Israel. By the end of the book, the nation is in the grip of horrible chaos. It is a time that bears many similarities to "those days" which Jesus and the prophets speak of and are later detailed in the Book of Revelation.

- *Read Judges 17:6; 18:1; 19:1; and 21:25. The phrase common to all these verses is*

  _____

  _____

Even a casual reading of the final chapters of Judges reveals a period of anarchy, confusion, and reprehensible public sin. This period in Israel's history foreshadows the future time of great tribulation of which Jesus and others spoke. I find it fascinating that in the book of Judges this period is not described as "that time," or "this era," or something similar, but consistently as "those days." Repeatedly we are told "there was no king in Israel and every man did that which was right in his own eyes." In the coming time of tribulation, the church will no longer be the restraining force in society as it is today. And, the King of kings will not yet have returned to earth—there will still be no king in Israel.

This is not to say that every single instance of the phrase "those days" in the Bible has a direct or indirect reference to the coming time of great tribulation. It does, though, give us insight into a phrase God uses multiple times to point to that future tribulation.

"A Woman in Childbirth"

The figure of a woman in childbirth appears in the form of several key phrases many of times in scripture. Like "those days," it is often found in the context of the coming great tribulation and the coming of "that day" or "the day of the Lord." Specifically, the figure refers to the nation of Israel in the coming tribulation to underscore the intense pain of that tribulation.

Nothing is more basic to our faith than the resurrection of our Lord Jesus Christ on the third day after his crucifixion.

- *Read the following diverse passages of scripture and write the phrase that represents the image of a woman experiencing the pain of childbirth, noting the relationship to the tribulation leading to the Second Coming.*

- *Revelation 12* _____

- *Micah 4:8–10* _____

- *Isaiah 13:6–9* _____

- *Isaiah 54:1–10* _____

- *1 Thessalonians 5:1–4* _____

Listening to the specific words of the Bible enables us to connect with other passages dealing with the same themes. This provides more information and allows us to compare scripture with scripture. God chooses his words with care and precision. In the verses surveyed above you can see the thread that connects them.

"Three Days"

Nothing is more basic to our faith than the resurrection of our Lord Jesus Christ on the third day after his crucifixion. It should come as no surprise that throughout the whole Bible, the phrase "three days" often alerts us to teaching, images, predictions, and applications of the resurrection power of Jesus Christ.

- *Read John 2:18–22 where Jesus himself gave a sign that would validate his identity and ministry. What was that sign?*

  _____

  _____

- *Read Matthew 12:38–40. Again, Jesus speaks of giving a sign. In your own words describe that sign.*

  _____

  _____

- *Read Genesis 1:1–13 where the first mention of life occurs. What is the day on which this first mention of life, plant life, occurs?*

  _____

  _____

- *Read Genesis 22:1–14 as God instructs Abraham to offer up as a sacrifice his beloved and only son Isaac. Dutifully obedient, Abraham makes the necessary preparations and journeys to the place of sacrifice with Isaac. Isaac was as good as dead as far as Abraham was concerned during this entire time of prepara-*

tion. On what day did God cancel Isaac's sentence of death and return Isaac's life to Abraham?

_____

_____

- What person in the New Testament would you say Isaac prefigures?

_____

_____

- Read Exodus 3:18; 5:3; and 8:27 as Moses asks Pharaoh for permission to go into the desert and worship God. Moses asks to travel a distance of how many days?

_____

_____

- In the Bible, Egypt is often a picture of the world system from which we have been saved by faith in Christ. The imagery of God delivering Israel from the bondage of Egypt is a picture of our salvation, as Stephen spoke about in Acts 7 before he was martyred. Considering the death, burial, and resurrection of Christ, what is the difference in days between believers in Christ and those who have not put their faith in him?

_____

_____

- Read Joshua 1:10–11 as Israel prepares to cross the Jordan River and march to victory in the Promised Land. Joshua instructs the people to prepare to pass over within how many days?

_____

_____

- Our victory in Christ depends not on our own efforts, but on what Jesus Christ accomplished. How many days separate his death and resurrection?

_____

_____

- Read Esther 4:15–5:3. Esther, a Jew, was queen of Persia. Her people were threatened with extinction because an evil man named Haman had tricked the king into signing an irreversible edict. By Persian law, not even the queen could enter into the king's presence unannounced. Esther is willing to risk her life entering the king's presence to plead for the deliverance of her *people. All depended on whether the king would grant her favor and spare her life when she entered unannounced into his presence. Like Isaac in Abraham's mind, Esther, in her own mind, is as good as dead for a period of time during which she is fasting and praying. On what day does Esther enter the king's presence and is granted life by the king's favor?*

_____

_____

• *Read Hosea 6:1–2. On what day do God's people find life in his sight?*

_____

_____

These examples do not mean that every mention of "three days" or "the third day" has to do with Christ's resurrection power. There are, though, many such examples. The ones you have seen here are only a few. The point is to learn to listen to the individual words of scripture to be able to say, "That sounds just like God!" Though using many human authors, God ultimately is the Author of the whole Bible and displays his continuity of thought and personality by using key words, phrases, and images throughout the Bible.

"Without a Cause"

Learning to listen for key words and phrases that connect to other scriptures has to do with more than the frequency of their use. The phrase "without a cause" is a powerful example occurring only a few times.

• *Read John 15. In verse 25 Jesus says that the Old Testament prophecy, "They hated me without cause," is fulfilled in him. In the context of this chapter, who do you think "they" refers to?*

_____

_____

• *Read David's Psalm 35. Christ is called the "son of David," and David often is a type(picture) or foreshadowing of Christ. Here, David speaks of his enemies and uses the phrase "without cause" twice in what verse?*

_____

_____

• *Several of the psalms are called "Messianic Psalms" because they clearly contain prophecies of the coming Messiah. Jesus has already applied the phrase "without cause" to himself.*

Can you find any other aspects of this psalm that might be fulfilled in the life and ministry of Jesus Christ?

_____

_____

• *Read Psalm 69, another Messianic Psalm. John 2:17 records the fulfillment of Psalm 69:9, when Jesus cleansed the temple of those who were making his Father's house a house of merchandise. What verse of Psalm 69 records the phrase "without a cause?"*

_____

_____

• *Read Psalm 109, a psalm of David. Compare Psalm 109:8 to Acts 1:20 and tell who it was who ultimately fulfilled this prophecy.*

_____

_____

• *What verse of Psalm 109 contains the phrase "without a cause?"*

_____

_____

Jesus applied the "without a cause" phrase to himself. Therefore, seeing this phrase in the psalms of David alerts us to the possibility those particular psalms are Messianic in their final fulfillment. Remember, each psalm has a historic application, a truth to teach, and an application for our daily lives.

"Innocent Blood"

"Innocent blood" is another seldom-used phrase that has great meaning because of how it applies to Christ's blood that was shed for us.

• *Read Matthew 27:1–8. Who uses the phrase "innocent blood," and whose blood was it?*

_____

_____

• *Read Hebrews 9:11–22. Why do you think Christ's blood is "innocent blood," and why is this so important to our salvation from sin?*

_____

_____

- Read 1 Samuel 19:15. We have already mentioned how David is often a foreshadowing of Christ. In this passage who had the "innocent blood?

  _____

  _____

- Is there another phrase in this verse that alerts us to the possibility that a word picture in some way portrays the son of David to come?

  _____

  _____

- Read Deuteronomy 19:1–13, which makes provision for cities of refuge for those who have committed manslaughter, not premeditated murder. In what verses do you find the phrase "innocent blood?"

  _____

  _____

- In Deuteronomy 19:10-13 what is God's concern for Israel involving innocent blood?

  _____

  _____

- Read Deuteronomy 21:1-9 where God gives provision to cleanse the land of innocent blood. Briefly, in your own words describe how the land was to be cleansed from innocent blood.

  _____

  _____

- From this passage, did the responsibility to cleanse the land of innocent blood belong to Israel's leaders or the people in general?

  _____

  _____

- In Deuteronomy 19:6 what were the elders of Israel to do over the animal sacrifice offered to cleanse the land of innocent blood?

  _____

  _____

- *In Matthew 27:19-25 what did Pilate do in response to the innocent blood of the Lamb of God about to be offered for the sin of the world?*

_____

_____

Obviously, Pilate had no idea of the significance of washing his hands in respect to cleansing the land of innocent blood. He probably was thinking only of himself. However, the fact that he did this in the presence of the elders of Israel, who were clamoring for the death of Jesus, will be a powerful testimony against them in the day when they stand in judgment before God. Judas was so desperate to be free from the innocent blood of Jesus that he threw the blood money down in the presence of the priests and then took his own life. Even though the nation as a whole and her leaders rejected the Messiah, God had a way for the entire nation to deal with the innocent blood and find God's forgiveness. To this day, any individual Jew can still find forgiveness of sin through the innocent blood of Jesus Christ that was shed for us.

This chapter has been about learning to listen as we study the Bible. First, we listen to the literal sense of scripture. Though the Bible has symbolism and figures of speech just like we use everyday, we start by listening to the literal sense of the Bible. We also listen to the Holy Spirit of God within us as he applies the truth of scripture to our lives. And, we listen to the very words of scripture as we are aware that a single word can make a big of difference and connect us to God's big picture.

Notes

1. James Orr, ed., *International Standard Bible Encyclopedia* (Grand Rapids: Wm. B. Eerdmans Publishing Co., 1939), s.v. "Parable," by G. H. Schodde.

2. A "disciple" is a "learner," and the word "apostle" means "sent one." Jesus selects 12 apostles from among his group of disciples to send on this mission.

3. Inductive Bible study has three key steps corresponding to the layers of understanding asked for by these questions: Observation: what does it say? Interpretation: what does it mean? And, Application: how do I apply this truth? This will be the focus of chapter eleven. I chose to include these questions at this time so the student can become accustomed to looking for these layers of truth in all scripture.

4. An interesting feature of the KJV is how the name "Jesus" is used instead of "Joshua" in Acts 7:45 and Hebrews 4:8, even though the Old Testament Joshua is clearly the historical figure intended in the text. The KJV translators obviously understood that the normal translation would be "Joshua" instead of "Jesus," which could easily be confused with the Jesus of the Gospels. However, they purposefully recorded the Greek "Jesus" instead of the Hebrew form "Joshua," perhaps to point out to the English reader that in both of these scriptures Joshua is a prophetic picture of Jesus' victory over Satan which is yet to be fulfilled.

Obviously, Pilate had no idea of the significance of washing his hands in respect to cleansing the land of innocent blood. He probably was thinking only of himself.

CHAPTER SEVEN

Learning to Connect the Dots

Loosely following a detective analogy in our discussion of investigative Bible study, we have talked about the importance of getting the "big picture," asking the right questions, and learning to listen carefully.

Other than the well-known, two-step "survey and search" we learned earlier, good detectives in real life don't follow any sort of sequencing, as though looking at a four-color laminated check list, "Key Rules of Good Detective Work." They treat each crime individually, based on years of training and experience, with principles and processes overlapping as the need and situation dictate.

Learning good principles of Bible study also requires training and experience. As we gain experience studying the scriptures, we become more spontaneous and free about applying good investigative principles. Each passage calls for an overlapping application of Bible study principles.

I recently read an article about police work in which the author mentioned the intuitive crime-solving skills of good police officers. Some people are naturally more intuitive than others. However, I think many "intuitive skills" are really the culmination of good analytical skills and habits developed over the course of a career. These skills and habits become such a part of an officer that observers label them collectively as because it seems so natural. Years of experience and good skills enable them to size up a situation, carefully analyze the evidence, and then "connect the dots." Those same officers probably didn't make it look so natural and intuitive their first year on the job!

So, have patience. Don't allow yourself to be overwhelmed by thinking you need to have instant recall of all we have learned. Keep at it, and many of these truths and practices will become second nature.

In the course of an investigation, whether of a crime scene or the Bible, there is room for all of us to improve our powers of observation and the interpretation of the data we observe. An officer may be asking questions, listening to a witness, or trying to grasp the big picture when something jumps out and catches his or her attention. An uncovered detail that previously had gone unnoticed, can change the whole direction of the investigation. An experienced officer may observe some minute detail a less-experienced investigator overlooks. Years of training, practice, and experience all contribute to enhanced powers of observation and the ability to "connect the dots" in an investigation.

Many "intuitive skills" are the culmination of good analytical skills and habits developed over the course of a career.

There is also an element called "intention to focus" that refers to the investigator's commitment to develop necessary skills of observation and analysis. In the law enforcement profession there is an old saying that officers and investigators can have ten years of experience or one year of experience ten times. A good investigator must have the desire and determination to investigate thoroughly, to honestly evaluate the clues, to try new approaches when former ones don't seem to be working, and to improve both knowledge and skill. A good investigator needs the ability to see both the big picture and the smallest details of a crime, almost at the same time. This skill is learned only by being committed to doing it, working at it, and striving to be better. It doesn't happen automatically.

Good Bible study takes the same effort and commitment. (See Proverbs 2:1-9.) Don't be discouraged. With time and experience, you can master these techniques and develop the ability to employ them almost subconsciously as you study the Bible.

In this chapter we continue our list of potential Bible study questions. The questions so far have focused on skills of biblical observation. The questions in this chapter apply more to proper analysis and interpretation than observation—connecting the dots rather than counting them. They are not questions you will necessarily ask in every investigation, but they can prove invaluable when you need to connect the dots. These questions are rooted in what many have called the principle of first mention and the principle of full mention. We will also learn how to compare scripture with scripture. Later, we will see how these questions, and those in the previous two chapters, fit together into inductive Bible study. Remember, "inductive" crime investigation and inductive Bible study both collect the little pieces of information and assemble them into a big picture just as you do with a picture puzzle.

You are studying the Bible and come across a word, phrase, doctrine, or topic and are wondering what it really means. You have a hunch this word or theme is so important that you need more information than a brief dictionary definition can offer.

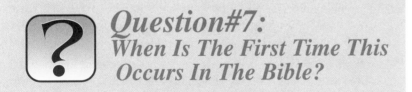

Question#7:
When Is The First Time This Occurs In The Bible?

Here's why. Many Bible students through the years have talked about a principle some call the "Principle of First Mention." The idea is to find the first time an idea, word, doctrine, or people appear in the Bible, then trace it through the Bible to discover if there is some particular pattern of usage and/or meaning.

> The "Principle of First Mention" simply suggests that the meaning of a figure, truth, teaching, picture, or other concept usually is consistent through the entire Bible. Here's another way to say it: if something is true, it is always true.

Trends and attitudes change, and in recent years this principle has become the object of ridicule by some who see it as rooted in ignorance. Some people legitimately leave themselves open to such criticism by looking at this principle from an almost mystical or magical perspective, expecting some hidden jewel of meaning tucked away in the first mention of something in the Bible. I have seen people check the first meaning of something in the Bible, read some strange meaning into it, and then totally disregard the clear teaching of the rest of the Bible. This is ***not*** the intent of the Principle of First Mention!

Another criticism of the principle of first mention is that the Bible is not arranged in purely chronological order and, therefore, something's first mention in the Bible has no particular significance. But, that is not the point. Of course the Bible is not arranged in strict chronological order! The point is the Bible's consistency of thought, not chronology. The principle simply suggests that the meaning of a figure, truth, teaching, picture or other concept usually is consistent throughout the entire Bible.

Here's another way to say it: if something is true, it is always true. Tracing something from beginning to end through the entire Bible provides a good understanding of that characteristic of truth..

Think of this principle from the perspective of a police investigation. We have suspicions while working on a case, but not enough information or evidence to turn a "person of interest" into a "suspect." What do we do? We might start by learning everything we can about this individual. Tracing this person's life from beginning to the present might reveal certain behavioral patterns, similar crimes or accusations. We might follow this individual for a time to see if we can more information, including habits or behavior patterns that would prove helpful. Sometimes someone may "snap" and commit a crime that is not part of that person's regular pattern. Often, though, people fall into patterns of word and deed. Tracing a person's life can lead to clues, evidence, or an M.O. (modus operandi or method of operation).

The same principle applies to Bible study. When attempting to understand a key doctrine, image, figure, truth, or whatever, a good technique is to get out your concordance (we'll talk about using a concordance later), and trace that particular through the whole Bible. You will most likely see a consistent pattern from beginning to end. Even the occasional exception to the rule can help you increase your skills of observation.

I have seen over years of Bible study that many of the "first mentions" in the Bible occur in Genesis, Matthew, or Acts. The reason is to understand. Genesis is the book of origins or beginnings. Since Genesis begins the Bible, we can expect many truths and principles to appear in it for the first time.

Similarly, Matthew begins the New Testament, and we might expect to see the first appearance of certain teachers and words particular to the New Testament. Since Acts makes the transition from the Old Testament

Jewish law to teachings and commandments for Christians in the church age, more first mentions can be found there, too. This is not, of course, a hard and fast rule. Again, we are not looking for some mystical, hidden meaning by finding the first time something is mentioned in the Bible.

We use first mention as a starting point to trace a subject through the whole Bible to assemble bits and pieces (scripture passages) into the big picture God wants us to see.

Doing this kind of investigative Bible study demands determined and persistent work as Proverbs 2:1-9 points out. God means business! If you really want to know and understand all God ahs for you and all he wants you to become, he requires you to mean business, too. A survey beginning with a concept's first mention in the Bible can give you a broad overview scripture and may provide some arresting details if you develop and use sharp powers of observation. Here are a few examples to practice.

The Serpent

- *Read Genesis 3:1. The Devil appears to Eve in what form?*

  _____

  _____

- *Read Revelation 12:9–17 and 20:1–3. Who is represented by the serpent?*

  _____

  _____

These passages encompass the beginning and end of the serpent's figure in the Bible. Now, let's examine a few of the instances where the serpent appears in-between. Tracing the serpent though scripture, you will see that the serpent appears in a negative connotation, provokes fear, or represents the Devil, sin, or those controlled by the Devil.

- *Read Exodus 4:1–3. What reaction did the serpent provoke in Moses?*

  _____

  _____

- *Read Psalm 58:1–4 and Psalm 140:1–3. Do you see any connection between the serpent in these verses and what we have already seen?*

  _____

  _____

- *Read Proverbs 23:29–32. Does the word "serpent" here have a good or bad connotation?*

  _____

  _____

- *Read Isaiah 14: Notice the word "serpent" in verse 29. Observe the appearance of Lucifer, another name for the Devil, in verses 12-17. What connection, if any, do you see with what we have observed?*

  _____

  _____

- *Read Isaiah 27:1 and 30:6. How might these verses fit the pattern we have seen?*

  _____

  _____

- *Read Isaiah 65:25 and note the comment about the serpent's "meat" or food. Read Genesis 3:14. What time do you imagine Isaiah 65:25 looks forward to?*

  _____

  _____

- *Read 2 Corinthians 11:3. Who would the serpent represent here?*

  _____

  _____

- *Read Numbers 21:4–9. Perhaps the use of the serpent as an instrument of healing seems to be out of line with the pattern we have observed (though this is where physicians get their universal symbol). But, read John 3:14–15 and 2 Corinthians 5:21. Explain in your own words the picture God is painting in Numbers 21:4–9.*

  _____

  _____

To sanctify is to set something apart, or to make it special, but not necessarily more spiritual or holy than another.

Sanctification

Have you ever heard of "sanctification?" Entire books explore this very important biblical idea. Unfortunately, as important as this concept is, there is much confusion and misunderstanding. Some have taught, for example, that sanctification is some lofty state of "sinless perfection" that one aspires to obtain in the Christian walk. Before jumping into definitions of various Greek words and wading through thick books of scholastic thought, let's apply the principle of first mention to see how this word is used in the Bible.

- *Read the first time some form of this word appears in the Bible in Genesis 2:3. Is this word used in the sense of some state of mystical "sinless perfection?"*

  _____

  _____

- *What do you suppose the word "sanctified" means in this context?*

  _____

  _____

Were we to consult biblical literature discussing the meaning of the Hebrew and Greek words translated into English as "sanctify" or "sanctification," we would discover they all have to do with the idea of "setting apart," or "setting aside as special."

After Genesis 2, the next time some form of this word appears is in Exodus.

- *Read Exodus 13:1–2. Do you think this is consistent with the same meaning we saw in Genesis 2:3?*

  _____

  _____

- *Read Exodus 19 describing the preparation for giving of the Ten Commandments. Mark each time some form of "sanctify" occurs in this chapter. What was to be sanctified?*

  _____

  _____

- *Read Numbers 8:17. What did God sanctify for himself?*

  _____

  _____

Considering this verse, it is hard to imagine that "to sanctify" means to make someone more powerful or spiritual than another. Here, God says he sanctified their beasts or animals. Certainly that wouldn't mean he gave their animals some special spiritual power or state of sinless perfection! If we follow the pattern we have seen from the beginning it all makes sense. To sanctify means to set something apart, to make it special, but not necessarily more spiritual or powerful. If I bake five pies to give to friends and decide to set one aside for my own family to enjoy, I just sanctified a pie!

- *Read Isaiah 8:13 and Isaiah 66:17. In light of what we have seen, what do you think it means for us to sanctify God and his name?*

  _____

  _____

- *In the New Testament, the first English appearance of a form of "sanctify" is Matthew 23:17–19 where it appears twice. Explain what you think the word "sanctify" means in this context.*

  _____

  _____

- *Read John 17:17–19, part of the prayer Christ prays to his Father. Explain what you think the word "sanctify" means in this context.*

  _____

  _____

- *Paul wrote his first letter to the Corinthians to deal with serious sin problems in the church. The Corinthians were far from "sinless perfection!" Read the following passages and then give your impressions of sanctification as it appears in 1 Corinthians 1:2; 1:30; 6:11; 7:14.*

  _____

  _____

- *Read John 17:17 and Ephesians 5:25–26. From a practical standpoint how can we live a life that is "special" or "set apart" in our daily walk with God?*

- *Read 1 Thessalonians 4:3–4 and 1 Timothy 4:4–5. What insights about sanctification can you learn from these passages? Do they seem to fit the same pattern we have seen?*

  _____

  _____

There are many other passages that mention sanctification and many aspects of this great doctrine of our faith, but this brief survey demonstrates how much you can learn from tracing a word or idea through the Bible, beginning with its first mention. Here is a final example of the use of the Principle of First Mention.

Worship

Years ago a friend of mine pointed out the first mention of an important word, and I never forgot this lesson. We often speak of worship. We hold worship services and we have a time of worship. Often we think of praise, prayer and church services when the word "worship" is used.

- *Read Genesis 22:1–19. Find the word "worship." This is the first time it occurs in the Bible. What is the context in which "worship" appears?*

_____

_____

Abraham headed up the mountain on a somber mission—to offer his beloved son, Isaac, as a burnt sacrifice in obedience to God. This is hardly what we have in mind for a typical church service! God intervened and prevented Abraham from actually going through with the sacrifice. Abraham and Isaac came back down the mountain changed forever.

I find it very instructive that the first time worship appears in the Bible, it is not amid scenes of angelic choirs and voices of praise, but rather in the context of a life-changing encounter with God. This knowledge of the first time worship appears in the Bible was not a substitute for a complete theological study of this important biblical concept, but it did give me a fresh perspective of worship and provided food for thought. It made me wonder how many times we really have a "worship service." Also, it caused me to pay more attention to the word "worship" when it appears elsewhere in the Bible to see if my understanding of that word has been too limited.

By the way, in this same chapter of Genesis 22, you can also find the first time the words "tempt," "love," and "obey" appear in the English Bible. You are now armed with the ability to study them on your own!

These have been just a few examples of tracing a word or idea through the Bible, but they are typical of the lessons we can learn by following this simple technique. Remember, this is merely a guideline or technique, and not a hard and fast rule. Not every word or concept follows the same consistency. Sometimes a word may have several definitions. Most of the time, though, you can reap great benefits by tracing a biblical word or concept from its first appearance onward through the Bible.

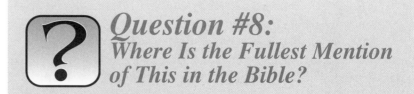

Question #8:
Where Is the Fullest Mention of This in the Bible?

Books on biblical hermeneutics treat this question as the "Principle of Full Mention." The thesis is this: somewhere in the Bible God usually declares his mind more fully in regard to issues of vital importance. These passages serve as a foundation for issues of great significance and set the stage for this doctrine throughout the rest of scripture. Here are some examples.

Born Again

We frequently hear references to the need to be "born again." Even non-religious people use the phrase in ordinary conversations to speak of a "born again" career or a "born again" experience, yet nothing spiritual is intended. The phrase has become part of our everyday language. As followers of Christ we understand that we are born again when we irrevocably place our faith in Jesus Christ as our Lord and Savior. Yet, what else does the Bible really teach about being born again?

- *Read John 3:1–21. Though the concept of the new birth is found elsewhere in the Bible, most people would agree this is the one place where the nature of the new birth is most fully developed. Thus, John 3 is the place of full mention of the new birth, to use the Principle of Full Mention. Summarize the key aspects of the new birth that you see in John 3.*

    _____

    _____

- *Read James 1:18; 1 Peter 1:3; 1 Peter 1:23–25; 1 John 2:29; 1 John 3:9; 1 John 5:1 and 5:18. All of these passages mention the new birth in some form. Can any of these passages really compare with John 3 in terms of breadth and depth of teaching about the new birth?*

    _____

    _____

This example of the new birth is typical of how the Principle of Full Mention works. One passage gives a good understanding of a certain doctrine. More information appears elsewhere in the Bible, but one passage is foundational and gives the most information.

> **The "Principle of Full Reference" is this: somewhere in the Bible God usually declares his mind more fully in regard to issues of vital importance. These passages serve as a foundation for issues of great significance and set the stage for this doctrine throughout the rest of scripture.**

- *Read 1 Corinthians 15. Many consider this passage to be the most complete treatment of a great doctrine of the Bible. What do you suppose that doctrine would be?*

_____

_____

Obviously there are many passages in the New Testament that mention the resurrection of Jesus Christ. This chapter, though, lays a foundation that supports and links other references.

- *Read 1 Corinthians 12–14. There is a single theme that ties these chapters together and many consider this to be the full mention of teaching on what biblical theme or concept?*

_____

_____

- *Read James 3. This might be considered the full mention of what topic in the Bible?*

_____

_____

Clearly, declaring a passage to be the "full mention" of a particular doctrine, topic, or theme in the Bible is subjective, and different people might have differing opinions about which passage is the fullest mention. Don't miss the point: God gave us "full mention" passages to guide us, as a crucial clue guides a crime investigator, so that we can understand a doctrine or teaching. We can benefit greatly from a passage of scripture where an issue is explained more thoroughly than in other passages and use our new knowledge and understanding as a big dot in a trail of dots leading to other places where it occurs in the Bible. If there appears to be two or more passages that might contend for the honor of being the "full mention" of the matter, fine! It's not important that everyone has to agree on which passage is considered the "official" full mention. What is important is to learn to benefit from it by looking for a passage that fully explains a doctrine and then use that passage as your point of reference to compare the information you find about that

In this age of the Internet, think of the Principle of Full Mention like the biblical "homepage" for a specific teaching or concept. A good homepage is the front door to a potential wealth of information.

same teaching elsewhere.

In this age of the Internet, think of the Principle of Full Mention like the biblical "homepage" for a specific teaching or idea. A good homepage is the front door to a potential wealth of information. If a homepage is well-designed, it has the basic organizational outline of that website and can lead you in many directions. Hyperlinks on the homepage allow a single click to transport the user to more information about an item. This is much like the use of cross-references in the Bible.

From one location, your doctrinal homepage, you can discover the other places a certain truth appears in the Bible. In this way, God turns a "line of dots" into a path leading you to the knowledge, wisdom and understanding of the truths he wants you to apply in your life. Like a homepage on the Internet, you can always come back to the homepage of "full mention" and go in different directions according to the information you are searching. A concordance or similar Bible study tool is a wealth of biblical "hyperlinks." If you do not already know how to use a concordance, you will learn that skill shortly.

Another way to look at this concept is to return to our investigative theme. The folder of information an investigator presents to a prosecutor is called a "case filing" (a verb used as a noun). Within the case filing are all the documents, statements, photos and lab reports related to the crime. Also included is a criminal case summary with notes in parenthesis to show links to the appropriate item in the file folder. When prosecutors read the case filing, they flip back and forth between the summary and the detailed information.

The case summary doesn't tell all the details of each report or statement, but provides an overview that puts the details in perspective. The detailed information doesn't tell the whole story but gives the prosecutor specific information that can be combined to build a case for court. The two components work together to present a big picture. When someone speaks of the Principle of Full Mention in a biblical context, that full mention functions very much like a prosecutor's criminal case summary.

The two questions we have learned in this chapter are complementary: "Where is the first time this word, phrase or idea occurs in the Bible?" and "Where is the fullest mention explanation in the Bible?" When you research or study a particular doctrine, theme, word or idea,

Question #9:
What Can I Learn By Comparing Scripture with Scripture?

ask yourself these two questions to guide you in "looking around" the Bible to discern the lesson God wants to teach you.

You might decide to use a concordance or similar tool to go back to the first time this matter appears in the Bible and work your way through scripture. Or, you can see if you discover a particular scripture passage that takes you deeper into God's mind and then use that as your "homepage." God's will is for your Bible study toolbox to contain both of these tools (questions) whenever you need them.

Several times in the previous chapter we mentioned the need to compare scripture with scripture. In essence, both questions we have learned in this chapter are ways to compare scripture with scripture. Whether using the principles of first mention or full mention, or just looking for any and every applicable passage to increase our understanding of a biblical concept, the objective is to learn everything possible about that particular doctrine or truth. Our mind should be constantly thinking: where else in the Bible might I learn more about this?

This concept is important because we learned earlier that understanding the Bible is not a matter of one's private interpretation. Instead, God wants us to allow the Holy Spirit to lead us into full knowledge in cooperation with the rest of the body of Christ.

A common way to express this principle is to say that the best commentary on the Bible is the Bible itself. Bible scholars have many great teachings to help us understand the Bible. God gives the gift of teachers to the church. But, nothing has a higher priority than simply allowing the Bible to explain itself by comparing scripture with scripture. Paul's words in 1 Corinthians 2 help us understand this principle.

- *Read 1 Corinthians 2:1–8. Paul contrasts two types of wisdom in this passage. What two types of wisdom are these?*

  _____

  _____

- *Read 1 Corinthians 2:9–12. What has God revealed to us?*

  _____

  _____

- *By what means does God reveal these things to us?*

The best commentary on the Bible is the Bible itself. Bible scholars have many great teachings to help us understand the Bible. God gives the gift of teachers to the church. But, nothing has a greater priority than simply allowing the Bible to explain itself by comparing scripture with scripture.

_____

_____

- *Are these things revealed to everyone, or only to a certain type of people? To whom does God reveal his deep things?*

_____

_____

- *Read 1 Corinthians 2:13. How does the Holy Spirit teach us these deep things of God?*

_____

_____

- *Read 1 Corinthians 2:14. Can one understand the deep things of God by human intellect alone? Why or why not?*

_____

_____

As we seek to discover God's wisdom in a passage of scripture, we constantly should be aware of how other scriptures might also shed light on our study.

Not every biblical theme or teaching merits a passage of full mention. There will be many times when we are trying to understand the meaning of a word, phrase or teaching, and the principles of first and full mention offer no help. The following examples show how examining various scriptures where the same word or concept appears can enlighten us.

- *Read 1 Corinthians 11:23–30 where Paul discusses the Lord's Supper and mentions those who participate "unworthily." He adds that some are sick and others sleep. The KJV and other translation use the word "sleep," and perhaps you wonder what he means by those who "sleep."*

- *Read John 11:1–14. Jesus' disciples also wondered what Jesus meant when he said his friend Lazarus was sleeping. How did Jesus define his use of the verb "sleep" in regard to Lazarus?*

_____

_____

- *Read 1 Thessalonians 4:13–16. Compare the phrase "them which are asleep" in verse 15 with a parallel phrase in verse 16. From this comparison, who are "them which are asleep?"*

_____

- *Read 1 Corinthians 15:51. Give your own paraphrase of what Paul says in this verse.*

The Bible interprets itself as we learn to compare scripture with scripture. This truth is the foundation of many aspects of Bible study.

By comparing scripture with scripture we see how it is possible to understand the way a particular word like "sleep" is used in certain applications. In the cases above, sleep is sometimes used to speak of the death of believers in Christ.

In practice, how does one know where to go in the Bible to compare other scriptures? Later, we will learn to use tools such as a concordance. You are probably already familiar with that book, and many Bibles have a limited concordance in the back, where you can find some of the other places in the Bible a word appears. We will also learn how to use other tools to trace a particular Hebrew or Greek word regardless of how it is translated into English. Many Bibles have center, bottom, or marginal notes that list a few cross-references to other scripture.

Sometimes, we learn cross-references listening to a preacher or teacher, reading a book or biblical commentary. There are other ways to discover cross-references, but for the moment we just want to establish in our minds this basic principle—the Bible interprets itself, as we compare scripture with scripture. This truth is the foundation for many aspects of Bible study.

Good Bible study demands we improve our skills of observation and pay attention to what we might otherwise overlook, just like a police investigator focuses on a crime scene. The three questions of this chapter all contribute to good Bible investigation.

Can we learn something by going back and tracing the word or idea through the Bible? Is there a passage that treats this subject in greater detail? Perhaps studying that passage can lead to others. Is there any other way that we can compare scripture with scripture to improve our understanding and arrive at correct interpretation of the Bible? These questions and others like them contribute to the growth of our investigative ability as Bible students.

CHAPTER EIGHT

Learning the Unknown from the Known

Life has taught me that I will never have all the answers. This statement is especially true when it comes to Bible study and is why I never get bored studying the Bible; I still have so many questions I want to explore. Sometimes in my Bible study, I hit a snag and need to adjust my approach.

At the point in an investigation when the investigator seems to be encountering dead ends in every direction, it may be time to sit down and say "What is it that we *do* know?" Sometimes, we become so focused on what we don't know, we fail to see how what we *do* understand can lead us to discover the unknown.

A friend of mine told me that an old-time detective sergeant once said, "I have no way of knowing all the things I don't know about a case. The only thing I know for sure is what I know for sure. That's what I spend the most time studying."

Parents and teachers also use this technique. Any good teacher learns to communicate truth and intangible concepts by comparisons to what is already known. Trying to communicate a new idea to a young child, the teacher or parent has to stop and consider, "What is it this child *does* understand? How can I use something already understood to teach something new?"

I asked my wife, Cheryl, about this. For years, every summer she has coached four-year-old girls in Tee-Ball. Most four-year-old girls approach baseball with an understanding level of about -5 on a 1 to 10 scale. "So, Cheryl, how do you teach a little girl to run to first base?"

"I say, 'Run like *a bunny!*'"

"Okay, I've seen even older girls try to throw a baseball without much success. Guys are always kidding about someone who 'throws like a girl.' So, how do you communicate to a four-year-old girl how to throw a softball?"

"I tell them to pretend their arm is like an elephant tossing out its trunk."

Think about it for a moment. That's not bad, is it? Bunnies and elephants fascinate most little kids. Imagine an elephant extending its trunk and try to imitate that with your arm.

Previously, we learned nine questions to direct our investigative Bible study. Now, we are going to add nine principles to our Bible study

> *"What is it that we do know?" Sometimes, we become so focused on what we don't know, we fail to see how what we do understand can lead us to discover the unknown.*

toolbox, four of them in this chapter. Not every one of these principles applies in every case, but most often one or more of them points us in the right direction, or keeps us from heading in wrong directions. They set the boundaries for our Bible study.

In chapter two I quoted a classic law enforcement textbook by Charles O'Hara discussing the two stages of investigation—survey and search. In the first four chapters we learned to survey to get the big picture. Since then we have been collecting tools and techniques to assist in the search. Regarding the search phase in investigation O'Hara says, "Method rather than intuition should guide the basic search…. The spirit of the investigation will be caught if the investigator assumes everything he finds will be the only evidence of the crime."[1]

The following principles will help us establish a solid methodology of Bible study. While intuition can be a wonderful thing, these principles protect us from intuition that is unchecked by truth and reality.

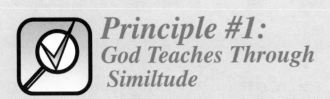

Principle #1:
God Teaches Through Similtude

Teaching by Similitude Is to Associate, Contrast, and/or Compare

- *Read Hosea 12:10. Through the prophet Hosea, God says he used the prophets to speak to Israel through visions and what other method?*

  _____

  _____

- *Look up the word "similitude" in a dictionary online, or the big one that sits on your desk. Then, define similitude in your own words.*

  _____

  _____

Teaching by similitude is to draw comparisons or contrasts to things or concepts already understood.

Teaching by similitude draws comparisons or contrasts to things already understood. As mentioned above, every good parent and teacher uses this technique repeatedly. Thinking about it, it should come as no surprise that God would use similitude to teach us his truth. God's truth is heavenly, eternal, and spiritual. Man's understanding is earthly and finite.

- *Read Isaiah 55:8–9. How does this passage characterize God's thoughts and ways?*

  _____

  _____

- *Read Romans 8:5–7 and 1 Corinthians 2:14. How would you characterize mankind's understanding in the natural, unconverted state?*

  _____

  _____

Like any good parent or teacher, God starts with what we know to help us comprehend concepts and truth beyond our normal understanding. To introduce us to eternal, intangible truth, he draws comparisons, contrasts, and associations of things tangible—a similitude.

Every one of the principles in this chapter has to do with God's use of similitude in the Bible. This first principle introduces us to the educational principle itself and to two little words that have the potential to revolutionize your understanding of the Bible.

Two of the Most Important Words in the Bible Are "Like" and "As"

Yes, you read it correctly. These two little words are powerful indeed. If you will cultivate the habit of looking for them and paying attention when they appear in the Bible, you will be amazed by how much you can learn. We will use a few examples to illustrate what I mean, but the concept itself is quite simple to grasp and apply.

- *Read Matthew 24:36–3. Underscore, highlight, or otherwise note the times the word "as" appears.*

- *If you are unfamiliar with this passage, read the entire chapter and see that the context has to do with Christ's Second Coming. By using the word "as" Jesus links his Second Coming to what other period of history?*

  _____

  _____

- *Think about the comparison between the Second Coming and the days of Noah before the Flood. What are some of the things you can learn about the Second Coming by comparing these two times in history?*

  _____

  _____

- *Keep in mind the intentional similitude between the Second Coming of Christ and the days of Noah as you turn your biblical investigative skills to the historical account of those days. Read Genesis chapters 5 and 6 and list any similarities you see between Noah's days and the day leading up to Christ's Second Coming.*

  _____

  _____

- *Read Luke 17:28–30. Underscore, highlight, or otherwise note the word "as" in this passage. Here, Jesus uses the word "as" to compare the time leading up to his Second Coming to what other period of Old Testament history?*

  _____

  _____

- *Read Genesis 19:1–26 describing the historical events in Lot's days that Jesus referred to in Luke 17. Comparing this passage in Genesis 19 with what Jesus said in Luke 17, what would you list as some of the similarities Jesus may have had in mind when he compared his Second Coming to the days of Lot?*

  _____

  _____

- *Read Ephesians 5:22–25. As you did in previous passages, locate the words "as" and "like." Here, Paul uses these words to establish a similitude between two things. What are they?*

  _____

  _____

Paul clearly teaches that marriage illustrates the relationship between Christ and his bride, the church. The Old Testament does not directly teach the New Testament church. The church was present, though, as a "mystery" waiting to be revealed through Paul (Ephesians 3:1-2). Armed with the knowledge that God intends marriage to illustrate his love relationship with his people, the astute Bible student will pay attention to ways marriage teaches us about our relationship with the Lord.

The Song of Solomon is the love story between Solomon and his Shulamite lover. Paul's use of "as" and "like" in Ephesians 5 should alert us to look a little deeper in the Song of Solomon. Solomon, the "son of David" (Proverbs 1:1) takes a Gentile bride much like Jesus, the "son of David' (Matthew 1:1) takes a bride, the church, that is currently made up of mostly gentiles.

Ruth is the love story of Boaz and Ruth, a gentile. Boaz, like Jesus, is a native of Bethlehem and, as a close relative to Ruth's dead husband,

While one must be careful not to look for "hidden" meaning or to read something into the plain sense of scripture, both Song of Solomon and Ruth are books rich in illustrations of the relationship between Christ and the church, thanks to Paul's judicious use of the words "as" and "like."

is able to redeem the Gentile Ruth, just like Jesus became a member of the human family to redeem us from our sin. While one must be careful not to look for "hidden" meanings or to read things into the plain sense of scripture, we can see that Song of Solomon and Ruth are books rich in illustrations of the relationship between Christ and the church, thanks to Paul's judicious use of the words "as" and "like."

These are only a few of many examples in the Bible where we discover similitude by observing the use of the little words "as" and "like." Discipline yourself as a good Bible investigator to look for these two words that can make you see the important use of similitude in the Bible.

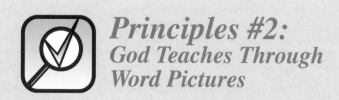

Principles #2:
God Teaches Through Word Pictures

The Old Testament Is a Picture Book

When parents first read books to their little children they often use books with pictures only, no words. Even if the book has words, the children are looking at the pictures and their imaginations are in overdrive. Most of us learned to read by seeing a multitude of pictures.

This is a gross oversimplification, of course, but it is helpful to see the Old Testament as a "picture book" to illustrate the intangible truths of the New Testament. The Old Testament is full of stories of real people and it describes all of their successes and sins, flaws and failures, and the wisdom and warts of personality. Nothing is held back. Even most of the great heroes of the Old Testament have serious problems and issues along with their victories. God uses real lives to illustrate life's truths and principles. In this whole process God uses the principle we have been discussing – teaching through the use of similitude.

> *It might be helpful to see the Old Testament as a "picture book" to illustrate the intangible truths of the New Testament.*

- *Read Romans 15:1–4. In verse three Paul quotes from Psalm 69:9. In verse four what is it Paul says these scriptures "written aforetime" were written for?*

  _____

  _____

- *Read 1 Corinthians 10:1–10. Paul is speaking of the Old Testament story of the Exodus. Read 1 Corinthians 10:11 and tell why God recorded this story in the Old Testament.*

  _____

  _____

The Old Testament, then, often acts as a "picture book" to open our understanding of the New. Here, though, we are not as concerned with a specific similitude introduced by words such as "like" and "as," but with pictures painted with words. Let's see some classic examples of the use of word pictures by paying close attention to words of Jesus Christ.

Word Pictures of Christ by Moses

- *Read John 5:39–47. Jesus discusses his healing a man by the pool of Bethesda with certain religious Jews. Look carefully at John 5:46. What did Jesus say Moses had done?*

_____

_____

This is a critical point. Jesus said Moses wrote of him. We have already learned that Moses is the human author of the first five books of the Bible. Yet, a search of those five books yields not a single reference to Jesus, Christ, or anything close. The only way to understand what Jesus is saying is to understand that Moses wrote word pictures of the coming Christ. And did he! Here are some examples:

Abraham's Offering of Isaac

- *Slowly and carefully read Genesis 22:1–14.*

- *Read the New Testament commentary on the Abraham-Isaac story in Hebrews 11:17–19. This event was a "figure" of what?*

_____

_____

- *Read Genesis 22:2, the first time "love" is mentioned in the Bible. Read John 3:16 and list any comparisons you see between these two verses.*

_____

_____

- *God tells Abraham to offer his only son in sacrifice, and Abraham commits to obey. Reading Genesis 22, especially verse four, how long is the period of time in which Isaac is "as good as dead" to Abraham before God tells Abraham to spare him?*

_____

_____

- *Thinking again of Abraham's faith mentioned in Hebrews 11: 17–19, can you see Abraham's faith in God's power to resurrect the dead in Genesis 22:5? Explain.*

  _____

  _____

- *Read Genesis 22:6. How does Isaac display his faith and obedience?*

  _____

  _____

- *Read Genesis 22:7–8. What does Abraham say God will provide for himself?*

  _____

  _____

- *Read John the Baptist's statement in John 1:29. What do you think is represented in prophetic form by Genesis 22:7–8?*

  _____

  _____

A prayerful reading of this passage in Genesis 22 will reveal even more parallels between Abraham's willingness to sacrifice his "only begotten son" (Hebrews 11:17) and God's offering up his "only begotten son" (John 3:16). The point of this exercise is to show how Moses wrote of Christ, not directly, but in word pictures such as these. Though Christ is not mentioned directly, most believers have little difficulty seeing Christ in word pictures such as in Genesis 22.

The Exodus

- *Read Exodus 12. This instruction for the first Passover is another word picture of the sacrifice of Jesus Christ, the Lamb of God.*

- *The key to understanding that this is a word picture of Christ is 1 Corinthians 5:7. Read this verse and what does it say Christ is?*

  _____

  _____

- *Read Exodus 12:2. What do we learn about the date of the Passover in this verse?*

  _____

  _____

- *Read Exodus 12:5. What are the requirements for the Passover lamb?*

  _____

  _____

- *Read 1 Peter 1:18-19. How does the Lord Jesus Christ measure up to the requirements for the Passover lamb?*

  _____

  _____

As in the case of Abraham offering up Isaac, the Passover also has many other elements that point to the sacrifice of Christ as our Passover, offered for the penalty of our sin. Perhaps you have observed some of those as you read through Exodus 12. Paul's words in 1 Corinthians 5:7, though, make it clear that Moses wrote of Christ, just as Jesus said in John 5:46. This does not mean that as Moses wrote the book of Exodus he was conscious of how his words prophetically pictured the Christ to come, but only that God was using Moses to draw these word pictures pointing to Christ.

Jacob's Ladder

- *Read Genesis 28:12. Then, read John 3:1–15 (especially verse 13a) and explain in your own words how the ladder Jacob saw was a prediction of Jesus Christ as he himself explained to Nicodemus.*

  _____

  _____

We already learned in the last chapter that the serpent is a consistent picture of the Devil through the Bible. You will remember that John 3:14 explains that the serpent pictures Christ "lifted up" on a cross where he was made sin for us, according to Paul's explanation in 2 Corinthians 5:21. Once again, we learn to be aware of word pictures in the Old Testament that portray aspects of Christ's life and ministry.

Before moving on, we need to remember that these word pictures are not invented in our imaginations. We discover them by comparing scripture with scripture, seeing how the Bible itself identifies and interprets them. We must be careful not to read pictures into the Bible that were never intended to be there. Our final authority is the Bible, not our imagination. That being said, however, our understanding of the Bible is deeply enriched when we are alert to the possibility of some of the stories of the Old Testament being word pictures of things to come.

We must be careful not to read pictures into the Bible that were never intended to be there.

163

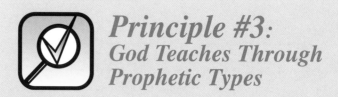

Principle #3:
God Teaches Through Prophetic Types

This principle is closely related to the Principle #2. The word pictures in the Old Testament contain people, events, places, or other things that symbolize or illustrate events or people to come. These prophetic symbols that look to a future fulfillment are called *types*. The person, event, or thing represented by a type is called an *antitype*.

In today's computerized world, biblical types are easier to understand than ever before. We speak of "icons" on our computer screens. That little trashcan picture on your computer screen is not really a trashcan but merely a symbol or icon of a trashcan's function. When you drag and drop a file onto that trashcan, it is erased. You don't really drop anything into a trashcan; you erase a file and the trashcan represents that function to help you better understand what you are doing.

When you arrive in the airport not speaking the local language and need to find something important, you look for internationally understood icons representing without words what you seek. For example, you might want to find the rest rooms, a money exchange, information, or a restaurant, which the icons represent.

In the Bible when a figure symbolically represents something else, it is often called a "type," and fulfills a function much like those airport icons or those computer icons Just as I have cautioned before, I cannot repeat forcibly enough: Don't let your imagination determine types in scripture. Let the Bible speak for itself.

The study of types in the Bible is nothing new. The word itself comes from a Greek word, *tupos*, meaning a print or mark made by beating, as in stamping an image into a piece of gold or silver.

Benjamin Keach ministered in the 1600's and wrote a classic book republished several times over the years. He defined types as "the images or figures of things present, or to come; especially the actions and histories of the Old Testament, respecting such as prefigured Christ our Savior in his actions, life, passion, death, and the glory that followed."[2]

In chapter six we spoke of biblical symbolism and saw the example of the sword representing the Bible. We looked at Hebrews 4:12; Ephesians 6:17; and Revelation 19:15–19, and saw this imagery defined in scripture. We can say that the sword in scripture is a type of the Bible.

Another example we have already seen in our study of the Passover from the book of Exodus and from Paul's statement in 1 Corinthians 5, is that Jesus Christ is our Passover lamb. We also saw John the Baptist's announcement about the "Lamb of God." In this word picture of the

In the Bible when a figure or person symbolically represents something else, it is often called a "type," and fulfills a function much like icons on our computer screens.

Exodus we can comfortably say that the Passover lamb is a type of Jesus Christ. Jesus Christ, then, is the antitype or what the type represents.

A few more examples illustrate how biblical types work.

Jonah in the whale

- *Read Jonah 1–2.*

- *Read Matthew 12:38–40 and 16:1–4. Jonah in the whale is a type of what?*

  _____

  _____

The Tabernacle in the Old Testament

- *Read Hebrews 8 and 9, paying careful attention to 8:2, 5 and Hebrews 9:9–11, 23–24. The Old Testament Tabernacle is a type of what?*

  _____

  _____

- *Remembering that scripture can have various levels of understanding, read 2 Corinthians 5:1–4 and 2 Peter 1:13–14. The Old Testament Tabernacle is also a type of what else?*

  _____

  _____

Manna

- *Read Exodus 16 and learn about the manna.*

- *Read John 6:30–59. Manna is a type of what?*

  _____

  _____

There are other types in the Bible. Entire books have been written about types in the Bible. Be careful, though, not to stretch the scripture beyond the meaning God wants us to have. Be careful to let the Bible itself define its types, and don't dream up types in your imagination or anyone else's. The study of types, though, can stimulate your mind and spirit as you grow in your biblical understanding and appreciate more and more the genius and glory of God in the making of the Bible.

Principle #4:
God Illustrates His Truth in Creation

Good parents understand another technique to teach their children an intangible truth by using a physical object lesson. Little children have done this in school for generations by playing "Show and Tell." Who hasn't used some physical object to illustrate a concept? Maybe you have used a small seed that grows into a massive tree to illustrate how our faith can grow into something much bigger than we can imagine. Good teachers love to discover effective object lessons to help students grasp difficult concepts.

- *Read Romans 1:18–20. How can we understand the invisible things of God?*

  _____

  _____

- *Read Psalm 19:1–4. What declares God's glory and handiwork?*

  _____

  _____

- *Re-read Psalm 19:4. Are there any geographical or linguistic limitations to this witness of God's creation? What does this passage say about that?*

  _____

  _____

God our Father is a both a great Parent and a wonderful Teacher. He is the Master of "Show and Tell." He uses his creation, the visible universe, to teach us truth about himself.

The Sun and Other HeavenlyBodies

- *Read Malachi 4:1–2. Most Bible students recognize this as a powerful prophecy of the Christ's Second Coming in judgment. In the second verse a figure is used to describe the Messiah's coming to those who fear God's name. What is the figure or phrase that represents Christ in this second verse?*

  _____

  _____

God our Father is both a great Parent and a wonderful Teacher. He is the Master of "Show and Tell." He uses his creation, the visible universe, to teach us truth about himself.

- *Read Psalm 84:11. Besides being our shield, what else is our God according to this verse?*

_____

_____

- *Read Luke 1:67–80, a prophecy given by Zacharias, father of John the Baptist. In verse 78 the dayspring is the dawn, the rising of the sun and connects Christ with the prophecy of Malachi made 400 years earlier.*

In these passages we see the sun used as a figure for God. No analogy is perfect in every detail, of course, but there are some strong comparisons between God and the sun.

One of the hardest teachings to understand or explain is the Trinity. As limited as that analogy is, many Bible teachers through the centuries have used the figure of the sun to help explain the Trinity.

- *Read John 4:24, Jesus spoke these words in reference to his Father God. God is a what?*

_____

_____

The sun we see in the sky is an unapproachable gaseous object, much like God as a Spirit is physically unapproachable. However, the sun is visible and felt by us through both visible and invisible rays.

- *Read John 14:8–9. In this passage Jesus claims to be equal to whom?*

_____

_____

Just as visible light rays enable us to "see" the sun, Jesus Christ enables us to "see" the Father.

- *Read John 14:15–17. Who is the Comforter that Jesus promises to send to his followers?*

_____

_____

If you stay out in the sun too long on a bright day, you discover that the sun also has invisible rays, but you can certainly feel them! God the Father is a Spirit far beyond our ability to comprehend. Yet, he made himself visible and knowable through Jesus Christ. Those who follow him receive his Holy Spirit to live within their inner beings. We cannot see the Holy Spirit, but we can certainly "feel" his presence in our lives.

This comparison between God and the sun reminds us of Paul's words in Romans 1:20 saying that we can understand the invisible things of God from his creation, *"even his eternal power and Godhead."*

• *Read 1 Corinthians 15:35–44, on the certainty and the power of the resurrection. Paul uses elements of God's creation to illustrate his point. Besides the sun that we have already considered, what are other elements of creation Paul mentions here?*

_____

_____

• *What do you suppose is the point Paul illustrates here with his mention of the sun, moon, and stars?*

_____

_____

You may remember what we saw in Revelation 1:20, where stars symbolize angels. There are many ways creation illustrates God's truth. As you continue studying the Bible, take notice when elements of creation illustrate some divine truth. When you struggle to understand or express some intangible biblical truth, stop for a moment to consider if there is some way nature illustrates that truth, in fulfillment of Paul's statement in Romans 1:20.

Trees

Trees are a common biblical figure to illustrate mankind, either individually or collectively as nations or peoples.

• *Read Matthew 3:5–12 as John the Baptist confronts some of the Pharisees and Sadducees when he was baptizing in the Jordan River. Explain the meaning of John's reference to "trees" in verse 10 and what they represent in this context.*

_____

_____

• *Read Matthew 7:15–20 and 12:33. Explain how Jesus used trees as an illustration.*

_____

_____

Remember this very important principle: types and other biblical figures do not establish doctrinal truth; they illustrate doctrinal truth.

Consider for a moment the similarities between people and trees. Trees receive their nourishment from water and sunlight. We receive our spiritual nourishment from the water of God's word (Ephesians 5:25–26) and from basking in the light of the Sun of Righteousness (Malachi 4:2). Some trees bear fruit and some do not, just like people. In temperate climates many trees illustrate the cycle of life each year, bearing fruit in summer, shedding leaves in the fall, and giving the appearance of death in winter, only to come to life in the spring.

Remember this very important principle: types and other biblical figures do not establish doctrinal truth; they illustrate doctrinal truth.

Some people make the mistake of trying to read something into the minor details of a biblical type and then construct some doctrine that is not found anywhere else in the Bible. The major teaching God wants us to have is clearly communicated in the Bible. The Bible is a divine revelation, not a divine secret. Types do not reveal doctrine; they illustrate doctrine.

In recent years, types have fallen into discredit in some circles as a reaction against those who go to extremes and push far beyond reasonable limits of understanding. The opposite extreme of ignoring types or denying their legitimacy is just as unfortunate. Understanding types and their uses bring the Bible alive, especially portions of the Old Testament. Just be careful to see that types are defined in scripture and are not figments of your fertile imagination.

- *Read Psalm 1:1–3. One who meditates day and night in the word of God (verse 2) is compared to what in verse three?*

  _____

  _____

- *In verse three what are three characteristics of a tree planted by rivers of water?*

  _____

  _____

- *Read Psalm 92:12. The righteous person is compared to two types of trees. What are they?*

  _____

  _____

This verse describes how the righteous flourish. The palm tree flourishes in desert places because it sends its roots straight down deep into the water table. Cedar trees grow in forests where they depend on each other. This verse describes two different aspects of spiritual growth, both of which are necessary. We need each other to grow properly, but we also need to have spiritual roots deep enough to flourish in those lonely, desert times of life.

Animals

Another aspect of God's creation is the animal world. The Bible also uses animals to illustrate spiritual truth. Here are a few examples:

- *Read John 1:32. To what does John the Baptist compare the Holy Spirit?*

  _____

  _____

- *Read Matthew 13:1–23, paying attention to verse four that speaks of the seed sown by the wayside and is then eaten up by fowls (birds). Then, see the interpretation Jesus gives in verse 19. It seems clear the seed corresponds to the word of the kingdom. What do you think is represented by the birds?*

_____

_____

The dove clearly represents the Holy Spirit. The Parable of the Sower, though, alerts us to the fact that not all birds in the Bible have such noble and pure symbolism.

- *Read Isaiah 34, a sober prediction of the day of God's wrath yet to come. How many different types of birds can you find in this chapter?*

_____

_____

- *Taking into account the context of this chapter, do you think the birds listed in Isaiah 34 have a good connotation or an evil one?*

_____

_____

- *Read Deuteronomy 14:1–20 where a distinction is made between clean and unclean animals. How many of the birds of Isaiah 34 can you find here in Deuteronomy 14?*

_____

_____

- *Are the birds from Isaiah 34 clean or unclean?*

_____

_____

Birds can represent pure forces such as the Holy Spirit, or they can represent demonic forces.

- *Read 1 Corinthians 9:1–10 where Paul defends himself and other ministers from the some charges that ministers have no right to expect financial payment. In this passage he quotes from an Old Testament passage and compares himself and other ministers to a certain animal. What is the animal Paul uses here as an example?*

_____

_____

Having personally observed oxen working on several continents, I find this an interesting comparison. Just as Jesus sent out his disciples two by two in Matthew 10, oxen often work in teams of two, yoked together by wood in the form of a cross. In tough, steep places I have seen them move forward on their knees. Clearly, there is something we can learn from this example.

The tenth and final plague God brought upon Egypt leading up to the Exodus was the death of every first born of Egypt, both man and animal. Those of Israel were spared if they applied the blood of the Passover lamb to the homes. Upon seeing the blood, the death angel would pass over that home. God instructed Israel in Exodus 13 to always remember that event by setting aside (sanctifying) the first born of all men and animals from that time on as a special offering to God. Rather than being offered as a literal offering, the first-born male child of an Israelite was to be redeemed by a substitute.

- *Read Exodus 13. Besides the first-born male child, a certain animal also needed to be redeemed by the sacrifice of a lamb. What was that animal according to Exodus 13?*

  _____

  _____

- *If the first-born of an ass was not redeemed by a sacrificial lamb, what was to happen to it?*

  _____

  _____

- *Read Zophar's comment about vain or empty men in Job 11: 12. To what does Zophar compare this man's birth? (Remember what we learned about the words "like" and "as.")*

  _____

  _____

The New Testament teaches our need for a new birth. Something is wrong with our first birth, and we must be born again (John 3). Mankind's problem, of course, is sin, and this is why we need to be redeemed, just like the first-born Israelite and just like the first-born ass.

- *Read 1 Peter 1:18–19. How have we been redeemed?*

  _____

  _____

We do not want to press our analogy too far, but it seems there is a similarity between lost man and a firstborn ass in the Bible. Both need to be redeemed.

The Bible is a book of real people, events, and objects that enable even a child to grasp the fundamental attributes of God and the basic lessons of life.

• *Read Deuteronomy 22:10 and 2 Corinthians 6:14. Keeping in mind what we have learned about the ox and the ass, what practical lessons can we learn from the comparison of these two verses?*

_____

_____

This chapter has shown how God employs the same basic teaching techniques used by effective teachers and parents. He teaches us the unknown and intangible by drawing comparisons and contrasts with what we do know. He does this by using similitude, word pictures, types, and even his creation to illustrate his truth—even truth as deep as "*his eternal power and Godhead*" (Romans 1:20).

These are but a few examples of learning the unknown from the known, but the Bible is quite full of this kind of teaching. How else could God make his wonderful truth available to us? Rather than a book filled with philosophical theory, the Bible is a book of real people, events, and objects that enable even a child to grasp the fundamental attributes of God and the basic lessons of life. As you improve your investigative Bible study skills, you can train yourself to be aware of the Bible's constant use of similitude, word pictures, types, and creation to illustrate divine principle.

Notes

1.   Charles O'Hara, *The Fundamentals of Criminal Investigation* (Springfield, MO: Charles Thomas, 1956), 43.

2.   Benjamin Keach, *Preaching from the Types and Metaphors of the Bible* (Grand Rapids: Kregel Classics), 1972, 226.

Learning to Think Clearly

Clear thinking is rare. Any effective investigative effort depends upon the clear thinking, common sense, and objective detachment of the investigators.

Returning to our detective analogy, a good crime scene investigator must be able to objectively survey and scrutinize the facts and the evidence. A detective must not allow personal distractions, emotional involvement or any other concerns to interfere with clear thinking. Intuition can be a powerful tool at times but must never be allowed to contradict facts, evidence and clear thought.

Studying the Bible is no different. A basic premise in our study so far is the commitment to see what the Bible really says, not to read into the Bible what we want it to say. This is hard and no one is exempt from the temptation to read his or her own ideas and desires into the absolute truth of the Bible. Objectivity is hard because it is impossible to have a dynamic relationship with God and the Bible without involving the emotions.

Honesty requires the admission that no one can be totally objective when approaching the objective truth of scripture. Sometimes what we call "intuition" is really a cover for our lifelong collection of experiences, presuppositions and biases that work against objective understanding every time we go to the Bible. We can, though, guard against this natural tendency by learning and using some basic principles in our Bible study.

The following principles build upon the four principles from chapter eight. They should lead to solid methods of Bible study. While intuition can be a wonderful thing, these principles protect us from intuition that is unchecked by truth and reality.

> *Honesty requires the admission that no one can be totally objective when approaching the objective truth of scripture.*

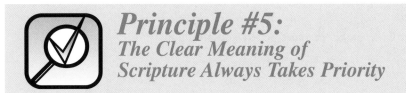

Principle #5:
The Clear Meaning of Scripture Always Takes Priority

When faced with the human tendency to read things into scripture that aren't there, this principle should fill our thinking; the clear meaning of scripture always takes priority over any obscure or complicated meaning. We have learned to begin Bible study by seeking the plain, literal, grammatical and historical sense of the words, never going beyond that to violate the clear meaning.

Some passages are hard to understand. But we must never abandon the clearest and most literal sense in order to discover some forced symbolism or imagined message. When the going gets tough, we must content ourselves with whatever we can understand on the surface and never force an interpretation that would conflict with or ignore the normal and natural sense of the passage. The clearest sense always takes priority.

- *Read Daniel 12. Daniel's prophecy has to do with the end time and the coming tribulation. In verse 4 what is Daniel instructed to do with these words?*

    _____

    _____

- *Even Daniel did not have full understanding and asks God for clarification in verse 8. What is the answer Daniel receives?*

    _____

    _____

- *Read 2 Corinthians 12:1–4 where Paul refers to himself in the third person to speak of a dramatic experience in his life. Many Bible students believe Paul has in mind the time in Lystra when he was stoned almost to death (Acts 14). Was Paul in the body or out of the body during this experience?*

    _____

    _____

The correct answer, of course, is "I don't know." Paul himself did not know. Only God knows. This, along with the passage in Daniel, is an example of scriptures that simply are "sealed," or unable to be known until God is ready to reveal the meaning. You should never press a passage for "hidden truth" and go beyond the clearest sense of the words. The clearest sense always takes the priority. You may learn more about the passage later, but you must not stretch or twist the clear meaning in order to make the passage say something else.

Principle #6:
Direct Statements Take Priority Over Questions

Some bad teaching has resulted from someone basing a doctrine on a verse of scripture that is a question, not a statement. Think about this for a moment. Questions are, not a statement of purpose or truth. You should never base a doctrine on a question. This is just common sense, but it is amazing how often this principle is ignored. Here's an example:

• *Read 1 Corinthians 15:29. There are two sentences in this verse. Are they statements or questions?*

_____

_____

The obvious difficulty in this verse is the phrase *"baptized for the dead."* What in the world does that mean? The Mormon Church has developed an elaborate doctrine based on this verse and spent millions of dollars to construct a genealogical data base so that they can be baptized for their dead ancestors.

Here are the facts of the case. This verse is the only time in the whole Bible the phrase *"baptism for the dead"* or its equivalent occurs. And, the only time it does appear is in a question.

Actually, this verse is a great illustration, not only of this principle but also of the previous one about giving priority to the clear meaning of scripture. The literal meaning of 1 Corinthians 15:29 is not in question, and none of the individual words of this short verse are difficult. What confounds us is the phrase *"baptism for the dead."* As mysterious as this phrase may be, there is no reason to construct some complicated teaching or ritual to explain the phrase *"baptism for the dead."*

According to Principle #5, we should take this phrase simply for what it says, even if we don't understand the phrase *"baptism for the dead"* or what it represents. Since the two sentences of 1 Corinthians 15:29 are questions, Principle #6 warns us against seeking some doctrine in them. This is the only time in the Bible the *"baptism for the dead"* appears, so it is unwise to read any doctrine into this phrase.

While we consider 1 Corinthians 15:29, let's apply some of the tools we have learned. Our first question should deal with context. 1 Corinthians is the New Testament letter Paul wrote to fix serious problems in the church at Corinth, in modern day Greece.

• *Read 1 Corinthians 15. Give the main theme of this chapter.*

_____

_____

Whatever Paul means by this phrase *"baptism for the dead,"* he mentions it in the context of reaffirming that the resurrection is the centerpiece of the Gospel. However, you may have worded your answer to the above question, 1 Corinthians revolves around the resurrection.

- *Read again 1 Corinthians 15:1–11. Whose resurrection is Paul stating as a fact confirmed by multiple eyewitnesses?*

  _____

  _____

- *Read 1 Corinthians 15:12–22. If Christ is risen from the dead, does this have any connection to his followers' hope of a future resurrection?*

  _____

  _____

The controversy in Corinth was not about someone denying Christ's resurrection. Christ's resurrection was an established and accepted historical fact, as Paul confirms in verses 1–11. The issue in Corinth was false teachers denying that believers would likewise have a physical resurrection (1 Corinthians 15:12). They were teaching that the promise of a future resurrection for believers was only meant to be symbolic. Paul, on the other hand, says that if Christ literally is risen from the dead, so will we.

In 1 Corinthians 15:29 he poses two questions about baptism in the context of teaching the certainty of God's promise to physically raise believers from the grave. Think for a moment of the powerful visual image portrayed by baptism by immersion (the only kind that appears in the New Testament). As the baptizer lowers the person to be baptized into the water, it is a picture showing that as Christ died for our sin and was buried, we have also died to our sin and our old way of life and are "buried" under the water. And just as Christ rose again from the dead, the believer is lifted up out of the water in a clear picture of resurrection. The simplest explanation of Paul's words in 1 Corinthians 15:29 in their context is that our baptism has no meaning if there is no hope of a literal resurrection. Whatever else Paul might have meant by *"baptism for the dead,"* it must have something to do with baptism as a confirmation of the truth of the physical resurrection of believers, because that is the context.

- *Read James 2:20. This verse has been used often to teach that grace alone is not sufficient for salvation. Some have said that James contradicts Paul's teaching of salvation by grace through faith. Is this verse a statement of fact, or a question?*

  _____

  _____

- *Read the whole chapter of James 2, paying attention to the context. How would you summarize the context of this chapter?*

  _____

  _____

- *Read the illustration in James 2:21 describing Abraham offering up his son Isaac as a living sacrifice. Read Genesis 22:1–18 to which James 2 refers. Do you see any place in Genesis 22 that says that Abraham believed God and it was imputed to him for righteousness?*

  _____

  _____

- *Read James 2:23 and then Genesis 15:1–6. Do you see something in Genesis 15 that corresponds to what James quotes in James 2:23? What is it?*

  _____

  _____

- *Read Romans 4 where Paul uses Abraham's faith as an example of our New Testament conversion. Reread Romans 4:9 where Paul says that Abraham's faith was counted (imputed) unto him for righteousness. Does this event correspond to Genesis 15 or Genesis 22?*

  _____

  _____

- *Genesis 15 and Genesis 22 are separated by at least 30 years. If the event in Genesis 15 corresponds to Abraham's salvation some 30 years before offering up his son Isaac as a sacrifice, do you think the main point of James 2:21 is to show how Abraham gained salvation from sin and eternal life?*

  _____

  _____

Putting it all together, it's pretty clear that James 2 doesn't teach the manner of how to get eternal life, but rather the need for your works to show evidence of saving faith if it is indeed genuine.

Taking James 2:20 alone could certainly give the false impression that to be saved you must add works to faith in order to be saved, so we went back and rechecked the context of James 2. We also noticed that verse 20 is a question. Therefore, that verse alone can't establish a teaching on how to get saved. Comparing scripture with scripture enabled us to piece together the context and intent of James's remarks.

Observe how the questions and principles of biblical investigative Bible study work together. There is no particular order in which to apply these investigative tools. The investigator takes into account the details and setting of the passage and applies the necessary questions and principles to arrive at the intended message of the passage.

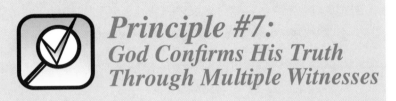

Principle #7:
God Confirms His Truth Through Multiple Witnesses

This is another principle firmly rooted in common sense. We should never base a doctrine or major teaching on a single verse or passage of scripture. Throughout scripture, God both uses and requires multiple witnesses to confirm truth.

In the case of the *"baptism for the dead"* in 1 Corinthians 15:29, we discovered that this mysterious phrase only occurs this one time in the whole Bible. If there was truly a ritualistic baptism for the dead, we would expect to find it confirmed elsewhere in scripture.

- *Read 2 Corinthians 13:1, Matthew 18:16, and John 8:17. In your own words summarize the principle common to these three verses.*

  _____

  _____

- *Read Genesis 1:16 and Psalm 89:35–37. What are two very visible and prominent witnesses God put in the sky to give testimony to his creation?*

  _____

  _____

- *Read John 20:1–12. How many witnesses were waiting in the tomb to testify to Jesus' resurrection?*

  _____

  _____

- *Read Deuteronomy 17:6 and 19:15 and observe that in the Old Testament law, two or more witnesses were required to settle a dispute.*

There is nothing complicated about this principle, which should protect us from accepting or spreading propagating doctrinal error. Before putting stock in any thread of biblical teaching we should ask ourselves where this truth is confirmed elsewhere in the Bible. If something is really important, we will see it confirmed by two or three witnesses.

> **Some of God's teachings take time and spiritual maturity to understand, and there are Bible passages we will never understand in this life.**

Principle #8:
Some Bibical Truth Requires Maturity to Understand

By this point in our study it should be abundantly clear that we will never understand everything in the Bible. We have also learned that the Bible is to be spiritually discerned, not merely be the object of intellectual curiosity and unsupported interpretation. Only a submissive attitude to God will yield the depth of riches and wisdom he wants us to discover in his Word.

There is more to consider. Some truth can only be understood with maturity. Understanding this principle requires we stop pushing and twisting when we don't understand something. Some of God's teachings take time and spiritual maturity to understand, and there Bible passages we will never understand in this life. We must never try to force the Bible to line up with what we think, but rather line up our lives to match the truth of the Bible. We do not go to the Bible to find support for our ideas; we should go to the Bible to form our ideas in line with God's ideas.

- *Read John 16:12. Jesus had other things to say to his disciples, but why did he choose not to say them at this time?*

  _____

  _____

- *Read John 16:13–14. What is the key to going beyond our current biblical understanding according to these verses?*

  _____

  _____

- *Read 1 Corinthians 3:1–2. What might sometimes be a reason you may not be able to understand certain spiritual truth?*

  _____

  _____

- *Read Hebrews 5:11–14. What are some other possible reasons why you might not be able to understand some of the deeper truth of the Bible?*

  _____

  _____

Learning the Bible is a life-long process. Do not get frustrated when there is something you cannot understand. Keep studying with an open heart and mind and you will understand everything God thinks you need to know at your level of spiritual maturity.

When I was about twelve years old, I became interested in electronics. I lived in a small town and there wasn't much to do. So, I went to the library and checked out all the books I could find on electronics one at a time. I read every magazine that talked about electronics, such as *Popular Electronics*. At first, I didn't understand much of anything. My passion to learn about electronics was so great, though, I just kept reading even though I didn't understand most of what I was reading.

A funny thing happened. The more I read, the more I understood. I decided not to worry about what I didn't understand and just kept reading. I never took a class in electronics, yet two years later I got a job repairing radios and televisions for a local repair shop. I just kept reading and never allowed myself to get frustrated by what I didn't understand.

Studying the Bible should be like that. Our passion to know God should far outweigh any frustration at not understanding some portion of scripture. The more we read, the more we understand. Some things just take time to understand. Some things we will never understand.

Principle #9:
Your Hand and Mind Are Connected

Watching crime investigation shows on television might give you the idea that investigation is all about standing at crime scenes talking to other detectives, wolfing down hot dogs while on surveillance or kicking down doors to make a dramatic arrest. It seems most television shows leave out the part about how much time detectives spend typing hundreds of pages of documents for a case, copying and stapling case files and going to court. Few detectives I know enjoy the paper work, but it is a necessary part of the job.

As we discuss principles to help us think clearly, one of the most important ways to think clearly is to write things down. Few of us have the brainpower to remember everything we see and hear. Neither is it easy to organize all our thoughts without putting them down on paper first. Here is where the paperwork of Bible study enters the picture. Sorry! (To those of you skimming through this workbook trying to gain information without completing the written exercises—shame on you! Go back and do the exercises. You don't know what you're missing.)

- *Read Habakkuk 2:2. What did God tell Habakkuk to do with the vision he received?*

_____

_____

The more we read, the more we understand. Some things just take time to understand.

- *Read Deuteronomy 17:18, part of the instructions given to the prince who would one day sit on the throne of Israel. What is it the prince was to do upon sitting on the throne of his kingdom?*

_____

_____

This is a very telling instruction. The one who sat on the throne could snap his fingers and command the finest scribes of the kingdom to make the most elaborate copy of the law imaginable. However, God command the prince to "*write him*"—for himself—a copy of the law. Why? God understands the powerful connection between our hand and mind. When you actually sit down and write out something, you force yourself to interact with every word.

- *Read Deuteronomy 27:1–8. Moses is instructing the people for the time when they would enter into the Promised Land. What is it he instructs them to do with the law?*

_____

_____

Countless psychological studies have confirmed that the more of your senses are involved in the learning process, the more you retain. Combining hearing, seeing, and writing is a powerful combination. The more you use your hand to write down what you are hearing and reading, the more of your Bible study you will remember and be able to apply. There are several ways you can do this.

Take Notes of Preaching and Teaching

Many years may have passed since you took notes in school. Maybe you were never good at it. Or, you might be an excellent note taker. Taking notes is a matter of personal style, and there isn't one right way to do it. If you are already comfortable taking notes I encourage you to increase your learning and understanding by taking notes whenever you hear the word of God preached or taught.

If you need help to become a better note taker, here is an outline to get you started. I suggest you copy it on a sheet of paper that will fit in your Bible. Or, you might want to carry a small notebook the size of your Bible and copy this list on the inside cover as a guide to what you should look for.

- *Title or theme of the study:*

_____

_____

- *Text or key verses used as the basis for the study:*

  _____

  _____

- *What are the main points the speaker is making?*

  _____

  _____

- *What are some of the ways I need to apply what I am hearing to my life?*

  _____

  _____

The above outline is about as basic as it gets, but it's a pretty good model for what you should look for when you take notes. Don't worry about writing down everything the speaker says or you will be working so hard trying to write every word that you may the main thrust of the speaker's message. Relax. Remember, this is not school, and no one is going to grade you on the quality of notes you take.

One way to test how good your notes are is to look at them a few weeks later. If you don't understand what you wrote, try to write less to allow yourself time to express your thoughts clearly. If you can write down and apply just one or two things every time you hear someone preach or teach, you will grow in your walk with Christ.

Make Notes in Your Bible

In the first chapter I advised you to begin making notes in a cheap Bible, so that you can make mistakes without them becoming too costly. The more serious and experienced you become in Bible study, the more serious you will become about making notes in your Bible. For that purpose you need a good, wide-margin Bible.

Let me give you more advice as you get started. First, before you write anything in your Bible make certain the ink from the writing instrument you use will not bleed through the paper. Remember that the paper used in Bibles is often very thin. Many ballpoint pens use ink that will bleed through the paper and become illegible in time. Some people prefer to use pencil. If you prefer ink, some inks resist the bleeding effect. I suggest you ask someone at a good art supply store or Christian bookstore for recommendations about specific brands of pens and the ink they use. You can also try out various point sizes to see which is best for your personal writing style. There are some pens that do quite well on Bible paper.

Next, ask some good Bible students to show you how they mark their Bibles. There is no one right system, and you simply need to discover what works for you. Some people have elaborate systems using different colors, diagrams, and pictures. I'm no artist and have to keep things simple. I use several colors of ink to represent different categories of notes:

- *Black—historical, background, and general information.*

- *Green—Doctrinal information.*

- *Blue—Personal applications*

- *Red—Dates and chronological information*

That little system is not too complicated, is it? I've used it for years and it works just fine for me. The only thing that's important is to find what works for you. Any system of making notes in your Bible is better than no system at all.

Journal

Another way to use your pen to enrich your spiritual life is to keep a journal. Maybe this is something you already do. If so, congratulations! I don't have to sell you on the benefits. If not, I can tell you that a simple journal is a great tool.

Just as in note-taking, journaling is a matter of individual taste and style. The journaling I am thinking of here is not like keeping a diary or even like blogging on the Internet. The journaling I'm talking about is simply recording what you are learning in the Bible, what God is doing in your life, what you are trusting God for now, and how he is answering your prayers.

As I said, I like to keep things simple. I write in my journal along with my daily Bible reading. I keep a schedule to read through the Bible several times a year, moving from Genesis to Revelation. There are plenty of other ways to read through the Bible (alternating Old and New Testaments, chronologically, etc.), but this works for me.

Before reading, I ask God to open my eyes to see what he wants me to see that morning. Somewhere in my daily reading, I expect God to impress some specific principle or scripture passage on my heart. There are times I have to go back and read again, but I continue until God speaks to me. Then, I write that verse or passage in my journal and maybe a few short thoughts about how I need to apply that to my life today. Finally, I list any particular prayer requests I have. As God answers my prayers, I go back and put the date he answers beside the prayer request.

All the principles in this chapter are designed to help us think clearly. The more we commit things to writing, the more clearly we think. A college philosophy professor once scolded me for saying in an oral exam that I knew the answer, but was having trouble finding the words to express it. He said, "Mr. Adams, if you really know something you are able to clearly articulate it in words."

He was right. By writing things down clearly, just as God commanded Habakkuk to do centuries ago (Habakkuk 2:2), we greatly increase our understanding. Make sure you have enough ink in your pen!

The more we commit things to writing, the more clearly we think.

CHAPTER TEN

Harnessing Technology and Teamwork

The principles and methods we have discussed to this point are timeless. These simple precepts of Bible study have been passed down from generation to generation. The first part of this chapter will be out of date the day after I write these words, though, because I want to make you aware of how technology offers exciting possibilities for Bible study. I also want to make you aware of books and other tools you might want to consider for continuing your adventure in Bible study. By taking advantage of the best of technology and available tools, we can benefit from the contributions of many gifted Bible teachers.

Bible study was never intended to be a purely individual affair, but as part of God's family. So, in this chapter we will learn how technology provides some wonderful Bible study tools, and we will learn to build upon the hard work and study of Bible students through the centuries.

I have often recommended a book to someone, only to have them express frustration later when they try to find it and discover it is out of print. Books frequently go in and out of print and new ones are published all the time. The same is true for technology. The latest and greatest technology of today is obsolete tomorrow. Despite the risk of being out of date, I want to talk with you about technology and books.

Other chapters of this book are very interactive; this one is not nearly as interactive. Bear with me. The technology and tools I want to discuss with you are extremely interactive.

The Computer Revolution

I think we will look back on the explosion of personal computers and the Internet during the final two decades of the last century as having been as revolutionary to Bible study as the invention of the printing press. Technology offers many advantages to the serious investigator of scripture.

As a new follower of Jesus Christ, right after I fell in love with the Bible, I fell in love with books about the Bible and the many reference tools available to help me. When I traveled years ago, I carried a separate case just for my Bible study books. I would always have

> *The latest and greatest technology of today is obsolete tomorrow.*

a concordance that allowed me to find all the places where a specific word appears in scripture. Also, I would usually carry an *Englishman's Greek Concordance* that allowed me to trace a particular Greek word through the New Testament and see the ways in which it is translated into English. In addition, I would normally carry several commentaries on particular books of the Bible I was studying at the time. Those days are over. Thank God!

Today, I carry all of that and more on my Personal Digital Assistant (PDA) that literally fits in my shirt pocket. In that little package I have two different English Bibles, two Spanish Bibles, two German Bibles, a French Bible and the New Testament in Greek. Also loaded into my PDA's memory are 10 complete Bible commentaries, six Bible dictionaries of various types, and a five volume Bible encyclopedia. Why would I want to lug around a 150-pound duffle bag when I can put all that in my pocket?

Bear in mind that just about anything you can buy in a book can be found online or otherwise loaded onto your personal computer. This statement is truer as you read these words than when I wrote them.

Today, the Internet is a gold mine of Bible study material. Entire libraries of rare, old books have been scanned and made available to any interested Bible student. Collections of sermons and outlines from wonderful Bible teachers are online. New riches of information appear daily.

However, let me offer a vital word of caution: *anyone* with a computer can put *anything* online, good or bad. Know your sources. Check things out. Verify what you see with other independent sources. Just because you see something online does not make it true.

Now, what is it you should be looking for, where should you look, and why do you want it in the first place? This is where we will begin.

The Basics: The Bible on Paper and in Digital Format

It will be some time before we get away from the warm fuzzy feeling of holding a leather-bound Bible in our hands. I love to see people carry their Bibles to church and hear the rustle of pages turned as they follow along with my sermon. Most people are still very comfortable with a Bible open on the table before their eyes as they study or read at home. I do not mean to suggest you do away with your "hard copy" Bible.

So, why should you care about all the Bible tools available on computer and on the Internet? As I write these words in the early years of the twenty-first century there are even now people who don't own a television and don't want to own one. Some people consider television an unnecessary, even dangerous distraction. I am just as certain there are still people who are happy not to have a computer and have no interest in buying one.

Keep in mind that every form of investigation, including the criminal investigation, we have used as an analogy throughout this book, has benefitted from technology. Sherlock Holmes, the famous fictional detective who "sleuthed" during the late 19th and early 20th Centuries. If he was being written about today, do you think his character would refuse to use a telephone, electricity, crime lab, word processor, fingerprinting or DNA sampling? Of course not! He knew that tools could help him achieve more than he could achieve on his own, which is why he always carried a magnifying glass. In some ways the technological tools I will discuss in this chapter are no more than magnifying glasses you can use to better see the details in your Bible study.

Give me a chance to make a case for having a computer, even if all you use it for is to study the Bible. (If someone reads these words 20 years from now, they will probably wonder why I wrote them.)

There is a wide variety of Bible software available, ranging from very simple to exceedingly complex. You can spend much money on sophisticated software, or you can download some programs for free or for a small contribution to the developer. Such programs can be easily located and downloaded onto your computer.[1] If you are not sure how to do that ask any thirteen-year-old.

No matter how much money you decide to spend, all Bible software aims to accomplish the same basic functions. First, there is the biblical text itself, usually available in a plethora of translations and languages. Even in "free" Bible software some translations require a fee to download them due to publisher royalties. This is another advantage of the KJV. Since it is in the public domain you can download it for free.

Most software programs allow you to open windows on your computer screen to compare languages and/or translations. Most of them also have the option of loading Bibles in different Hebrew and Greek versions as well. Being able to line up different languages and translations in parallel form is a great feature in itself.

Earlier, we talked about the importance of marking your Bible and making notes. One of the most important features of having the Bible on your computer is the ability to print out parts of the Bible to use as study "worksheets." If I want to study Ephesians 5, I can print out the whole chapter (or book!) on a cheap sheet of paper and make all the scribbles and notes I want without having to worry about making a mistake or messing up my "real" Bible.

I can make the print large or small, single space or double, and in any font my computer supports. I can print out the words in different colors, or highlight them digitally. I can put them on three-hole punched paper and create a Bible in a binder. Your only limitation is your imagination and the capacity of your computer and printer. We will learn why this is so important in the next chapter.

Once you have made your preliminary notes on a sheet of paper, you can transfer what you want to keep into your nice, leather bound Bible. Or, most Bible software allows you to keep and file all your Bible study notes digitally, if you choose.

All the software programs allow you to search for words and phrases as they appear in the Bible. The more sophisticated the software, the more tools and features are included—commentaries, books on different themes, dictionaries, devotional guides, charts, Bible maps and many more. Let's break these features down into some basic categories.

Concordance and Search Features

Besides the Bible itself, the most basic and important tool for Bible study is a concordance. Back in the stone ages of Bible study before computers, a concordance was a book that listed Bible words along with a list of verses where the word appears. Some Bibles have an abbreviated concordance in the back, listing some of the major words of scripture. The list of places where the word appears is not exhaustive, but merely represents some of the more important verses where that word occurs.

An exhaustive concordance is one that lists every occurrence of every word in the Bible. These are very big books! But some of them, including *Strong's Exhaustive Concordance*, are available in paperback.

However, a concordance is version-specific. This means that English words in the concordance are as they appear in a particular translation. For example, if you are using the *New American Standard Translation* you won't find a concordance based on the *King James Version* to be of much use, but would use the *New American Standard Exhaustive Concordance*.[2]

One of the most famous of concordances in the English Language is *The New Strong's Exhaustive Concordance of the Bible*.[3] This work is keyed to the KJV. The great value of Strong's concordance is not only that it is exhaustive, but also that each Greek and Hebrew word is assigned a number. When you look up the word "love," for example, there will be a number beside each verse where the word "love" is listed as appearing in the Bible. We will call these numbers the "Strong's numbers." That number tells you the specific Hebrew or Greek word that is translated into English as "love" in that particular verse. By the way, the *New American Standard Exhaustive Concordance* mentioned above also uses the same Strong's numbers, as do many other word tools used in Bible study. We will see some of them later.

Right now, let's practice.

Besides the Bible itself, the most basic and important tool for Bible study is a concordance.

- *If you have an exhaustive concordance with Strong's numbers, look up the word "love." You'll see that the words in the English Bible are listed in alphabetical order, as though it were a dictionary. Find "love," and you see a list of 281 verses in the KJV where "love" appears. In some verses the word appears more than once. In each row you will see the scripture reference followed by part of the verse and the italicized letter "l" where the word "love" occurs. To the right you will see a number, James Strong's labor of love tagging each individual Hebrew and Greek word in the Bible.*

- *If you are using Bible software, follow the instructions provided with the software to do a word search and search for "love." In all probability your software also has a way to indicate the Strong's numbers corresponding to the individual words of your English Bible version. See if you can discover how to do that. Each program is a little different but you **can** learn to do this. I have faith in you!!*

- *Remember that the Old Testament was written in Hebrew and the New Testament in Greek. Keeping things simple for the moment and dealing only with the New Testament, look in your concordance or software for the verses with "love" and tell what is the first time "love" occurs in the New Testament?*

  _____

  _____

- *What is the Strong's number that corresponds to the word "love" in this particular verse in Matthew? _____*

- *The word "love" appears again in Matthew 6:5. What is the Strong's number in this verse? _____*

Notice that the word "love" has a different Strong's number in Matthew 6:5 than in Matthew 5:43. This is because the Greek language has several words correctly translated as "love" in English. Each of these Greek words has a different shade of meaning. Even though you don't know Greek, you will now be able to appreciate the way these different words are used and the different shades of meaning.

In Matthew 5:43 where "love" appeared for the first time in the New Testament, the Strong's number is 25 (You might see it listed in some works or software programs as 0025). If you are using a paper version of an exhaustive concordance with Strong's numbers, you will find separate Hebrew and Greek dictionary sections in the back of the book.

- *In the Greek Dictionary section look up the number 25. Your Bible software will perform the same function. Either click on the Strong's number 25 (or run your mouse across it in some programs) and the information about that particular word will appear. Remember, each software program is different, so follow the instructions for your particular program. When you find the Greek word corresponding to number 25, you will see the word written in Greek letters followed by the same word transliterated into English letters.*

- *In this case, what is the Greek word that corresponds to 25?*

_____

_____

This Greek word is a verb meaning, "to love." Keep in mind that these Hebrew and Greek dictionaries in the back of the concordance are superficial and limited in the information they can provide about each word. There are other dictionaries, sometimes called "lexicons," that give more information about particular words and their various meanings.

Your Bible software, by the way, probably brings up much more information when you click the number or run your mouse across it than you find in the back of a concordance. Many of these programs link the Strong's numbers to a lexicon that provides much more information than *Strong's Concordance.*

- *Look up the Strong's number that corresponds to "love" in Matthew 24:12. What is it* _____

_____

- *Once again in the Greek Dictionary or from your software program, what is the Greek word from which "love" in this verse is translated?*

_____

_____

Notice that the reason there is a difference between numbers 25 and 26 is that 25 is a verb, "to love," and 26 is a noun, "love." However, you should also see that the dictionary indicates that number 26, *agape, a noun,* is derived from number 25, *agapao,* a verb.

- *In Matthew 6:5 you learned that the Strong's number corresponding to love was 5368. Look up this word in the Greek Dictionary. What is it?*

_____

_____

This, too, is a verb, *phileo*. This particular Greek word is used more to speak of friendly or brotherly love. Philadelphia's name, the "City of Brotherly Love," is derived from this Greek word.

Let me show you an example of why these distinctions of words can be important. Look at John 21:15. If you are using a KJV Strong's Concordance, remember that there is a difference between "love" and "lovest." Each is a different English word and each has its own listing. You will find both "love" and "lovest" in John 21:15 in a King James Bible and need to look up John 21:15 under the listing for each. With Bible software the process is much simpler and quicker. Just look up John 21:15 and see where Jesus asks Peter if he loves him. Then, note Peter's reply in the same verse.

- *In John 21:15 what is the Strong's number corresponding to "love" when Jesus asks Peter if he loves (lovest) him?* _____

- *In the same verse Peter insists that he loves Jesus. Yet, what is the Strong's number corresponding to the word "love" in Peter's answer?* _____

- *What is your initial impression as to the reason Peter and Jesus used two different words?*

  _____

  _____

Knowing the Strong's number assigned to a Bible word, you can trace that Hebrew or Greek word through scripture and see different ways it is translated into English. Just as the word "love" in English may be the translation of several different Greek words, the same Greek word might be translated different ways in English. This is just the way languages interact.

Working with the example of "love," you might learn that *agape*, one of the Greek words we saw for "love," is also translated as "charity" in the KJV (1 Corinthians 13:1, for example). That may seem hopelessly antiquated to you since charity suggests to most modern readers a philanthropic organization to which people give money and the organization in turn gives to those in need. Armed with that information, though, you can gain some insight into God's love, or *agape*. Biblical love in the purest moral sense is a love that gives.

In "the good old days" tracing Hebrew and Greek words by use of the Strong's numbers was accomplished by using still another thick book called The Englishman's Greek Concordance,[4] or its equivalent in Hebrew.[5] You would find the English word that appeared in the KJV in the concordance, note the Strong's number that appeared by it for a particular verse, then, you would look up that same number in *The Englishman's Greek Concordance* and see a list of the verses where that same Greek word appeared and the various ways it is translated.

That was then; this is now. No longer do we have to switch back and forth between thick, cumbersome books with fine print to trace a word through scripture. Now, we simply use a Bible software program and can get the same information and much more with the click of a mouse. In most software programs you can enter the Strong's number into the search field and the result shows you every time that particular Hebrew or Greek word appears in the Bible translation you use. By looking at the list of verses where the Hebrew or Greek word appears, you can see if there are different ways the word is translated into English.

The Bible software I use has a tab that opens what is called the *King James Concordance*. For every Strong's number it shows how many times that particular Hebrew or Greek word appears in the KJV Bible and lists the ways it is translated into English in the KJV followed by the list of all the occurrences of that specific English translation.

If I looked up Strong's number 25, for instance, I would see the different ways forms of *agapao* is rendered in English in the KJV. The list includes "love, loved, loveth, beloved, lovest, and lovedst," along with the verses where each appear.

Not only can your Bible software perform the same function as a paper concordance, it can do much more. You can look up the times when two or more words appear in the same verse. You can look up entire phrases. And, you can limit your search to just a book or portion of the Bible. What Bible software can do is truly amazing in comparison to a paper concordance.

I moved back to the United States from Central America in the early 1980's. I was resistant to technology, having come from a developing country where we were technology-challenged (at that time). One night, a staff member rang my bell, walked through my living room into my home office and, without asking permission, set up a small computer that he was carrying under his arm (At the time I didn't even know how to type!). He opened up one of the first Bible software programs available and showed me how I could enter in "God" and "love" and then tell the computer to find every verse in the Bible where those two words appear in the same verse. He pressed the search button and the computer began to search. We went and got a cup of coffee and about 20 minutes later we printed out the results. My mouth fell open. To do that manually with a concordance would have taken me days! I was hooked. Now, of course, I get frustrated when a similar search takes more than half a second or so. I haven't touched a hard copy concordance since.

Digging Deeper

Nothing is more important to Bible study than a concordance or its equivalent in Bible software. Not only have we learned how to search for words and phrases in the Bible, we have also learned how to discover the Greek and Hebrew words from which they are translated. This is just the beginning.

There are several books you might consider adding to your library early in your Bible study journey. Keep in mind much of this information may be available digitally, but some people do better with good old fashioned books. Here are some suggestions whatever format you prefer.

A Bible commentary is just that; someone's comments about a particular passage of the Bible, usually a specific book or group of books. There are some good general commentaries that cover the whole Bible or large parts of it. Most Bible software comes with commentaries built in to the program.

- *Take a moment and list the commentaries available on your Bible software. Writing them down will help you remember they are there!*

_____

_____

If you do not yet have Bible software, check out the various tools different software offers before deciding on which you will purchase.

Whether or not you use a computer in your Bible study, here are some volumes you may want to purchase to set on your shelf. They are that good. J. Sidlow Baxter's *Explore the Book*[6] and W. Graham Scroggie's *The Unfolding Drama of Redemption*[7] provide excellent overviews of the whole Bible and how it all fits together. Obviously, any book as general as a commentary on the entire Bible is going to be limited in the amount of detail about a specific scripture. The big picture view they provide, though, is tremendous.

A Bible Handbook is similar to a single volume commentary on the whole Bible and provides essentials to understand any portion of the Bible. Some of the best known and most effective are the three written by Merrill Unger,[8] Henry Haley,[9] and Henrietta Mears.[10] These well-known works have been issued in various editions and are readily available.

Other tools that you can find, either in electronic or paper form, are Bible dictionaries and encyclopedias. The difference between the two is the scope and the amount of information offered, with encyclopedias being the more complete. Both give information to define and explain the words, topics, places, people, and other key elements of Bible study. A great standard for many years has been the *International Standard Bible Encyclopaedia,*[11] originally published in five volumes, but commonly included in a number of Bible software programs. Zondervan publishes another fine encyclopedia.[12]

Earlier in this chapter I cautioned you that the Hebrew and Greek dictionaries in the back of a Strong's Concordance are necessarily limited. Even those definitions that may appear on your computer screen with the click of a mouse are often limited in the information they provide. Though they give you an idea of the meaning of the word, they cannot guarantee that is the meaning intended in the context you happen to be studying. Remember that the first principle of understanding the Bible is to take everything in its proper context.

You may have used a small, compact dictionary in your school days. That was usually enough to satisfy your homework requirements. And, at least once you probably had occasion to look up a word in one of the gigantic dictionaries in the library that weigh more than a medium size Collie dog. Only then do we become fully aware of how many meanings a word can have! And, we find the meaning is determined solely by the context. The same principle is true in any language. So, be aware of that before you look up the meaning of a Greek word in the back of a concordance and proudly proclaim with an authoritative voice that the word means such and such. The authoritative meaning of any word in any language is how it is used in the specific context, not what is written in a dictionary.

Not to confuse you, but as you dig deeper you will become aware that not only do many words have several possible meanings and shades of meaning, they also have tense, gender, voice, mood, person, number, and other linguistic quirks that affect a proper understanding within the context. Don't worry. There are books and tools to help you with that when the time comes.

Though many Bibles have a section of maps in the back, a book dedicated to biblical geography and maps is an excellent investment. Maps are available in electronic form, of course, and some offer sophisticated features, such as being able to zoom in and out, or to measure distances from point to point by dragging a line with your mouse cursor. However, many people still benefit from studying a nice, large map on paper. The first serious book of Bible maps I used is still available and still respected, the *Oxford Bible Atlas*.[13] More recently, Tyndale published an excellent book of maps with an interactive CD.[14]

All of the tools and features we have considered in this chapter are available in computerized form. In the past I have sometimes used expensive, sophisticated, academic Bible software rich in the capacity to research in both Hebrew and Greek. Frankly, the software I use daily is available for no charge on the Internet. It has most of the features of the more costly versions and it allows me to simultaneously load and compare Bibles in many languages and translations. Besides the search features we noted, this software has a number of basic commentaries and dictionaries. It also has several books of Bible maps and the foundation of a solid library of classic Christian books on theology, history, practical devotional living. All that and more!

There are impressive collections of Christian books and study aids available on disks, and I have even seen them offered for next to nothing in bargain bins at secular stores. I have mentioned the ability to access many works directly on the Internet. Some of the old classics, as well as many of the more contemporary Bible study aids, have been scanned and put on the Internet. We live in a wonderful new world!

I also would encourage you to read more books on the subject of Bible study itself. I wrote this book primarily to help the members of my own church and those who, for one reason or another, have been influenced by my ministry. I make no claim that this book is the final answer in Bible study.

One of the finest books I have come across in recent years is *How to Study Your Bible,* written by Kay Arthur.[15] She and her Precepts Ministries International have made a major contribution to encouraging and equipping people to study the Bible. Others also have written great books to help people understand the Bible.[16] Howard and William Hendricks recently wrote an outstanding book for beginning to intermediate Bible students called *Living By the Book.*[17] I mention this so you won't think I dreamed up all the principles found in this book.

Remember what I said earlier about Bible study being a team effort. God's Holy Spirit preserves truth by bearing witness through the testimony of believers. While none of us have all the answers and we will always agree to disagree on some details of Bible interpretation, there is great comfort and protection in knowing that you are in line with the godly students of the Bible down though history.

King Solomon said, "*And further, by these, my son, be admonished: of making many books there is no end; and much study is a weariness of the flesh*" (Ecclesiastes 12:12). Even today, there is no end to the books, and the lists of helps available to serious Bible students is a long one. This chapter is only a beginning reference to what I trust will be a life-long quest to study the Bible.

Notes

1. At the time of this writing *OnLine Bible* and *e-Sword* are two programs available on the Internet for minimal charge. There are others.

2. Robert Thomas, ed., *New American Standard Exhaustive Concordance of the Bible,* (Nashville: A.J. Holman, 1981).

3. James Strong, New Strong's Exhaustive Concordance of the Bible (Nashville: Thomas Nelson Publishers, 1984).

4. George Wigram, *The Englishman's Greek Concordance to the New Testament* (Peabody, MA: Hendrickson Publishers, 1996).

5. Laird Harris, ed., *Theological Wordbook of the Old Testament* (Chicago: Moody Press, 1980), is an excellent example of an Old Testament tool where the Hebrew words of the text are keyed to the Strong's numbers.

6. J. Sidlow Baxter, *Explore the Book* (Grand Rapids: Academie Books, 1966).

7. W. Graham Scroggie, *The Unfolding Drama of Redemption: The Bible as a Whole* (Grand Rapids: Zondervan Publishing House, 1972).

8. Merrill Unger, *Unger's Bible Handbook* (Chicago: Moody Press, 1967).

9. Henry Halley, *Halley's Bible Handbook*, rev. ed. (Grand Rapids: Zondervan, 1961).

10. Henrietta Mears, *What the Bible Is All About*, 2nd rev. ed. (Ventura, CA: 1997).

11. James Orr, gen. ed. *The International Standard Bible Encyclopaedia* (Grand Rapids: Wm. B. Eerdmans Publishing Co., 1939).

12. Merrill Tenney, gen. ed., *The Zondervan Pictorial Encyclopedia of the Bible* (Grand Rapids: Regency Reference Library, 1976).

13. Herbert May, ed. *Oxford Bible Atlas,* 3rd ed. (London: Oxford University Press, 1984).

14. Neil Wilson and Linda Taylor, *Tyndale handbook of Bible Charts & Maps* (Wheaton, IL: Tyndale House Publishers, Inc., 2001).

15. Kay Arthur, *How to Study Your Bible* (Eugene, OR: Harvest House Publishers, 1994).

16. Other good books on Bible study include: Irving Jenson, *Independent Bible Study,* rev. (Chicago: Moody Press, 1992); and Robertson McQuilkin, *Understanding and Applying the Bible*, rev. (Chicago: Moody Press, 1992).

17. Howard Hendricks and William Hendricks, *Living by the Book* (Chicago: Moody Press, 1991).

NOTES

CHAPTER ELEVEN

Putting It All Together

So far, you have learned about tools and truth to guide you in investigating the Bible. Now, it is time to put it all together.

Like a rookie detective fresh out of the police academy and ready for his or her first case, you can now get serious about a life of investigative Bible study.

This chapter will lead you to focus on the first chapter of Paul's letter to the Colossians. Rather than simply inform you about this short New Testament book, you will apply the principles you have learned and see that you can are quite capable of studying the Bible yourself. You will probably discover as many questions as answers, because the Bible is an infinitely deep book. In fact, you will discover questions you never knew existed! Don't let that worry you. The goal is to put you on the trail of clues in the great adventure of investigating the Bible. And, in the process you will learn some things about Colossians.

First, you will apply what you learned about starting the case with an overview of the book before diving into the details of the first chapter. Then, you will learn and practice the three basic steps of inductive Bible study that bring together in one process all the questions and principles you have learned. The first clue in this case is to understand the process called inductive Bible study, rooted in what is called inductive reasoning.

Inductive and Deductive Reasoning

Inductive Bible study has many champions, and well it should! Inductive Bible study is a time-tested method for serious Bible students. Before teaching you this method, though, we must agree on the meaning of the word "inductive."

In classical logic you learn the difference between inductive and deductive reasoning. There are many explanations and illustrations of these two types of reasoning. My purpose here is not to make you an expert in logic, but merely to help you understand two different approaches to interacting with the world around us, and specifically, with the information in the Bible.

Inductive reasoning is observing specific details and information clues leading to certain conclusions based on evidence. Inductive reasoning moves from the specific to the general. Some say inductive

The first clue in this case is to understand the process called inductive Bible study, rooted in what is called inductive reasoning.

reasoning moves from the bottom up. If you throw a basketball into the air, it always comes down. After doing this for a while, you would conclude that the next time you throw the ball up it will come down again. Your conclusion is based on inductive reasoning—repeated observations that lead to a general conclusion.

Returning to our detective model, a sleuth discovers clues that lead to solving a crime. That, too, is inductive reasoning.

In contrast, deductive reasoning moves from general and established truth to more specific details. Some say that deductive reasoning moves from the top down. For example, someone comes by about the time you conclude that the next time you toss the basketball into the air, it will come down. The passerby smiles and says, "That's just an example of Newton's Law of Gravity. What goes up must come down. Therefore, every time you toss a basketball into the air, it will come down."

That passerby is using deductive reasoning by starting from an accepted truth about gravity and how it affects material objects on earth and then applying it to a specific case – you and your basketball.

Consider a detective working a crime and who is finding little evidence. Stepping back to look at the big picture, the detective reflects on similar cases and perhaps consider a "profile" of people who might commit such a crime. This thought process may lead to a list of potential suspects or "persons of interest" that, in turn, set off a chain reaction that leads to solving the case. This is deductive reasoning.

Whether inductive or deductive reasoning, one approach is not right and the other wrong. They are simply two different ways to approach the same case. We have seen examples of law enforcement officers using both deductive and inductive thinking in their investigations. Everyone uses both deductive and inductive thinking daily to deal with issues of everyday life. Similarly, Bible study involves both deductive and inductive reasoning.

The first four chapters of this book were deductive in nature. We began with some solid presuppositions that definitely determine the direction of all future study. Those presuppositions centered on our faith in the divine inspiration of the Bible, its inerrancy, and its absolute authority. From this we deduced that the Bible has a unifying theme and purpose. We also deduced that if God is the Author of the Bible, then his Spirit guides us to understand and apply its truth. In these early chapters our goal was to grasp the big picture of the Bible. All this is in line with classical deductive reasoning.

Having laid this biblical foundation in chapters five through ten, we assembled an investigative tool kit of inductive questions and principles. We are now reading to use questions and principles in the process of inductive Bible study. This process examines biblical evidence inductively and arrives at solid conclusions that affect the way we live.

A sleuth discovers clues that lead to solving a crime.

The Three Steps of Inductive Bible Study

Chapter six posed questions to use in approaching any passage in the Bible. The fifth question was "What are the three basic understandings of this passage?" Those three layers of understanding concern the historical, doctrinal, and personal application of a biblical text.

We learned to study any passage of the Bible by first determining the historical, literary, and grammatical context of that scripture. Then, we look for the doctrinal understanding to determine what God wants us to know and why he included a specific passage in the Bible. Finally, all scripture has some specific lesson, which God wants us to learn and apply to our lives.

What is true in a principle we use to develop a snapshot of a certain scripture passage is also a method of Bible investigation. Those three basic understandings of scripture are at the heart of the "Inductive Method of Bible Study." As you worked your way through this workbook, you may have thought you would never remember all the questions and principles you have studied. Actually, the key to effective Bible study is simply to remember the three basic questions that we discussed earlier. These three steps of inductive Bible study are usually expressed as:

1. **Observation**—What does it say?
2. **Interpretation**—What does it mean?
3. **Application**—How does it work and how do I apply this to daily life?

Those three steps help you find key clues to a life of rich, investigative Bible study. If you can make these three steps your line of questioning every time you investigate a Bible passage, you will be amazed how easily the other questions and principles you learned will come flooding back to your mind. Really! You'll see that's true when you put all this into action.

Your first few assignments will explore Colossians as a whole. You have learned how important context is for proper understanding. Before looking in detail at the first section below, we will determine the context of the book. Before jumping into the three steps of inductive Bible study, here are some exercises to help you see the big picture.

The Overview

- *Spend a few minutes in prayer right now and ask God to guide you as you study Paul's letter to the Colossians. Tell him your goal is to know him better, not just to get information about the Bible. Ask him to show you aspects of his truth that will have an impact on the way you live life and relate to others.*

- *Read the whole book of Colossians no fewer than five times. Do this before moving on. Come back here tomorrow if necessary, but don't put this off too long. Colossians has only four chapters, and they are short.*

- *What category of literature is Colossians? History, prophecy, poetry, proverb, gospel, epistle? _____ _____ (Easy question, huh? The idea is simply to establish this thought pattern as a habit each time you approach the Bible.)*

- *After reading this book, what can you observe about the Colossians and the time and circumstances of Paul's writing? Remember, you are only looking at information in the Bible itself. There will be time later to consult other tools such as commentaries and Bible handbooks.*

  _____

  _____

  _____

- *Try to summarize in a single sentence what you think is the major message of each of the four chapters of Colossians. There is no right or wrong answer here. Simply state your first impression.*

  - *Chapter One*

    _____

    _____

    _____

  - *Chapter Two*

    _____

    _____

    _____

  - *Chapter Three*

    _____

    _____

    _____

  - *Chapter Four*

    _____

    _____

    _____

- *Now, put all this together in a single sentence that says what the book of Colossians is about.*

_____

_____

_____

We could, of course, spend much more time on an overview of Colossians. At this point, you may want to spend a little time reading an introduction to Colossians in a Bible handbook or a study Bible that has some introductory remarks about this book. You can find similar information on your Bible software.

Notice the pattern we just followed. You first went to the Bible directly before you consulted any helps. This prevented your opinion from being colored by what someone else says. Now, you turn to consider what others have learned.

This order of study not only provides you with information you may not have seen on the first pass through Colossians, it also enables you to compare your observations to those of others. That way you can be certain you aren't headed off in some false direction by having overlooked the obvious.

Now, let's turn our attention to a more detailed analysis of the first chapter of Colossians. We will follow the same pattern we used in the overview—first, observing the evidence in the Bible itself. If you have Bible software and a printer, you might want to print out this chapter double spaced and use it as a worksheet as you complete the following exercises.

Step One of Inductive Bible Study: Observation

- *Begin in prayer, remembering what you learned earlier about the Holy Spirit of God being our teacher. Ask God to open your mind, your eyes, and your heart as you study this part of his word.*

- *Read Colossians 1 no less than 5 times. (Yes, I know you already read it at least five times in the overview.)*

We are going through the questions and principles you learned in previous chapters. These are investigative, inductive questions to direct us to the right evidence to arrive at the right interpretation and application. In the back of this manual you will see a checklist of these questions and principles. You might want to cut out this checklist or copy it and place it inside the cover of your Bible or notebook.

Sometimes, your answers may overlap from one section to another, but don't worry about that. The more questions you ask and the more answers you find, the more you will understand. You may not have an answer for every question, and some simply may not apply, but the goal is to lead you through the series of questions and principles to establish a pattern of questioning in your mind.

- ***What is the context?*** *We already considered the context of the book as a whole. Now, let's consider the specific context of this chapter. Since you have read the entire book several times, don't be afraid to use what you observed in Colossians to answer these questions about the first chapter.*

  - *How does chapter one fit into Paul's purpose in writing to the Colossians?*

    _____

    _____

    _____

    _____

  - *Do you see any historical information or circumstances we ought to be aware of as we study this first chapter?*

    _____

    _____

    _____

    _____

  - *Where was the city of Colosse? (Look this up on a Bible map.)*

    _____

    _____

    _____

  - *Why would Paul have written this letter?*

    _____

    _____

    _____

  - *What was his relationship, if any, to the Colossians?*

    _____

    _____

    _____

• *Does Paul mention some event or circumstance related to his writing? You are doing detective work. Look for any details that may help you better understand what you are reading. Later, you will consult the work of others by using some of the tools we have discussed. Right now, we want to examine the biblical text itself. List anything that may be important to what Paul is saying, or that might deserve study later.*

_____

_____

_____

• **To whom is this chapter written?**

_____

_____

_____

• *Which of the three broad categories, Jew, Gentile, or church does Paul address this letter?*

_____

_____

_____

• *Paul is writing to believers in a church. Do they appear to be mature believers or new converts? And, do they seem to come from a Jewish or Gentile background?*

_____

_____

_____

• *Are there any people mentioned by name in this chapter? Can we learn anything about them from this chapter?*

_____

_____

_____

• *Consider circling the names of people in the chapter on your worksheet, highlighting or underling them with a specific color.*

- **When was this letter written?** *You already know that Colossians is from the New Testament, not the Old. But, is there any indication when Paul may have written this letter? Is there any way to tell if the letter was written early in Paul's ministry or later? Was it written on one of his missionary journeys or when he was in prison in Rome? Does it correspond to any of the events recorded of Paul's life and ministry in the Book of Acts? If you don't come up with any specific information, don't worry; just get into the habit of asking the questions and then keep your eyes open for the answers as you research.*

  _____

  _____

  _____

- **What does the passage say?** *The objective simply is to see the normal, literal meaning of Paul's words within the context we have just examined. We aren't looking for symbolism, types, hidden meanings, or anything beyond the obvious, normal usage of the words of this first chapter. The questions below will guide your investigation of the actual language of the passage.*

  _____

  _____

  _____

  - *In the overview above, you summarized in a single sentence what you think is the major message of this first chapter. Do you think you gave your best answer, or could you improve it now by modifying it? You aren't trying to "interpret" the passage, or go into any deep theological analysis. As best you can, summarize simply the main thrust of the first chapter.*

    _____

    _____

    _____

  - *Though you have identified your idea of the chapter's key emphasis, break the chapter down into several segments, each with a key word, phrase, or sentence for each segment. In other words, how would you do a simple outline of this chapter?*

    _____

    _____

    _____

- **What are the key words?**
  - *Are there any words in this chapter you don't understand or are uncertain of their proper meaning in this context? List them and then use some of the techniques and tools we have studied, including dictionaries, handbooks, commentaries, or Bible software to find the basic meaning of the word in this particular context.*

  _____

  _____

  _____

  - *Are there any words or phrases that are repeated?*

  _____

  _____

  _____

  - *Are there are words or phrases that seem to have special emphasis?*

  _____

  _____

  _____

  - *What do you consider to be the most important words or phrases in this chapter?*

  _____

  _____

  _____

  - *On your worksheet consider highlighting, underlining, or circling the most important words and phrases in this chapter.*

  - *Do you see any words or phrases that seem to be connected in some logical, chronological, thematic or other way? Do you see words and phrases that appear to contrast sharply with others in the chapter? What are these words, phrases and their relationships?*

  _____

  _____

  _____

  - *Consider drawing lines or arrows on your worksheet to show these connections, if any.*

To this point we have focused on asking, "What does this passage say?" Next, we turn to interpretation: "What does this passage really mean?" Making the right analysis of a Bible passage is hard work. But, the time you spend in observation will pay off in the next two steps of inductive Bible study.

Howard and William Hendricks express this point well in their excellent book on Bible study:

> The more time you spend in Observation, the less time you will have to spend in Interpretation, and the more accurate will be your result. The less time you spend in Observation, the more time you will have to spend in Interpretation, and the less accurate will be your result.[1]

Step Two of Inductive Bible Study: Interpretation

As we said in chapter seven, it's time to connect the dots. You have worked hard to observe the biblical evidence and determine prayerfully what the text says. Now, you must interpret the evidence and come to a conclusion as to what the text actually means. Once again, our old friend context is the foundation of our study. And, we will follow the same order of priority: we go first to the biblical text itself, and then to any interpretive helps we have available.

When you were observing, your concern was primarily to learn the proper grammatical and literary context of the words of scripture. You also looked in the immediate context for any hints of geographical, historical, or other clues that would aid in proper reading of the text.

Context is much broader than the immediate literary and grammatical concerns you have examined. There is a wider scriptural context as well as the historical and cultural contexts. To research these broader contexts you must often turn to outside resources for help.

Begin by using questions based on those you learned in chapter seven.

- *Is there a word, concept, person, place, or other item in this chapter for which you desire more information? Find where that item appears for the first time in the Bible and use a concordance or search feature to trace some of the other places it appears. Can you see a pattern or other lessons to be discovered to help you interpret Colossians 1 correctly? Do this exercise for each item important enough to be clarified in this way and record what you learn that helps you understand what Paul means by including it in Colossians 1. (Principle of First Mention) You may need more space than what is provided below.*

NOTES

Context is much broader than the immediate literary and grammatical concerns you have examined.

• *As you consider the most important teachings in this passage, are there are other places in the Bible where those same teachings may be more completely developed? You might use a concordance or search feature to check other Bible references or find a passage that teaches the same thing in much more depth (Principle of Full Mention). What do you learn to help you better understand what Paul says here in the first chapter of Colossians?*

_____

_____

_____

• *Looking over Colossians 1 again, do you recall any other passages of scripture that might complement, explain, amplify, contrast, or otherwise complete your understanding of portions of this chapter? You can use any cross references in the margin of your Bible. Most Bible software offers a help called* The Treasury of Scripture Knowledge, *R. A. Torrey's old and wonderful volume of cross-references.[2] List any significant cross-references here that help you understand a corresponding passage in Colossians 1.*

_____

_____

_____

The following exercises are based on principles you learned in chapter eight.

• *Do you see any use of similitude in this chapter? Look for words such as "like" and "as."*

_____

_____

_____

• *Do you see any word pictures in this chapter?*

_____

_____

_____

• *Do you see any use of types in this chapter that represent something else?*

_____

_____

- *Look for references to nature in this chapter. Think about any references to nature and determine if there is something in God's creation to illustrate and help you better understand what this scripture teaches.*

  _____

  _____

  _____

Next, consider principles learned in chapter nine as the basis for the following questions:

- *Is there something in this chapter that strikes you as rather obscure or hard to understand?*

  _____

  _____

- *Are you trying too hard to understand something and forcing an interpretation that would contradict other plain biblical teaching?*

  _____

  _____

  _____

- *Observe any question marks in this portion of scripture. Are you trying to make a question teach something out of context?*

  _____

  _____

- *As you reflect on what Paul says here and consider the cross-references you have explored, are you confident that your interpretation of this passage is consistent with the testimony of other scripture?*

  _____

  _____

- *If the meaning in any part of this passage still escapes you, take a moment right now to simply commit the matter to God. It could be that you don't yet have the maturity or information necessary for proper understanding. Or, this might be one of those passages that you will never completely understand in this life. Instead, thank God for what you **can** understand and commit the rest to him to be revealed when, how, and **if** he desires.*

We never stop learning the Bible.

You have searched the scripture using good investigative principles and used the Bible study tools available to you.

The focus to this point has been the biblical text itself. There is still important information to be gleaned from outside sources to help you understand the full meaning of the scripture.

- *Consult any tools you have available to learn what you can about the city of Colosse: Bible handbooks, commentaries, a Bible Atlas, Bible software or an Internet search. Did you find anything you feel worth mentioning as you consider the meaning of this first chapter of Colossians?*

  _____

  _____

  _____

- *Utilizing the same kinds of tools, what can you learn of value about the history of Paul's epistle to the Colossians, the history of that time, or the culture of the city of Colosse? What else was happening at that time? What other situation, events, places, or people should be taken into account to understand Paul's words here?*

  _____

  _____

  _____

- *Earlier, you took any difficult or key words and looked at how they were used in other portions of the Bible, applying what you learned in the principles of first and full mention, or comparing scripture with scripture. Which of these words merits more study? See if you can use the Strong's numbers to check how the same Greek words are translated elsewhere, or to get definitions of the Greek word itself that might be useful to your understanding of Colossians 1. Use the tools we discussed in chapter ten. Write out any important information you learn.*

  _____

  _____

  _____

- *You have searched the scripture using good investigative principles and used the Bible study tools available to you. Next, it is time to read the commentaries of others about their own investigations of this passage. Read any commentaries you have that cover Colossians 1 and/or any commentaries you have available on your Bible software or the Internet. You have already expressed your idea of Paul's emphasis in this chapter.*

*Now, combine your own thoughts with what you have learned from others and write a brief summary of the meaning of this chapter. Give some thought and prayer to this, and do the best job you can. Don't worry about the form, spelling, or grammar. This is **your** work. You may come to a similar summary as the one you expressed earlier, or you may have significant things to add or change.*

Finally, let me strongly suggest if you are new to Bible study that you sit down with a more mature and experienced Bible student to review the work you have done in this chapter. You may be using this workbook as part of a class or small group Bible study and have help available to you. The point is to learn to compare your work with that of others so that you can learn from each other. Since none of us have perfect understanding, it is very easy to overlook the obvious, or head in a wrong direction for some reason that simply slipped our attention.

We never stop learning the Bible. This brief and basic introduction to Bible study can either establish or add to your skills of biblical investigation. The next time you read Colossians 1, you will undoubtedly see things you missed this time. There is always more than what you see and understand at this moment. But, no matter how much you understand, it is meaningless if it does not affect the way you live. On to the next step of inductive Bible study!

Step Three of Inductive Bible Study: Application

Having been pastor of a local church for many years, let me share with you the most miserable (and sometimes mean!) creature I have ever met—the professed follower of Jesus Christ who knows much information about the Bible and yet, fails to apply that knowledge to daily living. I have seen this case many times.

There are people who can quote whole chapters of scripture, have ready answers for any and all controversies of doctrine, take a stand on the major issues of the day, yet they are completely irresponsible in the way they live. I am talking about those Bible know-it-alls who steadfastly refuse to let the Holy Spirit control their lives and have no clue what it means to live biblical truth in daily life. Any biblical understanding they gain only serves to reinforce their pride and arrogance. In fact, it seems the more they study the Bible, the worse they become!

Continue to read, continue to study, continue to be open to learning, and allow God to stretch you beyond your current understanding.

- *Read 1 Corinthians 8:1–3, and then explain why you think some people grow more arrogant the more biblical knowledge they learn.*

  _____

  _____

  _____

The section on application is where the proverbial rubber meets the road. Don't take this lightly. Prayerfully consider the following exercises.

- *Taking into account what you have learned in Colossians 1, what areas of your life should be affected by what you have learned? Your personal life? Your marriage and/or family? Your workplace life? Your church life? Your social circle of friends?*

  _____

  _____

  _____

Now, having considered the affected areas of your life, let's get specific about how to apply what you have learned.

- *Is there a decision or commitment I need to make based on what I have learned?*

  _____

  _____

  _____

- *Is there an example that I can follow and apply to my life based on what I have seen in this passage?*

  _____

  _____

  _____

- *Is there a way to apply something in this passage to my prayer life? Perhaps there is an example of prayer to follow or a promise I can claim for my own life.*

  _____

  _____

  _____

- *Is there a sin or mistake mentioned in this passage that I need to correct or avoid in my own life?*

  _____

  _____

  _____

- *Is there some truth here I can share with someone else in my life?*

  _____

  _____

  _____

Other ways to apply this passage may occur to you, but these examples are offered as ways to highlight the need to apply what you learn. These questions form the basis for an outline you can apply to any passage of scripture to make application to your life. As you continue your study of scripture, answers to these questions about application make good daily entries to a journal. Looking back over past journal entries confirms and reinforces the lessons God teaches us about life.

Conclusion

We have been on quite a journey! I wrote this book targeting in my mind the person just beginning a life of Bible study. You may be a veteran of investigative Bible study and are looking over this material for new ideas or reinforcement. Whatever the case, I pray your time spent here has been worthwhile.

More than anything, I want to say that wherever you are in your ability to study the Bible, there is always more to learn. Even after more than 35 years of Bible study I still get excited about learning new lessons from the Bible. Bible study is still fresh after all these years! In many ways I feel as though I am just beginning. Continue to read, continue to study, continue to be open to learning, and allow God to stretch you beyond your current understanding.

This is just one more book on Bible study. Throughout this book, I have tried to share with you what others have taught me and what I have picked up along the way. I can teach you the principles, techniques and methods that have become part of my life. I cannot give you my passion to explore the depths of God's word. That part is up to you.

Dr. Watson once visited Sherlock Holmes on a frosty winter morning as the famed "consulting detective" trying to determine the identity of the owner of an old felt hat. No crime was involved, but Holmes was up for any challenge. Watson expressed amazement that Holmes could discover anything significant from such an apparently insignificant object, but he also knew Holmes.

Watson said, "But you are joking. What can you gather from this old battered felt?"

Turning to him, Holmes extended his magnifying glass and said, "Here is my lens. You know my methods[3]."

Happy sleuthing!

Happy sleuthing!

Notes

1. Howard Hendricks and William Hendricks, *Living by the Book* (Chicago: Moody Press, 1991), 224.

2. You can, of course, buy this in book form. A recent printing is R.A. Torrey, John Cann, ed. *Treasury of Scripture Knowledge* (Peabody, MA: Hendrickson Publishers, 2002).

3. Arthur Conan Doyle, *The Adventure of the Blue Carbuncle* (London: Baker Street Irregulars, 1948).

Other Books By Jeff Adams:

In English:
Job
Psalm 119
Reality Living

In Spanish:
Salmo 119
Filemon

For additional resources, including audio of sermons by Jeff Adams, please visit the following websites:
realityliving.org
kcbt.org

KCBT